BIG IDEAS *in*
Primary Mathematics

SAGE was founded in 1965 by Sara Miller McCune to support the dissemination of usable knowledge by publishing innovative and high-quality research and teaching content. Today, we publish over 900 journals, including those of more than 400 learned societies, more than 800 new books per year, and a growing range of library products including archives, data, case studies, reports, and video. SAGE remains majority-owned by our founder, and after Sara's lifetime will become owned by a charitable trust that secures our continued independence.

Los Angeles | London | New Delhi | Singapore | Washington DC | Melbourne

BIG IDEAS *in*
Primary Mathematics

Robert Newell

Los Angeles | London | New Delhi
Singapore | Washington DC | Melbourne

Los Angeles | London | New Delhi
Singapore | Washington DC | Melbourne

SAGE Publications Ltd
1 Oliver's Yard
55 City Road
London EC1Y 1SP

SAGE Publications Inc.
2455 Teller Road
Thousand Oaks, California 91320

SAGE Publications India Pvt Ltd
B 1/I 1 Mohan Cooperative Industrial Area
Mathura Road
New Delhi 110 044

SAGE Publications Asia-Pacific Pte Ltd
3 Church Street
#10-04 Samsung Hub
Singapore 049483

Editor: James Clark
Assistant Editor: Robert Patterson
Production editor: Tom Bedford
Copyeditor: Andy Baxter
Proofreader: Camille Bramall
Indexer: Cathy Heath
Marketing manager: Lorna Patkai
Cover design: Naomi Robinson
Typeset by: C&M Digitals (P) Ltd, Chennai, India
Printed and bound in Great Britain by Ashford
Colour Press Ltd

Library of Congress Control Number: 2016933486

British Library Cataloguing in Publication data

A catalogue record for this book is available from
the British Library

ISBN 978-1-4739-1316-5
ISBN 978-1-4739-1317-2 (pbk)

Contents

About the Author

Robert Newell has worked at the Institute of Education (IOE) for 12 years; full time for the last four. He works with Primary PGCE (Postgraduate Certificate in Education) trainees and Teach First participants. His career started as a primary school teacher, taking responsibility in maths in several schools before progressing to two deputy head posts and then a headteacher role.

Primary maths teaching, though, has been his biggest passion. He has worked as a numeracy consultant and also delivered a PGCE Maths programme to a London SCITT (School-Centred Initial Teacher Training centre) for three years. He is now part of a small maths team serving several hundred trainees at the IOE, now merged with UCL (University College London). He has two passions that underpin his work. One is ensuring that primary maths children are taught in a way that engages them and focuses on understanding. The other is the belief that, in the main, it is only anxiety that stops more trainees feeling comfortable about teaching maths. Part of his working role at the IOE is linked to supporting trainees with less secure understanding and allowing them to see how much they can offer. Many realise that although anxiety has affected their self-perception about mathematical understanding, this process can be reversed.

His dissertation focused on the different ways trainee teachers can learn to use different levels of understanding effectively in their primary school maths teaching. Here, he commits to print a range of ideas and activities, refined over many years and linked to ensuring all primary teachers can teach for understanding.

Acknowledgements

I would like to thank Carol, my wife, for her belief in me and her encouragement; also my children, Rachel and Tom.

Publisher acknowledgements

SAGE would like to thank the following reviewers, whose comments have helped to shape this book:

Vicki Fitt, University of Hertfordshire

Catherine Foley, University of Reading

John Fox, Numeracy coordinator and classroom teacher, Geoffrey Field Junior School

Pauline Palmer, Manchester Metropolitan University

Nick Tinsdeall, University of Cumbria

Introduction: The conundrum of primary maths teaching

There is a conundrum about primary school teaching that has vexed a lot of people. Given that the vast majority of teachers feel very comfortable about planning for a range of curriculum subjects why should one of the subjects to confound, and sometimes terrify, teachers be maths? Starting to address and support this situation has become one of the challenges and goals of this book.

At the UCL (University College London) Institute of Education, where my work is based we have had a strong cohort of trainees for a number of years. Good subject knowledge is frequently accompanied by academic confidence, good qualifications and creativity. However, there are a significant minority, possibly a majority, who feel ill-equipped to tackle primary maths teaching. They say, with some apprehension, that when they studied maths themselves, they resorted to learning rules and methods that they managed to carry out to pass exams, but didn't understand. This book seeks to help teachers become more secure about why procedures are appropriate and when they are insufficient.

Many of these otherwise confident, capable and enthusiastic trainees are therefore apprehensive about trying to develop understanding in children. Such a disposition also exists within the teaching profession. Primary school teachers can often feel they aren't helping children to understand maths, but simply doing their best to teach children techniques that they are required to know. This can have come about through receiving teaching that placed an emphasis on procedural and 'instrumental' learning (Skemp, 1976). Also they cite damage done to their own confidence levels through group or setted stigmatisation (Boaler, 2009). The problem comes when children need to know how to apply such knowledge. When will the procedures they have learnt be needed and what happens if the problem requires them to adjust the knowledge they have obtained?

This book has been written to try to allow trainees and newer teachers to the profession to become clearer about what concepts and ideas are to be developed that will allow children both to complete the curriculum requirements and also become mathematical in their thinking.

In order to do this as a new teacher, you are going to need to have enough idea of what you would like children to begin to understand as well as what kind of learning environment and atmosphere you are trying to create. This involves moving out of your comfort zone to some degree. The point is stressed in the book that whenever a teacher feels this happening in the primary maths classroom they are likely to be near to some very necessary conversations and questions that will not go away if they are not asked and discussed. In short, tentative, small steps forward in children's understanding are better than no steps forward at all.

Why use the phrase 'BIG IDEAS'?

The use of the phrase 'BIG IDEAS' is not to suggest that the curriculum content and objectives are not big in themselves. It is to develop discussion about which significant ideas need to be addressed if an understanding of the curriculum is to be achieved by children. If this discussion does not take place then children may tackle maths work more by memory than by understanding. The aim of coining the term BIG IDEAS is to try to ensure an approach to teaching and learning that involves understanding as well as memory.

Teachers' own learning experiences in maths

Working on the theory that ability in maths is not fixed, other things must also be true: namely that a lack in confidence in maths has evolved during a trainee's life; in all probability through negative experiences in the classroom, possibly transferred by teachers whose own confidence in understanding maths is limited. Whatever the cause, many teachers feel less equipped to develop understanding in children in maths than in other subjects.

The conundrum is that teachers with self-doubt will need to overcome this to allow a wider range of confident mathematical reasoners to emerge than has been the case to date. We continue to produce some of the very best mathematicians in the world. Currently though, many of the adult population struggle to apply mathematical knowledge in their everyday lives (Bynner and Parsons, 1997). The PISA (Programme for International Student Assessment) research test results confirm the situation. As a nation we are ranked 26th in the world in maths tests for 15 year olds; the role of teaching and learning maths in primary schools being pivotal to such outcomes (PISA, 2012).

How will the book seek to help in the teaching of primary maths?

The relevance of naming BIG IDEAS is to emphasise how understanding can and should be at the centre of what we teach. Currently the recently initiated curriculum is very good at broadening the content to allow wider coverage. It needs to be accompanied by teaching and learning that stresses understanding, lightbulb moments and the application of knowledge. This is stressed less in the National Curriculum; hence the curriculum and the understanding are linked consistently through the notion of BIG IDEAS.

Each chapter begins with a section entitled 'What does the National Curriculum say?' which links the topic with the National Curriculum in England (DfE, 2014). The need to teach for understanding is only specified in a small section of the curriculum document. This focuses, commendably, on fluency and reasoning. Therefore, the references to the National Curriculum are to allow you to see where teaching for understanding can dovetail with the curriculum programmes of study.

Learning intentions and success criteria: How BIG IDEAS fit in

There is often discussion among teachers, trainees and lesson observers about how success criteria should be used to increase and develop children's learning. Quite so. However, with such a full and wide-ranging curriculum there is a slight risk that learning facts and specific pieces of knowledge could be at the expense of wider and deeper understanding of how and why this knowledge both works and links to other knowledge. The book seeks to assist the trainee and new teachers to consider what key learning for children might be. This is done in two ways. Firstly, the BIG IDEAS, captured in boxes throughout the book, emphasise intended learning rather than activities. They are thus suited to being used as a teacher prompt towards creating effective learning success criteria. Secondly, the activities given throughout the book include learning intentions; these are also intended for use by teachers and trainees to help them consider the kind of learning and understanding the activities are seeking to develop.

The impact of testing on teaching (and how teachers need to know their knowledge)

Clearly the content of national testing directly affects what is taught. Inadvertently it can also affect the way concepts are taught. The style of questions being used in tests is often looked at carefully by teachers; attempts are made to make children familiar with a range of specific ways that questions are presented in maths. This can be at the expense of spending time discussing issues related to deepening children's overall understanding about a given theme in maths. Part of the reason for this is that superficial understanding by teacher and child can allow test questions to be answered successfully some of the time. It doesn't lead to secure understanding that can be built on throughout children's time in school subsequently.

Examples of this include rules related to multiplying by 10, 100 or 1000, or division equivalences. It would also apply to using formulae related to solving percentage problems, or multiplication and division by fractions.

The book also seeks to provide some guidance regarding how such areas can be taught. In that sense the BIG IDEAS captured in boxes do not, in the main, replicate the curriculum content outlined. They support it by underpinning ideas that will support the teaching of the content. The exception to this is the area of the National Curriculum which stresses the desirability of children developing reasoning skills to go with fluency; it also stresses the process of learning to solve problems.

Chapter progression

The initial chapter on problem solving is placed first. It is intended that this will do two things. Firstly, it can serve as an insight into the pedagogy of teaching maths, which has a different role for the teacher than when teaching more explicit maths content skills. Secondly, it acts as a basis for application to teaching across the whole maths curriculum. The opportunity to apply knowledge in problem solving and creative contexts is the way to make maths relevant in the real world and provide meaningful contexts that support the mathematical structures being taught and discussed.

Maths Mastery

The approach to teaching maths captured through the mastery approach now being valued by the government and being rolled out by academy groups such as Harris and Ark is significant. This approach, pioneered in the Far East underpins the teaching in the top countries in the PISA rankings – Singapore, China, South Korea and others. It is specific and quite rigorous. Problems are discussed and represented in a multiplicity of ways with extensive discussion and modelling. Then the models are translated back into the real world context. Although mastery teaching is acknowledged as being from the Far East in origin, the ideas have roots in education theory promoted here for many years through the work of Piaget and Bruner. We need to experience the concrete form, prior to representing symbolically or pictorially. Only then can we really start to patternise and abstract. The book seeks to capture a range of mastery type representations. Structures of representing ideas and resources to assist are discussed in a way that complements the mastery approach which is becoming common in a range of schools.

Generating active thinking (letting the genie out of the bottle!)

If children are encouraged to discuss; if they are given tasks that invite connections to be made, then they are likely to ask questions, some of which you may struggle to deal with adequately straight away. Rather than fear this outcome I would like to encourage you to feel a sense of achievement at facilitating this moment. Sometimes it is fine to say 'I don't know … yet'. If, over a period of time, you learn to respond in a way that addresses the issue, or issues, raised by the child this is believed to be the point at which children are at their most motivated and focused (Rowland et al., 2009). They are ready to learn. The aim of this book is to support you the reader, as either a trainee or new teacher, and to give you a chance of allowing some moments like this to happen. This is the only way we will create confident children who have no fear of maths in the same way that they tackle many other subjects. The genie alluded to in the sub-heading above is the one in the classroom released by teachers teaching through discussion for understanding. It creates active minds in children and makes them question. Any teacher making this happen must be congratulated, regardless of any temporary concern about what the way forward is. It will come sooner or later. School communities are resourceful places. Teachers scaffold each others' learning.

Problem solving

 Learning objectives

By the end of this chapter you should:

* Know how problem solving relates to the national curriculum.
* Recognise the possible gains and challenges that problem solving work brings.
* Understand the importance and the possibilities in teaching for understanding as well as the development of skills and procedures.
* Be able to articulate the learning intentions of problem solving work and to understand how such work can be evaluated.
* Accept and be comfortable with the idea that what may seem unsuccessful in problem solving lessons is often a real improvement on not teaching in this way at all.
* Be confident that dilemmas in teaching in problem solving lessons often occur when understanding is close at hand.

 ## What does the National Curriculum say?

Unlike all the other chapters in the book this one does not relate directly to a particular content feature of the curriculum. Rather, it relates more to a style of teaching and learning that requires commitment to and belief in the benefits of such an approach. This will touch on some mathematical concepts that are explored in depth in later chapters as they demonstrate how problem solving approaches can benefit all aspects of maths teaching. In general terms the new National

Curriculum guidance is clear and yet it relies on an understanding and commitment that less experienced teachers may welcome support in.

National curriculum guidance states that studying mathematics is:

a creative and highly inter-connected discipline that is essential to everyday life, critical to science, technology and engineering, and necessary for financial literacy and most forms of employment. A high-quality mathematics education therefore provides a foundation for understanding the world, the ability to reason mathematically, an appreciation of the beauty and power of mathematics, and a sense of enjoyment and curiosity about the subject. (DfE, 2014)

It then goes to on to state aims for the maths curriculum which are worth repeating in full here in order to analyse what they mean for us as primary teachers:

The National Curriculum for mathematics aims to ensure that all pupils:

- become fluent in the fundamentals of mathematics, including through varied and frequent practice with increasingly complex problems over time, so that pupils develop conceptual understanding and the ability to recall and apply knowledge rapidly and accurately;

- reason mathematically by following a line of enquiry, conjecturing relationships and generalisations, and developing an argument, justification or proof using mathematical language;

- can solve problems by applying their mathematics to a variety of routine and non-routine problems with increasing sophistication, including breaking down problems into a series of simpler steps and persevering in seeking solutions.

Children are encouraged to 'make rich connections across mathematical ideas to develop fluency, mathematical reasoning and competence in solving increasingly sophisticated problems'. (DfE, 2014; National Curriculum, mathematics programmes of study)

Background context and theory

In one sense the above words have very deep significance. However, they would be very well supplemented by some interpretation of these worthy aims: some examples and discussion about how to both provide relevant experiences and attempt to ensure they become meaningful to the children.

Many new primary teachers feel eager to impact on children's learning. They often feel happier to teach safe, structured lessons where some learning is likely to take place. The evidence for this can often be found in work in children's books and answers to questions linking to the lesson's learning intentions. Problem solving does not lend itself easily to such a teaching approach. A different pedagogy and style of engagement is needed as the purpose behind adopting such an approach is to try to nurture children's ability to refine their own thinking. The intention of this chapter is to capture the flavour of what problem solving can achieve in a way that allows new and less experienced teachers to feel that this is something that they can learn to do.

A number of writers talk about children becoming mathematical in their thinking. What does this mean and can those who remain cautious about their ability to develop such thinking feel positive about what they should do? The highbrow terminology can be fairly easily unpicked. Let us focus on one of the avowed aims of the curriculum: '[to] reason mathematically by following a line of enquiry, conjecturing relationships and generalisations, and developing an argument, justification or proof using mathematical language' (DfE, 2014). The words referenced here are worth unravelling and exploring. If children are to develop these skills they will need to be put in positions where related learning, knowledge and confidence may ensue.

Generalising: Haylock (2014: 38) describes a generalisation as 'an observation about something that is always true' at least in a way that is specified. Leone Burton (1985: 38) defines generalisations as statements that emerge from 'the recognition of pattern or regularity'. She notes that these statements are used by learners to create 'order and meaning' out of data and experiences, with number or other learning opportunities. An example of a generalisation might be that 'whole numbers end in zero after they have been multiplied by ten'. It may or may not be true. Just as commutativity, where changing the order of numbers in a sum does not change the result, is only true for some operations (for example, it makes no difference if you add 3 to 7, as in 7 + 3 or 7 to 3, as in 3 + 7, but it would if the numbers were used in subtraction), there is a whole body of debate and discussion waiting to be had for the brave trainee teacher. Children will often think that the reverse to true generalisations will also be true, for example, 'If 3 goes into 12 then 12 goes into 3', which is clearly not always the case. Other qualities and skills related to this kind of reasoning, such as counter examples, deductive reasoning and proof appear in Chapter 7 on algebra.

Conjecturing: To conjecture means to form an opinion on something that is a hunch or feeling. This is an unproven assertion; a working theory. Haylock (2014: 39) argues that the process of 'conjecturing and checking is fundamental to reasoning mathematically'. Another view in mathematics is that conjecturing would tend to follow looking at a range of examples to see patterns and connections and beginning to formulate ideas. As Burton (1985: 38) puts it: 'through conjecturing, a sense of any underlying pattern is explored, expressed, and then substantiated'.

The development of these two skills in particular is heavily hinted at in the National Curriculum. However, my experience with a majority of trainee teachers (but not all) is that these ways of thinking and reasoning were not commonly experienced in their own schools and there is caution about knowing how to promote such thinking. This is understandable and new teachers' engagement with the reasons underlying reluctance to embark on such work just might be the catalyst to breaking the cycle. Reflective trainees and teachers are very motivated to break down barriers to learning – even their own – and hopefully this is something that you will encounter throughout your teacher training and early experience in the classroom.

The relevance of problem solving skills in teaching

Clearly these skills and qualities are important and need a different approach to the idea of focusing on pockets of knowledge to be taught, practised and understood. The emphasis here is on being able to draw on these various pockets of subject knowledge and to start to make sense, see patterns and be curious about mathematical ideas. Vygotsky, among others, would see the link to his notion of the zone of proximal development (ZPD) (Vygotsky, 1978) and it lends itself to children's discussion of ideas and strategies.

What does such thinking look like in practice and how is it brought about? Children often achieve deeper learning when they think actively rather than developing skills through carrying out procedures; however, the results may not be so immediately obvious. This links to both Askew's 'connectionist' teaching mindset (Askew et al., 1997) referenced below and Skemp's 'relational understanding' (1976). First-hand classroom experience shows me young children are very capable of active thinking of this kind. Leone Burton (1985) makes reference to Bruner's idea of resolving 'cognitive conflict' or dissonance as she describes the teaching and learning process related to problem solving. The teacher's role is to be as curious as possible about what children are able to articulate *and* to engage with how relevant it is; both features should guide the teacher into choosing their next action. As Burton describes, 'the key to recognizing and using mathematical thinking lies in creating an atmosphere that builds confidence to question, challenge, and reflect' (1984: 47–8). Behind such behaviour is an acknowledgement of the need to: query assumptions; negotiate meanings; pose questions; make conjectures; search for justifying and falsifying arguments that convince; check, modify, alter opinion; be self-critical; be aware of different approaches; be willing to shift, renegotiate, change direction.

The 'win–win' interpretation of such thinking is that in order to achieve relevant results with your class linked to the skills being discussed you have to possess some self-belief. If you doubt your ability to achieve this, something I tell new trainee teachers is: 'You are what we have. There is no-one else. Be brave. Anything you achieve, in some cases, will exceed what was achieved for you. How good is that?'

In many instances in life we find out two things when we are brave: that we know at least a little more than we thought we did and also, when we have a firmer grasp of what we don't know, we can explore more productively. The need to be brave and to engage directly with problem solving work links closely to the different styles of teaching in maths, highlighted by Mike Askew (Askew et al., 1997). He referenced three main teaching styles common to the primary classroom:

- **Transmission approach:** here the teacher transmits knowledge through instruction, and often exercises and worksheets, to check if the instruction is understood. Many training and practising teachers recognise this as the method of instruction that characterised most of their own school experience of being taught maths.
- **Discovery approach:** here children, possibly through carefully selected tasks, gradually discover through curiosity, knowledge or by solving problems that can be supported by an enlightened teacher.
- **Connectionist approach:** this involves a little of each of the previous two strategies. The teacher focuses their teaching on trying to allow children to see, make and discuss *connected* mathematical knowledge so that the skills and knowledge learnt have a greater chance of being applied in real world problem situations.

Many student teachers, though not all, recognise the transmission of knowledge as the process by which they were taught. Many also cite this as a reason why they feel they were able to pass exams but they don't feel equipped to teach the knowledge effectively. They have strategies to tackle particular work but may not feel clear about why (or if) such strategies work. In short, they feel ill-equipped and ill-prepared to teach effectively for understanding. It's an understandable feeling and one that may ring true with you. Pleasingly, many such student teachers are very motivated to understand the background to their knowledge and to learn how to teach effectively: many would like to teach for understanding. Is it possible? You bet it is! Often, even fleeting moments of achieving something we felt insecure about are the most pleasurable of all.

In problem solving work it is the connectionist approach which is vital. That is not to say that children don't need skills and knowledge to tackle it. They clearly do and much of that knowledge may have been obtained through closed, procedural teaching. However, they need exposure to active thinking. This brings a range of potential pedagogic and emotional challenges for teachers. It also brings the possibility of 'golden moments'.

Big idea

Children's ability to generalise is considered to be indicative of 'genuine mathematical ability' (Haylock, 2014: 45), more so than prowess in routine calculation.

I concur fully. Furthermore a real threat to children attempting to conjecture and generalise is the fear of being wrong. Or, viewed positively, if children are able to see the accuracy and relevance of a generalisation as more important than whether they are right or wrong it seems that this is a key learning strength.

It is the self-belief to think you might be able to think this way and the 'robustness' to learn to deal with the inadequacies of your thinking that are key and have very little direct linkage to maths but everything to do with success in mathematical thinking, success as a learner and possibly professionally, socially and emotionally too in life. I believe this to be one of the main reasons we as teachers *will* strive to overcome our fears of teaching problem solving skills: because we want all children to have this chance. It represents the resilience we all have in our most favoured subject area, in all probability. We are merely beginning the early steps towards this in maths. If children are to deepen the way they know maths they have to be engaged in active thinking. This is where we currently often fail children: by depriving them of the chance to think and make sense of what they are being asked to do. Even if children conjecture, attempt to generalise and get no coherent response they are definitely *no worse off*: they are likely to be better off for the process of thinking that they have been through.

Child development

Fostering problem solving in maths is no different to any other developmental issues with children (and adults). Young children make connections through physical experiences, by being active and having the chance to reflect on their experiences. When given the chance they are never short of ideas to voice; these can be naïve, underdeveloped, relevant, logical or sometimes startlingly profound. Some children will need more visual and, perhaps, practical representations to allow their thinking to develop for subsequent problem solving. Many more sophisticated problems actually draw on a range of skills that can be developed one by one at an earlier stage. For example, young children have both to see the point of a task, or problem, and be interested in tackling it. With older children the same thing applies but they start to get more used to the idea that they are going to be tackling problems anyway as part of their schooling and sometimes the motivation to explore something further emerges as they work.

In primary mathematics problem solving revolves around four main ideas that can be categorised as follows:

* Identifying relevant starting points (this is particularly important in logic problems).
* Sequencing, identifying and illustrating patterns.
* Working out all possibilities.
* Representation (are problems represented visually, or can they be made to be this way?).

Children tackling problem solving work in mathematics will be dealing with one or more of these concepts. We will now explore a number of selected problems and activities that explore the potential merits and dilemmas of teaching and learning related to problem solving. Many of these will touch on the four ideas listed above, for example, the problem named 'Got it/21' shows how three, if not four, of these qualities could be present in one problem.

Two of these problems, 'Bipods and Tripods' and 'Card Sharp', first appeared in the document 'Mathematical challenges for able pupils in Key Stages 1 and 2' (DfEE, 2000), which offered teachers practical activities to support the then National Numeracy Strategy. Although the national strategies are no longer current policy, many of the activities designed to support them are equally useful today in exploring key concepts in the classroom. In discussing these we set out the initial problem and explore the problem solving in greater depth.

 ## Activity: Bipods and Tripods

Learning intention: Understanding patterns and reasoning with concrete resources

This is a classic maths problem with a space theme that should be appropriate for children in Key Stage 1 and lower Key Stage 2.

Problem: Some Tripods and Bipods flew from planet Zeno. There were at least two of each of them. Tripods have 3 legs. Bipods have 2 legs. There were 23 legs altogether.

How many Tripods were there? How many Bipods? Find two different answers (DfEE, 2000).

This problem has several themes that can be explored:

- It explores the different combinations that can be made with multiples of 2 and 3.
- It is context-specific in as much as it has a real life relevance (or would do if aliens existed).
- There is scope to discuss the different combinations of odd and even numbers as Bipods are even and Tripods are odd.
- There is a clear opportunity to create early forms of abstraction in children's thinking by using physical resources to represent the aliens and support reasoning and deductions.
- It is an example where all four features of problem solving listed above could be present.

There are several possible ways to develop or structure children's investigation of this problem.

One way is to identify a total number of legs that children have to make in different ways, for example:

8 legs

Solution 1 = 2 Tripods and a Bipod = 3 + 3 + 2

Solution 2 = 4 Bipods = 2 + 2 + 2 + 2

12 legs

Solution 1 = 4 Tripods = 3 + 3 + 3 + 3

Solution 2 = 2 Tripods and 3 Bipods = 3 + 3 + 2 + 2 + 2

Solution 3 = 6 Bipods = 2 + 2 + 2 + 2 + 2 + 2

An alternative option is to find ways to make different totals and to see which totals can be made the most ways. This could be developed further to allow children to take control of their own learning. For example, having established the nature of the Bipods and Tripods concept, children could be invited to think about other things they could investigate such as:

- How could Numicon resources support the investigation? (Numicon is a popular mathematical resource, or manipulative, that will be covered in greater depth in later chapters.)
- Which other numbers of legs could we investigate for the aliens?
- Are there any combinations of alien legs that won't work for certain numbers?
- What is a 'real life' situation where you might want to know this information? For example, if a group of aliens were at the bottom of the garden and you could see their legs under the fence, but not their heads, you would have an idea about the possible number of aliens there were.

Patterns in children's thinking are so crucial and big moments happen for children at different times. For very young children in Reception and Year 1, Numicon pieces (Figure 1.1) or colour-coded Multilink patterns offer many possibilities. The odd pieces are recognisable with the isolated extra square.

A. Odd + Odd = Even
B. Even + Even = Even
C. Even + Odd = Odd
D. Odd + Even = Odd

As we can see with the Numicon pieces the only way to end up with an odd number (of legs) is if there are an odd number of tripods (Numicon piece 3). Encouraging children to make these connections can be grown visually through the use of physical objects (Numicon, cubes, matchsticks and so on) and through discussion.

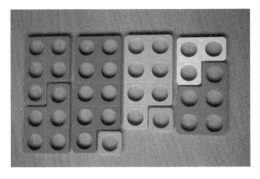 

 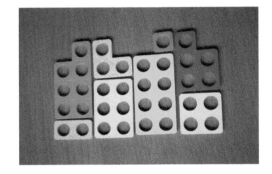

Figure 1.1 Numicon arrangements of numbers demonstrating, visually, the proofs in the relationships between odd and even numbers with addition

It is important wherever possible to allow children a chance to have a go and to see how they get on. If they are doing this and seem to be making progress, some positive remarks catching good moments could be useful. If they are struggling there are two basic choices.

One is to clarify and scaffold the task again. For example: 'Who thinks they have an idea of what is needed here?' Then, depending on the response you receive, add to it. Alternatively, simply decide what they are not getting and guide them towards understanding. For example, when working with the problem is possible to say something along the lines of: 'Here are two choices to make 8 legs. One is wrong, one is right. Talk to your partner about which is which: 2 + 2 + 2 + 2 and 2 + 2 + 4' (the latter method being impossible because neither Bipods nor Tripods have 4 legs).

Children don't all make connections at the same time in the same way. Different triggers assist different children. Many children need time to allow themselves to become immersed in the issue in front of them; even then understanding and discovery are not guaranteed. Therefore, although complete mastery by the teacher of the related mathematical thinking involved could be of assistance, in reality it is not a guarantee; discovery can be present in any learning situation, whether the teacher realises it or not. The best we can say is that enlightened teachers may be able to prompt and guide better but sometimes this can be at the expense of children thinking independently.

Activity: Got it (also known as '21')

Learning intention: Reasoning and justifying through game situations. Identifying key information

This is a strategy game that is appropriate for children in Key Stage 2, although simplified versions with smaller targets could be used in Key Stage 1. Alternative playing instructions including a playable online game appear on the NRICH website (http://nrich.maths.org/1272).

How to play: Two people take it in turns to raise a total from zero up to 21. Each player may add 1, 2 or 3 to the total. The winner is the person who gets to say the total 21.

You might present a worked example at some point to see if the rules were understood. For example: 'Here is how two children played. Here are the numbers they said. Player A calls the numbers in black. Player B calls the numbers in red. Talk to your partner to see if you think there is a problem with either game. One game has been played correctly, the other has an error in it' (Table 1.1).

Table 1.1   Two examples of Got it/21

Game 1	2	3	5	8	11	12	13	15	17	19	21
Game 2	2	4	7	10	14	16	17	18	21		

In the second game to jump from 10 to 14 is not allowed using these rules because the maximum jump size is 3; so 13 would be the highest number reachable from 10.

The purpose of this game is to begin to get the children to see that it isn't luck that decides the winner. There are patterns involved that link to the rules of the game.

 ## Big ideas

- Children (and adults) often make connections when they actively participate and have to buy into the point and purpose of what they are doing.
- They will often instinctively start to make connections, even without being asked to, when they are actively involved.
- Children are often the sum of their journey in life. They may be afraid to be wrong, they can lose heart. They may be determined or canny, they may squirrel ideas away or they may share them. Handling these phenomena is an important pedagogical issue; these life skills go way beyond problem solving in maths.

Many children start to realise that by saying 18, 19 or 20 you then lose the game. Others can state that if you can say 17 you can win. This articulation will often be hesitant as children reach for language to try to explain things that cognitively they are starting to make some sense of. This is valuable territory and teachers should seek to avoid filling in the gaps to move things along. You may find that children start to draw on other ideas which may or may not be correct, such as 'You can't predict what the other person will say and so it is a chance game'.

A typical interaction involving children starting to grasp the concept could be as follows:

Annabel: 'You win when you say 17. I can't explain ... but you do.'
Bilal: 'It's because you can say 21 but they can't. They can't reach it ... but you can.'

These ideas are a long way from the following, robust articulation.

Charlie: '17 is a number to say. If you can say this number your opponent only has 3 choices to say: 18, 19 or 20. Whichever of the three they say I can still say 21.'
Teacher: 'That's very good Charlie.'
Charlie: 'Not really because I haven't yet worked out how to make sure I can be the one to say 17. Kelly is beating me 3–2 at the moment!'

It is not only Charlie's articulation of his thinking that is relevant but his ability to start to judge effectively, for himself, the relevance of his strategies and ideas. To my mind these are all versions of positive remarks. They are a work in progress; a journey towards confident conjecturing. Any nurturing, objective teacher interventions are to be welcomed, but not solutions because the journey stops then. If nothing is offered by the teacher (perhaps because they don't know what to say) then so be it. Nothing has been lost.

Got it/21 can involve three of the big problem solving ideas mentioned earlier in this chapter:

* It is an example of a logic problem. It needs a significant piece of information for us to begin to unlock the problem. In this instance knowing that we are only able to add 1, 2 or 3 is a starting point that can lead to realising that if the other person says 17 you should lose.
* It is a problem that can be represented visually. The target score of 21 can be made visual through recording your numbers on a numberline or using physical resources such as a 100 square or Numicon pieces.
* Identifiable patterns and sequences exist which can help us to understand how the game works. The totals or the numbers added on may change (for example, you could play 'Got it/18' and add 1, 2, 3 or 4 each turn) but there are relationships that can be captured and adapted.

When the total is 21 you are able to win by plotting a pathway through these 'magic' numbers: 1, 5, 9, 13, 17, 21. These numbers can be controlled because they have a difference of 4, which is one more than the most that can be added in any single turn. There are 'magic numbers' regardless of the total or numbers allowed to be added. The link is between the maximum add-on (M) and the 'destination total' (DT) in this case 21. This can give us a winning formula $= DT - (M + 1) - 2(M + 1) - 3(M + 1)$, etc. (Algebra is covered in depth in Chapter 7.)

Big idea

The teacher's role is to allow active participation and wherever possible to ask questions that move children's thinking forward. It is not necessarily to give them the answers.

Questions to ask, which touch on some of the teaching strategies discussed above might include:

- Is it just luck who wins?
- Can you tell if you are going to win or lose? If so, when?
- Does it make a difference to go first?
- Are you able to explain what you have found out?
- What would happen if we played up to a different total? (Lower totals can be useful with young or less secure children.)
- What would happen if we allowed a different maximum number to be added, such as just 1 or 2 or 1, 2, 3 or 4?

One way of encouraging active participation would be to organise a tournament that would take place between different tables after a period of time. This would allow group discussion and give an overt purpose to the activity. Whole class discussion can take place after the tournament when everyone is ready to discuss their experiences. An important point to stress here that will apply across all maths teaching is that there will be times when children say ideas that you aren't clear about yourself. You may not be able to respond appropriately straight away. Do not worry. This is *important* territory. What might you say if a child says something that you are unclear about the validity of? Here are some options to consider:

- Certainly it's good to use a 'play for time' option and say something like 'Oooh, that sounds interesting. Say it again.'
- You can also ask for other views on the point made.

- You can express interest and say 'I'm going to make a note of that and see how relevant that is. Thank you.' (Physically writing the comment down is validation in itself.)
- Further than this, it is good to have another member of staff or friend, partner or parent who you could discuss it with. If you are able to get back to any comments in a later lesson this shows the children that you run an active, ongoing learning environment. No child, teacher or parent is the font of all knowledge.
- Challenges such as 'I wonder if Kelly is right. I wonder if adding consecutive numbers always gives an odd total' could be explored independently. Connections of any kind are often not explored deeply in school and they need to be to develop confidence in children's understanding.

Big ideas

- It is far, far better to generate thinking and ideas in your classroom that you aren't totally sure about than to stick to your comfort zone. The process of active thinking in maths in this country is very underdeveloped. Any progress here is to be welcomed.
- You cannot predict what children will say but you can commit to applying a particular strategy or philosophy to what they say.

Activity: Solving codes

Learning intention: Further reasoning and deduction in problem solving within game situations

This activity can take the form of the Mastermind board game that has been popular since the 1970s. In essence though, whether it has visual codes or numerical ones, the real skill being developed is clear and it is deep. This is an appropriate activity for Key Stage 2. Children have the opportunity to make multiple connections, to make deductions from a series of interconnected pieces of information. It is a logic game that can function at a very high level. The beauty of it is that there is the real opportunity for children to learn by doing and to operate at a level suited to them. In addition, the articulation of the deductions being made by children is excellent, not only for their own mathematical thinking but also as a catalyst to develop the thinking of those around them. Thus, codes of different levels of complexity can be tackled by children of different current abilities: crucially, as a catalyst to active mathematical thinking paired work in solving such problems is proven strategy. This problem certainly fits paired work well and

Figure 1.2   Code cracking symbols

having partners with slightly different ability can be very productive. Vygotsky's zones of proximal development (ZPD) (1978) are relevant here as the less secure partner latches onto the thinking of the more knowledgeable other. The ebb and flow of being near enough in ability means that the pendulum of confidence can swing as one learns and then leads. The problem is set up as follows.

Four of the six symbols in Figure 1.2 have been arranged to make a code.

The task is to identify which of the four have been arranged to form a code and to decipher the order that the four symbols have been placed in. Figure 1.3 shows a solver's attempt to crack the code. A '√' indicates a correct symbol in a correct position, a '?' indicates a correct symbol in an incorrect position. The correct solution that you see at the bottom has been concealed from the code solver.

Turn	Solver's guess				Results				Commentary
#1	¥	◉	☼	♣	√	?	?		Random guess. One is correct but it isn't clear which one. Two have been identified but the placing is incorrect. One symbol has yet to be identified.
#2	◉	◉	♣	♣	?	?			Strategy. Two symbols have been chosen to try to gain more information. There are now two symbols incorrectly placed.
#3	♣	♣	◉	◉	√	√			Swapping symbols around means we have now two correctly placed but it's not clear which symbol is correct.
#4	▮	♣	☼	◉	√	?	?		Two other symbols are tried. There are now 4 lines of information to track back over. Still only three choices are correct.
#5	¥	♣	◉	▮	√	√	√	√	The red symbol must be involved and a mixture of deduction and luck solves the code
	¥	♣	◉	▮					CODE

Figure 1.3   An annotated example of the code cracking game

The same problem can also be set using the numbers 1, 2, 3, 4, 5 or 6 (Figure 1.4).

You could also shorten the code to three digits and limit the range of numbers to 1, 2, 3 and 4 (Figure 1.5).

Turn	Solver's guess				Results			Commentary
#1	1	3	5	6	?	?		Wild guess. Only two correct, which means the missing two need to be tried.
#2	4	1	2	3	√	√	?	Getting more information.
#3	4	5	2	1	√	?	?	
#4	4				√			Just putting 4 in to see if it is in the right place. This proves to be correct.
#5	4	1	1	1	√	√		I find out that 1 is in the code and then I look back to Line 2 to find out it must be in the same spot.
#6	4	1	6	2	√	√	√ √	2 is in the code and looking back at Line 2 it must be in a different space leaving the 6 to go in this position.
	4	1	6	2				CODE

Figure 1.4 Playing the code cracking game with digits instead of symbols

Turn	Solver's guess			Results			Commentary
#1	2	3	1	?	?		3 Numbers so a free run at it.
#2	4	2	3	?	?		Only two in the first line are in the code and so 4 is definitely part of it. Guesswork about which one it replaces.
#3	1	2	4	√	?	?	Finally found which 3 numbers make the code and one of them is correctly placed.
#4	1	4	2	√	√	√	2 was incorrectly placed in Line 1 and Line 2 so has to be correct in this line. Therefore the 4 in Line 3 isn't in the correct place. This means that the 1 must have been correct in Line 3.
	1	4	2				CODE

Figure 1.5 Playing the code cracking game with three digits (selected from 1–4)

An online version of this problem is 'Crack the Code' at the echalk website (found at: http://bit.ly/1nd0Acs). It serves as a visual basis on a screen where lots of shared discussion can take place. There is a lot of scope for reasoning and conjecturing here. The articulation of thinking is an important part of this experience.

Activity: Card sharp

Learning intention: To begin to solve mathematical problems or puzzles. Know addition facts to at least 10. Solve a problem by sorting, classifying and organising information

This activity is appropriate across Key Stages 1 and 2. To start we need a set of 10 cards numbered 0 to 9.

1. Pick three cards with a total of 12. You can do it in 10 different ways. See if you can record them all.
2. Now pick four cards with a total of 12. How many different ways can you do it?
3. Can you pick five cards with a total of 12? (DfEE, 2000)

The answer to the first question here should be the following combinations: (0, 3, 9), (0, 4, 8), (0, 5, 7), (1, 5, 6), (1, 4, 7), (1, 3, 8), (1, 2, 9), (2, 3, 7), (2, 4, 6) and (2, 5, 7).

This kind of problem is vital to the process of being able to organise work to find out all possibilities. This is crucial to all life situations involving a finite amount of possibilities. This has real world links with probability and planning and calculation linked to this, for example, insurance. It is part of coherent, logical thinking. You can share with your class how many different possibilities there are. This can either give them a goal to aim for or impede them as they move towards another significant goal of 'knowing when they have finished the task'. Potential pitfalls for the Card Sharp activity include children struggling to sustain momentum, and they can lack a strategy to know when they are repeating combinations (for example, 0, 3, 9 or 9, 0, 3) unless the order is significant. Clearly the total could be changed to a different one.

It is generally thought that when there is a real dilemma that has to be resolved then children are more receptive to analysing such problems more closely as the relevance of the work impacts on their understanding. Therefore, consider designing problems relating to, for example, school photos, the school tuck shop, school dinners, playground rotas, that have real immediate relevance to children whose world is affected by the issue being investigated. More sophisticated real world links could be made to teaching about number combinations; for example, if you want to predict the first three home in a running race do you just want to say who they will be or do you want to know the order in which they will finish? Or, does a company simply need to know the bestselling three products on the market or the specific order in which they are ranked to be able to analyse why a particular brand or product is doing so well?

Pedagogical issues with teaching problem solving

What knowledge does the teacher need?

The main thing required from the new teacher, is not confidence, but the willingness to expose children to problems and thinking of solutions. Try to allow them a chance to make links and develop some strategies.

Does it matter if I don't know how to respond to comments from children or assess their relevance?

It helps if you are able to make a meaningful response, better still if you can bring in other children to offer responses; but it isn't crucial. The process is everything. Reflective and conscientious teachers will note comments they can't resolve for themselves and find ways after the lesson to clarify their understanding further; this is modelling excellent practice with regard to learning.

Motivating and sustaining attention

Effective teaching of problem solving requires a range of problems to cover and develop thinking in a range of situations. It emphasises trying things out that may not work. Elimination of certain ideas needs to be stressed and valued, for example, 'Well done you've found out something that definitely isn't relevant' is a positive statement that allows a teacher to reward a child's observation and also move the lesson on. This is a generic teaching attribute which many teachers become very good at quite quickly. They understand how children need nurturing and how to engage them. It is why knowledge of child development and generic teaching knowledge are essential to good primary maths teaching. Subject knowledge is needed too but can be learnt and added to; without the generic knowledge it is almost redundant.

How to avoid telling (including questioning skills)

If we accept that, in the main, telling children strategies and solutions in open-ended work is counterproductive to the purpose of the task, then we need to engage with the pedagogical issue of how to move children's thinking forward, and refine their ideas, without telling them the answer or 'leading the witness'. This can be done by adopting a not-knowing position, or 'leading from the back' (a developed example of using a deliberate mistake-making puppet is explored in Chapter 2 on maths in the early years). The aim of problem solving work is for children to develop strategies and ways of thinking that may come in useful. They need to be able to make mistakes and to put their thinking into words. This requires curiosity and interest from the teacher even when what they are saying may be incorrect. Too often classroom dialogue lapses into children trying to guess what the teacher wants to hear. You don't learn what the children really think and understand when this occurs. Sometimes you see something clever and you may want to draw reference to it; if children are struggling then this can be really useful. Another approach is getting them to talk about what it is they aren't sure of. This can allow you to evaluate and possibly assist. Can they put into words what they are finding hard to do or to understand?

Prompts to provoke thinking and activity (as opposed to telling)

Knowing how to prompt, generate discussion and disagreement to deepen thinking and understanding are desirable. Skills and strategies learnt, personally, by children in one situation often have relevance to other problems. Relevant teacher behaviour to establish and maintain this kind of classroom atmosphere is reflected in the use of questions such as:

- 'Why do you think that?'
- 'What do you notice?'
- 'Is there another way?'
- 'What if …? Can you convince a friend?'

(Burton, 1984: 48)

A typical teaching interaction involving these principles could be as follows:

Teacher: 'Ah. As I understand it, I see you think that adding 10 will always make the number end in zero, as in 30 + 10 or 70 + 10. OK. I follow that, but what if the starting number was 13 or 64 and you add 10. Does it still end in zero?'

In this example children are then given further time to conjecture and reason about what happens when you add 10 to a number. In our base 10 counting system adding 10 means an adjustment of 1 in the 10s column and maybe the creation of a new multiple of 100. The units column (and other columns) remain unchanged (a detailed discussion of our number system and these related concepts is covered in Chapter 3 on place value).

One way of supporting children here is to ask 'Can you find a counter example?'. In fact the previous example from the teacher is a counter example, as 13 + 10 and 64 + 10 don't fit the child's conjecture about adding 10 creating a number that ends in zero (see also the discussion of 'Never, sometimes, always' probability work in Chapter 9 on statistics).

The role of the teacher is to generate the above circumstances by fuelling curiosity and embodying a suspended state of not quite knowing while allowing the children to evaluate things for themselves. Some teachers find this hard, and guide and scaffold too much, although this is understandable if they want to maintain enthusiasm and avoid children feeling inadequate and unsure. If you find that you are falling into this trap remember there *is* a place for instruction, skill development and basic learning and understanding in maths. However, problem solving is about giving children the chance to develop ways of making sense of situations and problems. This means helping them towards a real ownership of what they are doing. Opportunities to do so should take place in all areas of maths; however, there is an actual pedagogy of engagement specific to the process of problem solving.

Finding the right question

This skill is one that can be worked on over a period of time, and is likely to be one that as teachers we can in fact refine over a whole career. Children are often motivated to disprove something; it can stimulate and provide a focus and energy for them. They sometimes struggle to distinguish between knowing whether something is sometimes or always true. Therefore the ability to ask a question that allows them to focus on an inconsistency in their thinking is important. So our teacher in the 'adding 10' discussion above might have said: 'That's a good discussion. I follow your thinking. Can you think of any numbers that your idea won't work for?' or alternatively 'Do you think it is possible to halve a number and get an even number?'. In doing so the teacher is using content and subject knowledge to move the discussion forward as well as evaluating what the children are able to do independently. Following this latter line of investigation, a further prompt might be to say: 'Yes, I can see 13 is half of 26 and 15 is half of 30. Good. You can get back to your starting number by doubling the odd number you got when you halved. So won't doubling an even number work in the same way?'.

These are just possible examples of guiding children's thinking; there are many questions or comments that could be helpful in developing understanding and if, when starting out in the classroom, you manage none of them then nothing has been lost. The children are applying something they have discovered that works in some cases and assumed the relationship will apply in all circumstances. It is good that they are attempting to conjecture. The skill, for us as teachers is to move the child's thinking forward by prompting, facilitating, provoking. Vygotsky might refer to this as allowing a child or peer to act as a scaffold. This is often effective at a deeper level than the teacher telling or judging. Vygotsky argued that this worked best when the gap between the two peers is not too great; this is also supported by the work of Howe and Mercer (2007) related to effective small group work.

How to structure and organise teaching sessions

We have considered content and the role of the teacher. It is also useful to have a rationale for how the children will work. Listed below are some of the possible options for inclusion in your lesson planning:

- Competition, working in pairs or threes to encourage collaborative thinking and motivation.
- Either a) naming the final outcome number to clarify the goal or b) deliberately avoiding making the final total clear.
- In 'find all the solutions' problems, such as the 'Card Sharp' activity discussed earlier, consider investing time to check combinations that are repeated or highlighting where children have repeated any combination.
- Follow-up activities that are similar or that allow children to think up their own similar-style investigation. For example, on work concerning number combinations, choose six of your friends to work out all the ways that they could be split into two dormitories on a school journey, one with four in it the other with two.
- Checking other groups' work for repetition.
- After clarifying the outcomes, a debriefing talk could be very useful, with children sharing, discussing and evaluating strategies.
- Less confident children can be supported through resources (such as Numicon, cubes, a more confident peer and so on).
- Consider ways to extend more confident thinking. This would involve either more challenging tasks or allowing children to apply their own, newly acquired knowledge to think up related activities either for other children to tackle or to be the basis of a whole class discussion through a visualiser at the end of the lesson.

Being clear on the purpose and valuing the journey as much as the outcomes

This means devoting time, commitment and validity to what children actually think and giving yourself credit for asking questions and generating discussion. I have been known to punch my fist, quietly, in triumph, when I ask a question rather than tell, or when I resist personally responding to what a child has said but manage, instead, to ask what other children think about what they have just heard. Good teaching is often linked to having an appropriate level of challenge; encouraging an atmosphere of problem solving as a work-in-progress. Given that the aim is to develop styles of thinking and ways of working, the temptation to tell answers or give leading clues is a real one.

It is of course a challenge to move children's thinking on when the traditional standard approach of 'telling them what to do' has been ruled out. Rather, teachers developing problem solving techniques or resilience in children are attempting to develop qualities in them that are ultimately going to serve them well in working independently where they have to decide for themselves if something is relevant or valid; whether it will be a discovery or strategy that unlocks a particular problem is only partly relevant. One classroom motto that can be beneficial is that 'You often have to be wrong to be right'. It is through adapting the flawed ideas that more rigorous ones are allowed to emerge. Any progress that is made here means the teacher's choice of lesson and content has been a good one. If no obvious progress has been made (and we don't always know whether this is so) nothing has been lost. As the saying goes, you can't catch a fish without throwing in a line!

Haylock (2014) references the process of children problem solving as 'bridging the gap'. The gap relates to what the children are sure about and what they need to know. Regarding convergent thinking (where different paths end up in the same place) and divergent thinking (different solutions as well as strategies are possible) some problems lend themselves to one and some to others. In a problem such as 'Cost out a two-week holiday for four people in the south of France' there could be a multiplicity of ways of both organising and tackling the problem (divergent thinking). In a problem such as Got it/21, discussed earlier in this chapter, we are talking about a strategy game that is moving towards a multi-part solution that can be understood on different levels. This is an example of convergent thinking in as much as it is the same idea accessed in different ways. This is a challenge for some teachers as they seek to be clear what the outcomes of the lesson should be. In addition, we are often expected to identify different learning outcomes for different groups of children; a more detailed discussion of learning intentions and success criteria will be explored in Chapter 3 on place value, and we will link activities.

Types of problem to use

Having discussed pedagogical issues and strategies to consider in lesson planning it makes sense to reiterate the four main variations on problems, discussed earlier, as a guide to the range of different problems we can use in teaching.

- *Working out all possibilities* (possible activities include: 'How many ways can 20p be made?' or Card sharp).
- *Identifying relevant starting points* (this includes logic problems such as the code cracking game, Got it and Sudoku).
- *Sequencing, identifying and illustrating patterns* (again, Got it can be tackled as can the 'Handshake problem', discussed in Chapter 7 on algebra, that asks how many hands are shaken when *x* people shake hands).
- *Problems that are represented visually or can be made to be this way* (the Handshake problem, Got it and Cracking the code all apply here).

It isn't that children need to know how to work out the specific solution to the Handshake problem or any other classroom activity in order to gain a life skill. These kinds of problem come up time and again in life situations, including later in the world of work. The experience of tackling similar problems means that it is the *process*, rather than any one formula, that can be applied to finding solutions. This approach forms the belief that solutions are possible.

What if they don't discover anything of any significance?

Discussion about problems can begin from a very young age. Reception children can follow visual, and sometimes complex patterns. However, clearly they won't always make all of the connections that you might hope for. Sometimes they may make very few. It does give you a chance to evaluate what they are struggling with. Younger children can have less 'staying power' and so perhaps designing an activity so that some success is guaranteed is often more necessary. However, an important teaching skill is being able to adapt a task to increase the difficulty to provide more challenge and active thinking when it is needed.

Linking problem solving work to learning outcomes and evidence of progress

Table 1.2 lists the main activities from this chapter and suggests potential learning intentions that would underpin each of them, and success criteria that can be used to assess children's learning.

The activities discussed in this chapter are only a small selection of possible tasks you can use in your classroom, and the learning intentions and success criteria will change depending on the nature of the problem you are setting. However, they should relate to any of the important skills and mathematical thinking that we are seeking to develop through problem solving and applying knowledge (Table 1.3).

Table 1.2 Learning intentions and success criteria for problem solving activities

Problem	Learning intentions	Success criteria
Bipods and Tripods Year 2 or Year 3	Children learn to use and adapt trial and error methods to problem solve. Children learn to listen to and articulate their own ideas to problem solve. Children begin to use conjecturing and argument to understand and explain problems and solutions.	Children can *all* use Numicon or cubes to help solve Bipod and Tripod investigation. *Some* children can devise ways to avoid repeating solutions. Children can begin to articulate why some combinations of alien legs work better than others. (This may have been preceded by children choosing their own alien leg numbers to investigate; it may not all get covered in one session.)
Got it/21	Children are able to play Got it independently. Children develop and adapt strategies. Children learn to match their own thoughts with those of their peers.	All children can collaborate to discuss and articulate strategies. Some children can distinguish between worthwhile conjectures and only partly relevant ones and prove why they work. Some children can adapt the strategies if the rules are changed (for example, if more or less numbers are to be added or a different total).
Card sharp	Children are able to adjust solutions to make new ones. Children are able to create methods to avoid repeating solutions. Children can adapt strategies to tackle amended tasks, such as making 11 or 9.	For this activity the learning intentions can also function as success criteria. Some children will, in all probability only be able to use trial and error strategies, or follow patterns with Numicon. Review whether children can articulate why some totals have more solutions; conjecture and reason likely patterns with larger numbers.

Burton (1984: 38) captures other features and qualities that can be used for two things: one is to justify why we are teaching in this way; the other is to inform what we might be seeking to evaluate in the children we teach; our assessment of and for learning. Primary children should be developing these kinds of qualities. Initially they may well need a strong scaffold, support using visual or physical representations of mathematical problems and various kinds of discussion to draw out their thinking. Their voices have to be heard and valued; even if their thinking is sometimes flawed.

Table 1.3   List of related skills and mathematical thinking we are seeking to develop through problem solving and applying knowledge

Solving problems	Testing
Representing	Abstracting
Enquiring	Generalising
Reasoning	Modifying
Communicating	Reasoning
Searching for patterns	Modelling
Patterning	Recording
Conjecturing	Justifying
Verifying	

This chapter has aimed to put some flesh on the worthy aims of the new National Curriculum, with an emphasis on problem solving and reasoning skills; skills such as conjecturing and generalising that assist the finding of successful solutions. The aim has been to allow an insight into what planned and accountable learning outcomes would look like in a theme where it is the process as much as the outcome that is being developed and that will need evaluation. Although work in this area can leave us on the edge of our comfort zones we would do well to remember we can do little to harm children in encountering areas where neither we nor the children are completely sure about the validity of what has been said. This can be both scary and exciting but it is ultimately rewarding for both you and the children that you teach because any clarification, then or in a future lesson, means that real active mathematical thinking is or has been taking place.

Here is a list of reflective activities that you should consider as a means to further develop your teaching skills relating to problem solving in the classroom:

1   Select an example of a problem for children to solve from the list of resources at the end of this chapter, or something similar. Consider the discussion on learning outcomes and think what learning intentions might be appropriate for the chosen example.

2   Observe a problem solving lesson. What examples of children's ideas are part of the lesson? How are their ideas voiced and what value is given to flawed thinking? After the lesson note any areas that you feel went well and any which may have been less successful.

3   Once you have read the rest of this book consider how you can apply your new thinking to the topics covered in other chapters, so that work that perhaps starts out as procedural and skill-based can be turned into something more creative and open-ended.

4   Make two lists on a piece of paper. Title one of them 'Reasons why you might be reluctant to tackle problem solving work', title the other 'Developments that would make you more willing to try to teach these kinds of lessons'. Share your lists with colleagues to discuss ways in which their lists would differ and why.

5   Consider what may happen if no work of this nature takes place for a class of children across the year.

Conclusion

We have looked at the references to the National Curriculum regarding problem solving in mathematics. It is clear that it is seen as crucial to life chances, although the details on how to teach it through everyday work are less clear in the document. We have explored some theory, which you may wish to look at more closely, surrounding the teaching pedagogy of problem solving. It is different to more traditional maths as the focus is on developing styles of working rather than specific content. We have used some activity case studies, both as a basis to explore the teacher role in context and as a basis for being able to articulate problem solving work through lesson plans and learning outcomes. Hopefully you have taken on board a key message: *engaging children in active thinking through problem solving is vital*. Any gains in this area are special. There are numerous possible ways to respond to different situations. If you feel you chose the wrong one or get stuck then so be it; there's always next time. Whatever you do or attempt is likely to be a lot more beneficial than sticking to a diet of teaching procedurally the whole time where no active thinking takes place.

Resources

NRICH (nrich.maths.org): Interactive and non-interactive website with a vast array of investigations and activities relevant across all ages from early years to degree level and beyond.

BEAM – Be A Mathematician (beam.co.uk): Application of knowledge publications. Supported by a wide range of primary mathematician specialists.

CAME – Cognitive Accelerated Mathematics Education Programme (http://bit.ly/1PXFCpD): A range of mathematical activities closely linked to mathematical thinking, reasoning and collaboration.

Mathszone (http://mathszone.co.uk): A wide range of interactive maths programmes including application of knowledge, drawn from different websites.

Mathematical understanding in the early years

✓ **Learning objectives**

By the end of this chapter you should:

- Be aware of the mathematical requirements in the early years curriculum.
- Have a clear understanding of the role of an adult in young children's active maths learning.
- Be able to distinguish between children taking part in maths and taking control of their own understanding.
- Understand the need to both model and interact with young children to move their mathematical thinking forward.
- Appreciate the benefits of encouraging young children to represent their own mathematical understanding as well as to learn and use standard symbols and representations of mathematical meaning.
- Recognise that a wide range of contexts exists that children can access to develop mathematical understanding further.

The chapter will focus on a range of issues related to pedagogy for maths teaching and learning, suited to the early years. It will discuss topical tensions about understanding, teacher knowledge, telling or facilitating and ownership of learning by children. It will explore a range of activities across the maths curriculum with reference to both what might be achieved with young children and how.

Teaching and learning mathematics in the early years is a beautiful challenge to adults. It involves revisiting the earliest part of our own lives; it also involves trying to split ourselves off from the sense and understanding we made of the world afterwards so we can understand the world as it exists to young children.

Hopefully, when we were young we prospered and learnt to think mathematically with confidence; sadly this is not a given. A lot of excellent teachers, trainees and aspiring teachers had an indifferent or minimal experience of maths as a young child. This was often followed by a confusing and at times unhappy experience of secondary school maths, encountering a range of teachers from the knowledgeable but unenthusiastic through to the inappropriate and impatient. Thankfully, through all stages of education there have been pockets of extremely effective and inspiring practice led by committed teachers with knowledge, understanding and emotional intelligence. At times these kinds of people have been involved in shaping early years maths experiences at national level.

What can we glean from what we are required to teach in the early, or foundation, years of school to assist us as we strive to initiate the process of promoting sound mathematical understanding and thinking? Well, in fact, as you will most likely have realised, the process begins well in advance of young children ever arriving at school. In fact it starts arguably from the moment we are born.

Key considerations that will underpin this chapter include: the main issues linked to young children learning maths and how can we make them more confident and motivated to enjoy and achieve in maths. How do we overcome some of the anxieties and inadequacies many of us felt? How can we avoid transferring such unhelpful feelings and experiences?

What does the Early Years Foundation Stage say?

Valid from September 2014, this document lays out in three fairly short paragraphs the general expectation of what maths in the Foundation Stage should be looking to achieve.

Mathematics involves providing children with opportunities to develop and improve their skills in counting, understanding and using numbers, calculating simple addition and subtraction problems; and to describe shapes, spaces, and measures.

Numbers: children count reliably with numbers from 1 to 20, place them in order and say which number is one more or one less than a given number. Using quantities and objects, they add and subtract two single-digit numbers and count on or back to find the answer. They solve problems, including doubling, halving and sharing.

Shape, space and measures: children use everyday language to talk about size, weight, capacity, position, distance, time and money to compare quantities and objects and to solve problems. They recognise, create and describe patterns. They explore 12 characteristics of everyday objects and shapes and use mathematical language to describe them. (DfE, 2014: 8)

The debate about the content, such as has been stated here, is not really the issue; the knowledge requirement has been made reasonably clear. The real debate is about how to engage young children so that they are able to understand what they are doing as well as follow instructions about how to address a given task or problem. For this to happen children have to be engaged in what they are doing and be given the opportunity to take control of their own learning.

Developing and consolidating mathematical understanding with role play

One of the key features of early years settings for 3, 4 and 5 year olds is the opportunity to experiment with role play. Engaging, context-specific situations have been set up by creative early years practitioners seeking to facilitate fantasy and reality play and experiments by young children that would draw in mathematical issues in context. This might include shops (amounts and prices), cafés (money, amounts), hospitals (measuring), train stations and airports (money, time). These could inspire writing opportunities, mimicking or copying numbers or writing, counting and estimating. Although this has potential it can be problematic. Perceptive early years teachers and adults have often valued the quality of play and exploration that can emerge here but, ultimately, have been disappointed with the quality of maths output from the children.

To intervene or not to intervene?

Some early years practitioners have been reluctant to guide the development of mathematical thinking and activity in role play areas feeling that they are stifling children's creativity and, in turn, their understanding if they impose things on children who may not naturally have undertaken things in that way. This *laissez faire* approach can fail to assist mathematical understanding and a more proactive approach is often needed. Young children in role play situations will naturally reach for language and emotional exploration and fantasy; yet they only reach for mathematical language and discovery in a spontaneous way very, very rarely.

Sad though this appears to be it doesn't mean that there isn't a rich vein of interest and discovery to be harvested; however, it may require a more proactive adult approach than the idealists among us might like.

The pedagogy of 'not knowing' versus the process of telling and instructing

Looking back to the content to be covered in the curriculum we can see content such as 'children learn to double and halve'. I have seen many competent teachers giving children experiences of collecting two groups of objects of the same size, discussing whether they are the same and pooling them together as a basis for sharing out to demonstrate that the result will be equal amounts of the same size as was originally there. This is often too much for young children to take in and is often not scaffolded in a way to allow children to take ownership of what is happening.

Many early years educators (see, for example, Gifford, 2005; Siraj-Blatchford et al. 2002; Skinner and Stevens, 2012), have advocated an approach that sees adults develop conversations with children in a curious way rather than an informed one. This is in contrast to the idea that the adult knows and the child does not yet but will if they listen, and isn't thought to empower children and allow them to make connections. A typical teaching interaction using this curiosity-led approach could go as follows:

Teacher: 'OK children … look at Alex's choice. Alex has doubled the eggs he chose. How did you do that?'
Alex: 'I took another box of them.'
Teacher: 'That is interesting. But now you have to share those eggs between the two bears who want to make their pancakes. Can anyone see how we are going to do that?'

(Children either take eggs out and share them or simply give one box each to each teddy.)

Teacher: 'Wow. You doubled the eggs and then gave one box each to each teddy. That is amazing. Surely that won't always work will it? What about you Dileep?'

I have seen teachers reaching for resources that build on the discoveries that children then start to make. For example, children realising that doubling an amount and then sharing the whole lot between two people results in the original amount are supported by Numicon pieces and cubes that can represent sweet packets.

Skinner and Stevens use the term 'enabling questions'. Possibilities include 'I wonder why …', 'I wonder if …' or 'How could we …?' (2012: 75). These kinds of questions can tap into children's willingness to investigate, meet a challenge, discover or simply be curious. Sometimes they can lead to spontaneous discoveries.

💡 Big ideas

- Open-ended and prompting questions often stir curiosity and engage in a way closed ones may not.
- Young children are stimulated by a sense of challenge and adventure.

For example, had the children not come up with a suitable solution to sharing the eggs then the teacher could have modelled, speculatively, by saying, for example: 'I wonder if we could just give one box to each bear … that seems to work. I wonder if it will always work? Shall we try it with yours Marlon?'. Older children benefit from this approach although the context may need to be realistic if they are to believe there is an authentic challenge.

Many early years practitioners have an excellent sense of how to relate to young children and nurture them. They sense how allowing children to stay in tune with what they are feeling, have experienced and how it can relate to learning in school is likely to be rich territory. I believe they are right. Fundamentally so. It may be that many feel less secure in applying this belief consistently in many ways to maths in early years but they manage it well in a number of ways.

Early counting

The process by which children learn to count and add up effectively has been well documented by a number of writers. Gelman and Gallistel (1978) captured key skills of children in their five counting principles:

- The one–one principle – ascribing one number as each separate item is counted.
- The stable-order principle – being able to use the number order consistently without omission or variation.

- The cardinal principle – knowing that the last number counted denotes the total of the whole set or group of objects.
- The abstraction principle – understanding that this method is not specific to just one experience but can be and is applied when counting any group of objects.
- The order-irrelevance principle – knowing that the order in which objects are being counted does not affect the total so long as each object is counted once and once only.

Carpenter and Moser (1984) identified in words ways in which some kind of progression and efficiency takes place in gradually using known knowledge to deduce the unknown.

- Count all.
- Count on from the starting number.
- Count on from the larger number.
- Recalling number facts.
- Deriving number facts.

These statements build on the Gelman and Gallistel counting principles. They describe efficiency in combining sets (addition) that allows the young child to start to take control; counting each set and then repeating the count after two sets have been combined. This can be taught through careful use of concrete resources as we will see. Carpenter and Moser also acknowledge the importance of either (and preferably both) remembering number facts or deducing them. This involves developing memory and understanding.

Visual contexts to number with embedded meaning

In 1981, Lord Cockcroft led a review of maths in England and Wales concluding that isolated references to mathematical ideas with little context were hard for children to understand and that opportunities for them to acquire and use knowledge in real life situations were required. This was at a similar time to reviews of some of Jean Piaget's ideas about suitable ages for children to begin to apply knowledge beyond physical situations. Many of Piaget's beliefs about what stimulates active learning and curiosity in children remained unchallenged. Martin Hughes (1986), a psychologist with a keen interest in fundamental maths, writing in the 1980s, seemed to pull together some of the key issues that often left young children feeling confused and unclear about number; in addition teachers felt frustrated. Hughes's belief was that adult-driven language and instruction, rather than lack of child understanding, lay at the root of limited progress in understanding maths that had been a feature of primary school education for many children for a long time. His video and recorded evidence about young children's ability to understand and apply knowledge in embedded contexts was part of a key shift in a whole wave of beliefs that 'embedded context' within mathematical experiences could help bridge the gap between the concrete and the abstract.

Songs, rhymes and stories with visual stimuli had always given the opportunity for children to make connections. Now, also they seemed to give some meaning to maths ideas being discussed, and the opportunity to visualise as a basis for moving from the concrete to the abstract and starting to reason mathematically. There is quite famous video footage of Hughes bringing to life the understanding of a pre-school boy seemingly lost when asked addition and subtraction questions involving small numbers. Through seeing combinations of bricks being put into a box or removed the boy is able to reason and answer, correctly, questions involving addition and subtraction because the context of the question is clear to him. Therefore, it has come to be accepted that songs, rhymes and stories involving situated mathematical content allow children to understand a real life situation which they can comprehend through visual representations. They can begin, as Hughes's observed child did, to make connections based on visualising what has already been. The nursery rhyme 'Five little ducks went swimming one day' initially needs ducks on a screen, or cubes, representing ducks. In the end the familiarity of the known context allows children to take the place of ducks. Finally, these known contexts allow the visualisation and ultimately the acceptance that 1 less than 5 of any given context will result in 4. Within the same research Hughes (1986) also demonstrates the importance of allowing children to represent numerical amounts that they can understand but do not remember or know the accepted symbols for.

Should children use standard symbols initially or mark making to establish their own understanding?

This question is both controversial and fundamental to understanding what it is that young children have to offer the process of being taught mathematics at school. The answer is that in some schools there is currently no choice. The policy will be to familiarise children with standard numeral symbols, 1, 2, 3 and so on, rather than engage children in activities that allow them to arrive at their own understanding and interpretation of how these ideas and amounts can be represented. The early counting principles, attributed to Gelman and Gallistel (1978) are at the heart of this issue. It is possible that children can have all five counting principles and still be unfamiliar with standard symbol representation. This is because there is a difference between knowing and using the value of an amount and recognising the standard symbol used. After all there is no real reason why we should use 1, 2, 3, 4. We could use I, II, III, IIII (or IV) or anything we want. The main issue is that in the end we all need to be able to understand and use a commonly recognisable set of symbols.

Hughes (1986), Gifford (2005) and Carruthers and Worthington (2004) all stress the benefits linked to deeper understanding if children are allowed to invent their own systems initially to represent mathematical situations they are dealing with. Here are some examples.

Example 1

In a cooking activity a spoonful of honey and 2 spoonfuls of oat mix seem to make a pretty tasty biscuit. Many 3 or 4 year olds would be able to record something that would allow them to remember or pass this information on to someone else so the recipe is safe.

Example 2

Captured on the BBC *Horizon* documentary (Ginsberg, 1986) around the time of his 1986 book, *Children and Number, Difficulties in Learning Number*, Martin Hughes uses his boxes to allow a boy to put amounts of 0, 1, 2 and 3 bricks into separate boxes. There are 4 boxes in all. The recently turned 3 year old has no difficulty making marks that distinguish the different amounts so that the next day he can identify the amounts in the different boxes.

A common progression in children's mark making processes includes moving from randomness to some kind of physical representation of, for example, sweets or apples. This might be followed by 1:1 correspondence, of some sort, to a mixture of the idiosyncratic and commonly used symbols, which may not be used correctly. Carruthers and Worthington reference the term 'binumerate' (2004: 33) as children gradually adapt their own terminology and start to reach for standard symbols that are referenced, shown and modelled in school and elsewhere around them outside school.

Harnessing children's prior knowledge and natural curiosity for life

Sometimes it is possible in early years settings to encourage and foster mark making and personalised sense making and recording of early mathematical problems and situations. Sometimes it isn't. Many theorists, Sue Gifford among them, would suggest this process can assist children's understanding of recording and understanding purpose. Carruthers and Worthington (2004) have described children using 'implicit symbols'. Without it we rely on being able to convince them of the merits of the existing system and bypassing their ability to think it through and reason it out for themselves. Many schools are faced with exactly that situation and mark making isn't encouraged. There is a need to appreciate certain ideas as young children are inducted into mathematical thinking and symbol usage.

Most children get there one way or another but the process of mark making, with children taking control of their learning, clearly fits in with theories about child development. Children are using personal understanding and reaching for the language and symbols to express what they are seeing and understanding.

Big ideas

- It is the five counting principles (Gelman and Gallistel, 1978) that are really key to early number work.
- Children can struggle to see number symbols as having a discrete meaning unless real world situations emphasise this.
- Children are very capable of finding meaningful ways of recording real world mathematical happenings themselves. Their attempts to do so form a deep part of their understanding and they often naturally reach out for standard symbols they have been exposed to in time.
- Standard use of symbols can be encouraged early so long as the initial alien nature of it is acknowledged along with children's ability to make sense of their world anyway if they are encouraged to do so.

Songs, rhymes and stories: Why are they significant for young children?

Young children have been encouraged to sing and say counting songs and rhymes. The possible benefits are many and their use seems to have been adapted as we have come to value how important it is that children understand number values and patterns through situations that are meaningful to them.

At the ages of 3 and 4, children are really not very old. They are constantly shaping their understanding of how their world exists. Their toys and belongings often have deep significance to them alongside the personal relationships with close family members who help to keep them grounded. It is the feeling of wellbeing and love that allows them to feel ready to explore, invent, imagine and fantasise. Into this set of circumstances the themes of nursery rhymes, sung songs and maths stories can resonate, interest and slowly make sense at a deep level.

Word rhymes such as 'one' and 'begun'; 'two', 'shoe' and 'you'; 'three', 'tea' and 'see'; do all connect in a way that is pleasing to the ear. The songs often relate to *do-mi-so-sol-fa* notation patterns and are accessible and rewarding to hear and sing. The repetition of a story involving biscuits and cookies such as Pat Hutchins's *The Doorbell Rang* introduces a situation that is both reassuring and very familiar – in this instance a tray of 12 biscuits being shared among an increasing number of children, as new ones arrive. The links work on many levels. Gifford (2005) alludes to the emotional, cognitive and social levels of learning and these experiences tick all three boxes. Out of meaningful experiences of the song children have something to relate to and in time to visualise. Many teachers will use visualisation, prediction and other, scaffolded experiences to deepen the way children can access the experiences, gradually starting to move from the concrete into the abstract. Here is a typical scenario returning to the earlier example of 'Five little ducks went swimming one day' in which a teacher is using children to represent the ducks.

Teacher: 'Hmm, yes now there are only 3 little ducks left. Here we have them: Katy, Marlon and Cherelle. Now how many will there be left if Katy swims away? Good lots of hands up. Well, let's see what happens when she does swim away. Yes, there are 2 left … so now we sing "two little ducks went swimming one day …".'

It was only as a teacher I started to realise the gradation or challenge in counting songs. Other useful examples include:

* 'One man went to mow' adding one each time (you could use 'one person went to mow', but it doesn't scan so well).
* 'Two, four, six, eight, Kalpesh at the cottage gate', a rhyme based on going up in twos.
* '10 fat sausages sizzling in the pan, one went pop and the other went bang', a rhyme about counting down in twos.

Once children are able to add and subtract more than 2 or 3 they are almost ready to start making up their own songs.

Role of the adult

Thoughtful young children, who are very active and receptive to stimulus, are in need of a teaching pedagogy that relates to the nature of how they develop, think and need to act. So, we now consider the adult role in general and then in more specific detail around activities.

Should we tell or leave the children to find out?

Picking up on this earlier theme, Gifford (2005) and many other experienced and able early years practitioners know that good mathematical thinking with very young children doesn't really seem to happen without a bit of a poke or a prod. Young children are keen to draw in what they see and hear from their lives into their play and interests. However, some thought processes need to be developed and neural pathways have to be grown. This view draws from the work of people like Kathy Sylva (1980, cited in Gifford, 2005), whose research noted that the quality of young children's interactions seemed to increase simply by having an adult around; they didn't necessarily have to be shaping and organising events as many have felt reluctant to do. Siraj-Blatchford et al. (2002) named the process 'sustained shared thinking' whereby the adult cues into the activities and conversations of young children to try to enhance or sustain the quality. Linked to scaffolding and Vygotsky's zone of proximal development (ZPD) it has been acknowledged that this is clearly a sound move, although there could be reasons, regarding mathematical development and readiness to learn, why deeper understanding may not emerge.

Gifford's (2004: 22) identified roles for the adult include: demonstrating, instructing, connecting and exploring, finding examples, discussing, using mathematical language, representing, visualising, problem posing, confronting errors and misconceptions, modelling and encouraging reflection. No pressure there then! Gifford cites the work of Bliss et al. (1996) and Sarama and Clements (2004). To this I would add the work of the US academic Herbert Ginsburg. These people all make the point that an understanding of child development and early learning with a specific emphasis on mathematical understanding is necessary to apply the adult qualities rightly emphasised by Gifford. The work of Siraj-Blatchford et al. (2009) related to the variable impact of teaching assistants in the classroom goes alongside this debate about how the adult needs to know their own knowledge and use it to support young children in their learning.

Using emotional understanding and knowledge of child development to plan and manage effective maths activities

Number

There are so many nuances to counting but the only real requirement is that we are able to get children to talk to show us how much they really do understand. It is important is to know what they don't understand so as to allow us to cue in to help. Gelman and Gallistel's five counting skills (1978) are by no means a given. The number order may seem long or it can be difficult to know where it starts or ends. Gifford (2005), along with Skinner and Stevens (2012) both reference 'number-string' delivery by young children, who see counting as a string of number sounds rather than one name to represent one amount. Some teachers will have a number focus, for example, 'this week it's the number 3'. Part of the reason for doing this is that it specifies one particular amount, what it looks like with cubes, apples, what the numeral looks like, finding '3 of a kind', feeling it in clay, sand or finger writing. For a related activity children in a circle could be given different numbers up to 5 and told to swap places with each other when they hear or see their number. Skinner and Stevens' (2012) idea of the parachute to run under would clearly enhance the engagement so long as the learning purpose is maintained.

The deliberate mistake

Part of the brief with early years children is not to tell. It just doesn't work. So we look for variations on this, one of which is to introduce deliberate mistakes in order to stimulate discussion about key concepts. This needs to be tackled carefully; if you as the teacher keep making mistakes some children may actually think you really are no good. Thompson (2008: 205) approaches this by using a puppet, Little Miss Count, who can introduce deliberate counting mistakes into teaching. Other teachers use different toy pets or motivating creatures. This can serve to distance any errors from you as a teacher but allow an important interaction to happen. The puppet or fantasy object fills the gap beautifully. For example, our puppet could say: 'That sounds good but I don't know what comes next. How did you know to say 8 after we counted 2, 4, 6? Why didn't you say 7 or 5? How did you know it is 8?'. This could be developed further to lead on to specific questions such as 'So, do we say 8 now on this one? We have counted 3, 6… Is this one 8? What do you mean no?'.

This type of dialogue is probably sounding familiar. Young children are very motivated to support in public the puppet who is struggling and of course the teacher has the freedom to keep asking questions and 'acting dumb' to probe the thinking and understanding without telling.

Big idea

Telling doesn't guarantee active thinking. Making mistakes does because children have to evaluate the errors.

Matching symbols and amounts

Matching amounts to number symbols, for example, asking children to match 3 sweets with the number 3, may or may not be fun for a young child. However, a puppet in trouble saying 'Oh, help me please! I have matched these objects with the symbols and I am pretty sure Naughty Nigella has changed one but I can't see which one' immediately becomes a more interesting task for the children and a more informative exercise for the teacher. You can take this further if our puppet says: 'Now let us trick Naughty Nigella by setting up some more biscuit plates and numbers and make just one of them wrong to trick her'. Here again the child has the chance to be creative and take control of the situation.

Relevant activities for the early years

Let us now explore a range of further activities that are appropriate for children in the early years.

Big idea

It is the style of interaction between children and an adult who is provoking and inviting rather than telling which is key to making mathematical connections.

What's the time Mr Wolf?

Learning intention: To develop one-to-one and cardinality counting principles as well as estimating skills with number and distance

In this old game children respond to the wolf's invitation. The wolf has their back to the other children. The children in turn ask 'What's the time Mr Wolf?'. They have to take one step for each hour they are told. If the wolf says '4 o'clock' they take four steps towards the wolf. If the wolf says 'dinner time!' then everyone runs back to base. If a child gets to touch the wolf they become the wolf. Useful prompts to use during this activity can include:

- Holding the number up to match the time, perhaps with the sequence, so for '3 o'clock' a 3 could be held up on one side and 1, 2, 3 on the other side.
- Asking children 'I wonder how many steps it is until you reach the wolf'.
- Making line marks on the floor to indicate where children step to as some have longer legs than others.

Number Bingo

Learning intention: Developing 'counting and matching'; the 'abstraction' principle of counting as the counting skills are applied to a range of objects or animals

This activity will require number boards with a range of numbers from 1 to 4, or 1 to 8 depending on the children, and laminated pictures with different amounts of different things, for example 4 cows, 3 pencils, 2 eggs and so on. To play children take it in turns to pick up a picture, turn it over and identify the amount. They then look on their card to see if that number symbol is there.

Useful prompts to use during this activity can include:

- Allowing children to help each other.
- Asking children to each fill in their cards for every go.
- Discussing the picture cards to assess their understanding, 'Do we think this is 3 cows? Shall we count them together?'.
- Encouraging children to subitise. Subitising is a term, introduced by Piaget, for the skill of being able to identify the number of objects in any small set instantaneously without having to manually count them out. 'Can anyone tell me how many are there without counting? Wow. Let's check. Yes. How did you know?'

Giant-sized jumping numberline with dice

Learning intention: Ordinal understanding of position. Counting out. Counting on

With adult guidance children play a race game to get along a giant-sized, playground number track. This requires a large dice, ideally with both number symbols and dots on it, and drawing a large numberline, outside there is often a large number track. One could be made inside, for example, on several sheets of A3 paper taped together that can be laid on the floor. Each child chooses an object to act as a game marker, for example, a teddy, a doll or toy car. They take it turns to roll the dice and the child jumps the right amount of spaces along the number track and places their object in the appropriate square. Useful prompts to use during this activity can include:

- After each round an adult can scaffold learning through questioning: 'Who is in in first place?', 'What position is the horse?', 'How many more jumps does the teddy have to make to finish?'.
- Mistakes should be questioned not corrected, for example: 'Who thinks teddy has 2 jumps to get from 9 to 10? Who thinks something different? I wonder which it is. Let's see.'

Problems that invite thinking

Learning intention: Developing reasoning through active participation problems

There are many ways to introduce age-appropriate mathematical problems for children in the early years that encourage them to explore reasoning and calculation in an understandable and meaningful way. Young children do learn from each other although they are just developing theory of mind; they are just starting to understand multiple perspectives and their view and understanding of the world is a personal one. Therefore, the impact of discussion can vary. However, the BIG IDEA is that we learn by doing and the ability to abstract and patternise feeds off this experience or experiences. Examples of relevant problems that could be used include:

- 'Which bowl has the most cubes in it?'
- 'How could we give these 6 biscuits out so all 3 of you have the same?'
- 'Is there another amount of sweets, apart from 6, that we could share out so all 3 of you have the same?'
- 'Is 4 the only number you could throw to win the game?'
- 'It took you 3 goes to get to 10. Is that the quickest? Could you do it quicker? Slower?'
- 'Listen carefully as I drop the cubes into the box. Does anyone know how many are in there before we empty them out to look?'
- 'We are going to put your shoes in a line to see how many of them fit across the table. We will see who makes the closest guess.'

Useful prompts for activities such as these include:

- Asking questions that invite active thinking.
- Showing an emotional understanding to support children's feelings and help start to develop their resilience, for example:
  - 'If I were you I might have wanted to be the one who had the closest guess. However, it is also about realising what helps you to get better.'
  - 'I've noticed that you have got much better at knowing when 10 seconds have passed. How did you do that?'

It really is such a life skill to focus on what we need to help us be ready to learn and to get better, that it should underpin a good PSHE (personal, social, health and economic) Curriculum. Emotional wellbeing and the understanding of how to improve are about as big as primary school issues get and are important beyond primary level too. There is further discussion related to this in Chapter 1 on problem solving.

Shape-based activities

Learning intention: Exploring shape properties in 2D and 3D

It is important that activities that focus on shapes allow for discussion and develop an understanding of shape properties as opposed to shape names. These properties represent the powerful knowledge. Young children need multi-sensory experiences to build up the way in which they know, experience and understand things. Activities that can support this include: feeling shapes, matching similar shapes up and discussing differences.

Children can often be fascinated by the task of matching up two-dimensional nets with three-dimensional shapes. Polydrons, a popular geometric classroom resource, score well here as do food cartons and containers. Opportunities to describe 2D and 3D shapes hidden in feely bags can provide a real focus, for example, by asking children to identify which shape has been taken away and what its properties were. Games that let them find and locate specific shapes can also be valuable. There are all kinds of possibilities for tapping into what children are on the verge of making sense of.

Useful prompts for activities such as these include questions that invite children to respond to visual and physical stimuli, for example:

- 'Does the shape under the red box next to the computer have 3 corners?'
- 'How many sides does the shape in the plant pot by the door have?'
- 'How many different corners can you feel on the shape you are holding in the feely bag?'

- 'Which of the shapes on the desk here does the shape you are holding feel like, even though you can't see it? What makes you think it is this one?'
- 'Children, Bobby is holding a shape that she can't see and we can't see. We know it is like one of these ones here. What questions could you ask her to help her work it out?'
- 'Are these shapes the same or different? I agree the colour is different.'
- 'Which solid shape will this flat net make do you think?'
- 'Which net will this solid shape make when we lay it flat?'
- 'Who thinks they might be able to make 2 versions of a shape; a flat one and a solid one?'
- 'Try these nets out to see which ones make a cube. Do you think they will all work? Why do you think this one won't Harry? Do we all think that? Hmm. It's going to be interesting to find out.'

The book *Knowledge under Construction* (Ness and Farenga, 2007) gives significant insight into what children are capable of achieving through exposure to 3D modelling resources. It exemplifies further the idea that young children in particular are making sense of the world through direct experience. They need exposure to discovery and confusion in an engaging way. The perseverance of young children in this text exemplifies this.

Length and measure

Learning intention: Establishing the difference between measure and position

A straightforward exercise on the topic of length can involve children being asked to find out which objects are longer. For example, you can place two chairs, a small chair and large chair, behind a display board. Stand a tall child on the smaller chair and a small child on the larger chair so that both their heads come over the top of the board. Take a digital photo to discuss with the children.

Useful prompts to use during this activity can include:

- 'How did you find out which objects are longer?'
- 'Who is taller out of Billy and Khalil?' (depending on the response) 'Ah! So you think Khalil is taller. Look at this photo. How can this be true?'
- Ensuring that children are clear about what is being asked of them. Quite often children's application of knowledge increases dramatically when they are very clear on the task.

An alternative measuring activity could involve placing pencils so they are in a line touching each other and using this as the basis for discussion. For example, 'As you can see it takes 6 of them to cover the length of the desk, 1, 2, 3, 4, 5, 6. See. I wonder which of these other objects (for example, rulers) will only take 3 to cover the desk. Have a think and a guess. I wonder which it is?'.

This could also be framed using a deliberate mistake-making puppet as discussed earlier in the chapter (Thompson, 2008). So our 'dozy monkey puppet version' could be framed as follows:

> Hello boys and girls. I worked out how many of each of these items it takes to make a line across the table. But I have got all the numbers mixed up. Could you help me please? Could you work out which number goes with which item? It might help if you made a guess first because you will be more likely to know if you make a mistake. Do you think you could do that?

In trying out the ideas we have covered in this section the BIG IDEAS relating to early years mathematics should start becoming clear. Don't tell. Be curious and engaging. Find a purpose to motivate children to try something, because if you can find a relevant purpose they will usually be motivated to try the task at hand.

Types of knowledge in early years mathematics

This chapter ends with a discussion of different types of knowledge and how they can apply to early years maths teaching. The first we will look at is 'situated knowledge', this refers to knowledge that is specific to a certain context. It is often associated with the theorists Lave and Wenger (1991) in their work looking at how people learn in organisations. In applying this to teaching mathematics we should be asking whether or not learning about number in one situation is an experience that can impact on other related situations. Clearly the ability to tackle certain situations in which mathematical knowledge is required must relate to how a child or adult has understood some similar variables in a previous situation. Thus the thinking, the adjustments, the connections, often at a fundamental level can form part of a cognitive shift as the child is immersed in a particular learning situation.

Big idea

The knowledge and reasoning achieved at a fundamental level relates to how a child makes sense of a particular activity but also builds neural stimuli that can probably affect thinking in subsequent situations.

This idea is true for participating in songs, rhymes with action, music, questions, as well as dice, domino, estimating, problem solving situations. It is true so long as the children are made to think and reason, not merely to follow instructions.

A further type of knowledge, specific to teaching is Pedagogic Content Knowledge (PCK), a term coined by Shulman (1986). This is based on what teachers know about the area they are teaching (subject knowledge) and what they know about *how to teach* that subject (teaching knowledge). It is relevant to our discussion in this chapter about how we as teachers need to know our knowledge in order to assist children in their developing thinking. Learning how children think and how resources can assist their thinking and understanding are important factors in becoming an effective teacher. Clearly, when teaching children in the early years, 'pretending not to know' is an important tool in the interests of sustaining curiosity and furthering active thinking. Pedagogic content knowledge is an important aspect of teaching, and although developing across all areas of mathematics may not be feasible for every primary teacher, consider the following BIG IDEA.

Big idea

Better to have good Pedagogic Content Knowledge in one or two areas only rather than not at all.

Conclusion

What we learn from this explanation, and throughout this chapter, are a number of key things.

There is a place to model and show; to demonstrate. However, this is more effective if accompanied by curiosity and the need to enlist the children's thinking skills. Role play situations involving children's interests, rich dialogue and interaction opportunities are both interesting and worthwhile. They will, in all likelihood need subtle adult intervention to ensure mathematical thinking and exploration gets a valid outing. Siraj-Blatchford's idea about sustained shared thinking (Siraj-Blatchford et al., 2002) between adult and child is a key pedagogical point regarding maths development in the early years. The adult's role is to be curious; to ask questions, generate thinking through wondering and curiosity. They do this by not giving answers but by knowing or developing ways to take children to fruitful areas of experience. This can be the reason, for example, why less experienced, or less qualified, teaching assistants can struggle to move beyond the telling stage into active thinking territory. Some teaching assistants can do this but it is less common. Teachers can also find this skill hard to develop, but it is definitely worth pursuing because the results can be life-changing for children. Active thinking generates confidence and belief that maths is an area for explanation, exploration and discovery. 'Not knowing' and curiosity can be assisted by 'dozy puppet' scenarios. This is because young children are, in the main, multi-sensory people who often need situated, embedded contexts to explore from which they may be better able to make more abstract deductions. The deepest connections are made when children either take control of what they are doing or fully understand the purpose. Using conventional number symbols or inventing their own straddles this issue. Children are creative. They will reach for efficient symbols in the end. Some schools don't pursue this, which is fine. Wherever you are at, I hope you believe, and see, that young children can be very mathematical when we encourage them to be so.

3

Place value

Learning objectives

By the end of this chapter you should:

- Be able to identify progression in both content and understanding linked to place value.
- Know how manipulatives can be used to deepen place value understanding.
- Know the rationale behind activities that help children to develop an understanding of how digits are used to mean different amounts.
- Know how to teach for understanding through using manipulatives and also planning for their absence as the National Curriculum is both followed and interpreted.
- Be aware of how the calculator can support learning and understanding in place value.

What does the National Curriculum say?

The theme of place value is fundamental to any mathematics involving number value beyond 9. For older readers the system of teaching maths prior to recent years tended to involve understanding place value without any real focus on what it includes; a process of absorption or osmosis. The idea of different bases to base 10 was often covered at secondary school as something of a curiosity rather than a key feature to understanding our counting system and how to use it efficiently.

Children encounter the need to make connections about place value when they start to record numbers with a greater value than 9. It is at this point that the placeholder zero starts to be used and allows for the repetition of digits whose value is determined by the position where they are placed.

In Year 1, or Reception, children start to group objects in tens and explore patterns in the ways such groupings are recorded; this develops an early understanding of place value and avoids the pitfalls of earlier teaching methods, most prevalent in the 1960s and 1970s, which relied on remembering values, albeit with a focus on physical resources.

The grouping in tens and ones is followed, in Year 2, by the need to recognise number values shown through manipulatives, physical objects that can be used to represent mathematical concepts, as well as create groups that are represented by the digits. We will discuss manipulatives in more detail in the next chapter on addition and subtraction, and they are an important teaching tool that we will return to throughout the book. This gets expressed through the ability to partition numbers, which then allows children to work out the answers to calculations without having the manipulatives there as individual objects or groups of tens and ones.

Children in Year 2 also begin to build on number bonds through place value links. In Year 3 pupils extend partitioning to 3-digit numbers and order up to 4-digit numbers. In the main manipulatives are now being used less although they can still be extremely useful in modelling and developing understanding through discussion at a fundamental level. Children here are also introduced to some early place value patterns involving multiplication and division.

In Year 4 children learn to add on powers of 10 up to 1000, to 2-, 3- and 4-digit numbers, securing an understanding of digit value. They are, by now, exploring inverse operations and they use known facts in multiplication and division with place value knowledge to derive connected quotients and products.

Year 5 brings in applying knowledge to include decimals, although money can be an area where superficially children would seem to understand place value with decimals well (we will consider this in specific detail later on). Finally, by Year 6, children are working with all numbers and the teacher is generating discussion around a range of formal written methods, stressing the value of digits being used in different positions, trying to ensure the procedures are both remembered and understood.

Number systems

A sizeable minority of adults were not taught the context in which our number system works and have tended to pick up a version of it rather than get to grips with what it really is. They may have missed some key features of it and therefore cannot fully relate to the kinds of questions and queries primary children experience, if they are able to put them into words.

We have only a certain number of symbols, known as digits. They originate from the Hindu-Arabic counting system invented in India. It includes symbols that resemble those used in our system, these are 1, 2, 3, 4, 5, 6, 7, 8, 9. These get used in different positions and denote groupings around our base system of 10. That is to say on the tenth item we group so that the digits can be reused. The 0 is an extremely useful and flexible additional symbol that allows an understanding of other digits in context. For example, it allows a distinction between 26 and 206. This function of 0 has become known as acting as a placeholder so that the value of the other digits can be easily established without having column headings such as HTU (hundreds, tens and units). The other guiding feature of our system is the decimal point, which distinguishes whole numbers from part whole ones.

This hasn't been the case with all counting systems. The Mayan people used a placeholder a long time ago, in the form of an eye symbol (a little bit like this: ℮, their number representations were mostly carvings). They grouped through line and dot representations up to 20. For example:

$$. . . . = 4$$
$$\underline{\quad\quad} = 5$$
$$\underline{\quad\quad}\ \underline{\quad\quad} = 10$$
$$\underline{\quad\quad}\ \underline{\quad\quad}\ . . . = 13$$

Our column headings read Th H T U for whole numbers (thousands, hundreds, tens and units). Working in base 20 their headings would show:

$$400(20^2)\ 20\ 1s.$$

Therefore, the Mayan representation in Table 3.1 would show the value we know as 1214.

The comparison between our system and the Roman number system is also interesting. The Romans used symbols that were repeated but there was no means of the symbols signifying different amounts in different positions as a result of grouping (as in our base 10 system or, say, the Mayan base 20 system). Table 3.2 shows how some of our numbers are represented.

Although used widely and still referenced today the system meant that new symbols were needed as numbers got bigger and some fairly small amounts required a lot of symbols, for example, LXXXIV= 84, DCCCLXXXVIII = 888.

Table 3.1 The Mayan number system

400	20	1 s[AQ2]
...	℮	$\underline{\quad}\ \underline{\quad}\ ....$
3 × 400	Nothing or zero	14 (2 × 5 + 4)

Table 3.2 The Roman number system

Roman number system	Our number system
III	3
V	5
VII	7
X	10
XVII	17
L	50
LXX	70
C	100
CLXVI	166
D	500
M	1000
MCCLXIV*	1264

*A symbol with a smaller value could be placed in front to denote a subtraction. For example XL would be 10 less than 50 (40) whereas LX would mean 10 more than 50.

Counting systems normally reflect, it seems, the needs of the people who are going to use them. In an age where large calculations and recorded numerical amounts are part of life the idea of repeating digits and symbols is relevant, manageable and has served us well. There may come a time, if it hasn't already arrived, where modification or change will take place. Clearly that happened in the UK in the early 1970s when we harmonised our counting system so that measurements, including money were standardised around base 10. Previously part whole fractions had a variety of denominators rather than just base 10, for example 12 inches made a foot, 12 pennies a shilling and 20 shillings one pound. The fact that a lot of our world deals with base 10 means that there should be a clearer path to understanding our current number system than was the case for children in the early 1970s.

Early years progression with place value ideas, including partitioning and overlay cards

Children in the early years should be busy enjoying number and being immersed in its everyday uses through songs, rhymes and practical activities such as multi-sensory bonding with the numerals themselves through clay, sand, moulds, mud and so on. Early recognition without stress is vital as is the ability to match symbol recognition to physical contexts such as counters, sweets, children, cats and many other things. In doing so we quickly encounter the issue about what happens when we get to 9. Where do we go next? In daily life children will often encounter objects in groups of tens and it is important that our teaching offers children experience of grouping and counting amounts *more than ten* where an actual group of ten objects is grouped together, for example, 10 straws, 10 pencils, 10 cubes, 10 marks. This is to allow several things to happen. Firstly, it shows us a way to count items efficiently. It is clearly beneficial to count out a large amount of objects if they have been grouped in tens and ones. It is far quicker than counting all the objects one by one. Secondly, it provides an opportunity to introduce 2-digit numbers and to interpret the newly positioned digits. It is clearly a huge step to comprehend that there are two digits to interpret. The standard route is to allow children to experience one group of ten some additional ones. This often involves children sorting an amount of between 10 and 20 objects into a group of ten and however many more, so that they can record '1 group of ten and 6 cubes', or some similarly scaffolded activity. Sometimes the conversation may be verbal with no recording. Children often need to interpret similarly recorded or spoken tasks.

Some Year 1 children will take to this process very quickly once the BIG IDEAS have been internalised.

Big ideas

- We group in tens. Each collection of ten ones makes a 'ten'.
- The digits in a number relate to groups of tens and ones.

Later comes the significant seismic follow up to this:

- Each column represents how many groups of ten have been made from the column to the right.

Table 3.3   Base 10 columns

TH	H	T	U	1/10	1/100	1/1000

Thus, a ten has the same value as ten ones; a hundred has the same value as ten tens. A thousand has the same value as ten hundreds. This BIG IDEA holds true for any link in our counting system including part wholes and across the division point of wholes and part wholes. Ten tenths make a whole unit and ten hundredths make a tenth.

The links between the second and third BIG IDEAS here relate well to work with Dienes blocks where the column values can be easily represented.

Place value cards

Many schools have place value cards which can be used to reinforce the idea of collecting groups of ten and exchanging for the equivalent grouping, mainly units into tens or sometimes the inverse of this when subtracting. Dice throwing and counting games with the place value board are strong ways to reinforce understanding of key concepts, particularly when children interpret and record the amounts they have collected. By Year 2 children can support and scaffold each other in these activities; sometimes this is possible at an earlier stage.

A multi-digit number is represented by its constituent parts.

Children need to have the experience of grouping in tens and relating this to the digits of a recorded number. This idea can be supported by 1-, 2-, 3- and even 4-digit overlay cards, which are a common classroom resource for teaching place value (Figure 3.1). All cards are multiples of 1, 10, 100 or 1000. When the digit values are combined, the individual value of each digit is emphasised.

Figure 3.1 Overlay cards

Different bases

Some schools choose to group in different amounts rather than always emphasising 10 using, for example, 6 eggs in a box, 3 apples in a packet and encourage the children to group in for example, 3 lots of 3. This thinking underpinned the Nuffield Resources from the 1960s, which were an important influence on maths teaching in the UK. If schools have committed themselves to base work before considering base 10 in depth then that is fine and with training and consistency will probably lead to deep understanding. However, this isn't the way current government initiatives seem to be going. So we will serve the children best by good quality base 10 activities, discussions and interactions at a fundamental level as outlined.

Early development and ideas

Ruth Merttens (1989) outlined some beautiful ways that early deep understanding of grouping in any one specific amount can be understood and used by young children. Clearly, to access place value effectively the one BIG IDEA, already expressed is that we repeat the use of digits in different positions that signify they are no longer single digits but a similar amount of groups that have either a larger or smaller value. Merttens referenced some examples of contexts in which young children could access this concept without being overwhelmed by grouping in tens, which is larger and unwieldy and takes the emphasis away from understanding and gets hampered by errors. We can think of other examples to go with hers that included children collecting legs on a beetle and beetle families where we could have 6 legs on a beetle, 6 beetles in a family. An alternative could be 4 legs on a cat, 4 cats in a family. We can take this further and add 4 cat families in a block of flats and 4 blocks of flats in a street. So in 'catland' the number 201 would be 2 families, 0 incomplete cat families and 1 random leg needing 3 more to make a cat. Similarly '213' in 'beetleland' would be 2 families of beetles, 1 surplus beetle and 3 legs waiting for 3 more to make another beetle. Other contexts can reflect children's interests or preferences such as: 6 soccer star stickers on a page, 6 pages in a sticker album; or 3 apples in a row, 3 rows in a pack, 3 packs in a box (Figure 3.2).

6 eggs in a carton can be used to explore a base 6 number. So the right hand picture would be written as 12; 1 box of 6 and 2 left over. The left hand picture has one missing when grouping in 12s. We would need another symbol to show this because in our counting system we have already started to repeat digits by the time we get to 11.

As Merttens (1989) correctly points out the logistics and the connections are emphasised in smaller, more manageable group sizes. Also maintained and developed is the idea that repeated digits and symbols work for any base. This underpinned the whole column system around base powers that the Nuffield resources emphasised.

Figure 3.2

We can use the different bases as a context for setting questions, for example, if we return to our soccer star sticker album: 'If 2 pages' worth of soccer star stickers and 3 other soccer stars are owned by Colby and 1 page's worth and 5 other soccer star stickers are owned by Jamie, who has more?'.

The misconception of thinking the child with a 5 must have more is overcome by both the physical experience and the visual link that 2 pages and 3 will have more than 1 page and 5. It is fundamental understanding of basic concepts such as these, pitched in an appropriate form to match the development of the children you teach, that provides the strong foundation for the (much) later move to abstract discussion and deduction. Primary teachers have sometimes kicked against tackling work with different bases with children of any age. With older children with no previous base experience other than base 10 this can be confusing. For young children, however, there is a compelling case for developing this understanding. They aren't yet familiar with base 10 methodology other than in passing. Grasping the fundamentals of different repeating group sizes means they are in fact more ready to be inducted into what repeating digits mean in base 10. The transition should be straightforward to manage, For example,

Teacher: 'Here we have the number 23. If we are collecting soccer stars how many pages of a sticker album would this fill? If we are playing cat families what would this look like?

'Well. Now we are going to start grouping things in tens, like these pencils in this packet, and 10 pencil packets make a box. The reason we are now doing this is that in everyday life when we see numbers they are using the idea that 10 means a group of ten ... not 6, 4 or 3.'

Often the response of young children in this situation is pretty much to the point such as 'Can't we play the beetle game anymore!' (Of course we can!), or 'Couldn't we make 10 soccer stars on a page?' (What a great idea!).

Moving from horizontal to vertical layout to establish understanding

By this stage, as children have experience of partitioning numbers into their digit value, they are able to explore emerging ways of adding together 2-digit numbers efficiently. Initially, the physical representations of numbers allows children to solve problems using manipulatives and equipment such as Dienes or Numicon or simply cubes made into blocks of tens. It is the linking of this knowledge to the value of each digit that gradually allows them to partition, group efficiently and recombine that is the essence of successfully carrying out addition and leads onto confident place value calculations. An important step here is moving from a horizontal layout for addition to a vertical one which emphasises place value. For example:

Horizontal layout

$$26 + 32$$
$$20 + 6 + 30 + 2$$
$$(20 + 30) + (6 + 2)$$
$$50 + 8 \rightarrow 58$$

Vertical layout

This, in turn, becomes:

$$26$$
$$\underline{32} +$$
$$50 \ (20 + 30)$$
$$\underline{8} \ (6 + 2)$$
$$58$$

… And then:

$$26$$
$$32 +$$
$$\underline{58}$$

In teaching place value we need to stress the value of each digit. This is enforced by activities and mental addition/subtraction procedures emphasising column values.

It makes sense to let children work with a horizontal layout in addition when they partition initially to emphasise the digit values.

$$34 + 23 \text{ partitions to}$$
$$30 + 4 + 20 + 3$$

This combines to

$$50\ (30 + 20) + 7\ (4 + 3) = 57$$

Care needs to be taken to manage the numbers initially to avoid the need to group the units as another partition but this can be added.

$$47 + 25$$
$$40 + 7 + 20 + 5$$
$$60 + 12\ (10 + 2)$$
$$72$$

The use of manipulatives, such as Numicon, Dienes and place value counters denoting 100s, 10s and 1s, in recent years does mean that there may be less misunderstanding of how the following algorithm needs to be interpreted.

$$8 + 126 + 40 + 7.3$$

This requires a lot more than the manufactured teaching of procedures that can limit understanding. Below are two attempts at working it out vertically; the left hand version is correct and arrives at an answer of 181.3, the right hand version misunderstands the place value of several of the addends, leading to an incorrect answer.

```
          8              8
      1 2 6          1   2 6
        4 0          4   0
          7 . 3      7 . 3
      ─────────      ─────────
      1 8 1 . 3      2 0 5 6
        2
```

I think this kind of error is slightly less prevalent today in, for example, Year 5 classrooms than it used to be due to how teaching methods have changed over time. However, this will only be the case, if, as stressed by people like Ryan and Williams (2007) the use of manipulatives and other strategies to develop this understanding takes place.

Use of Dienes and Numicon with a 100 square to establish patterns and reasoning behind why those patterns exist (Figure 3.3)

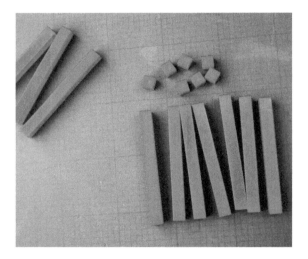 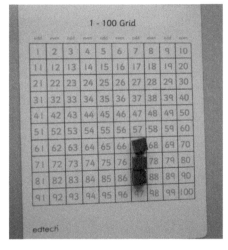

Figure 3.3

The Dienes form part of the mental image by which children understand the concepts of grouping in tens and ones as well as the patterns within that structure. The understanding is deeper in children if they experience a range of resources over time so that the resources become a means to abstracting the concept rather than the knowledge in themselves. For further development of this line of thinking see the activity to develop these skills in Chapter 4. The following objectives and success criteria also hint at how to frame and develop key ideas linked to place value.

Learning objectives linked to place value

Let us consider some objects linked to place value. Some are specific, others less so. All of these can be used as the basis for learning activities in the classroom. Many of these will link to tasks discussed elsewhere in this chapter and they should assist you as you plan to engage children and to teach for understanding.

a   To identify value of digits.

b   To interpret Numicon representations of 2-digit numbers.

c   To predict what '10 more' or '10 less' will be (while looking at Numicon arrangements of 2-digit numbers).

d   To count in patterns of 10 more from numbers ending in zero (and then not ending in zero), for example: 10, 20, 30, 40, 50, 60, followed by 7, 17, 27, 37, 47, 57.

e   Counting across the 100 border (80, 90, 100, 110 and so on) or backwards (120, 110, 100, 90, 80).

f   To use a 100 square to add on, go back in 10s and 1s.

g   To count on in 10s with Dienes and Numicon and match to numbers on a 100 square with cubes.

h   To estimate using knowledge of rounding off and place value. For example, being able to estimate 19×7, by using knowledge of 2×7 to find 20×7.

i   To demonstrate knowledge of column values through converting from horizontal layout to vertical layout (see example earlier in this chapter).

j   To know equivalent values related to different group sizes. For example, 3 units = $30 \times 1/10$, 2 hundreds = 20 tenths, 20 tenths = 2 units.

k   To be able to relate decimals to part whole representations. Such as in an activity that asks children to shade in 1/10 of the cake, or colour in 0.3 of the 100 square.

l   To represent up to 3-digit numbers using Dienes blocks.

These learning objectives are meaningful tools to ensure teaching of place value focuses on ideas that relate to understanding and the application of knowledge. As you spend more time teaching with different age groups you should start to experience the difference between superficially covering learning objectives and getting to grips with the ways children need to experience and discuss ideas to achieve understanding. Objectives c) and d) are both referenced in Chapter 4 on addition and subtraction. They seek to tease out the difference between emerging and real understanding behind adding and subtracting multiples of 10, 100 or 1000.

Big idea

When adding a power of ten it is only the value in that column that increases. For example:

$$28 + 10 = 38$$
$$38 + 60 = 98$$
$$231 + 100 = 331$$
$$1743 + 2000 = 3743$$

A question to help children to explore this BIG IDEA could be: 'Why don't all the digits change when you add multiples of ten or multiples of 100 or multiples of 1000?'. This could, and perhaps should, be tackled using base equipment, calculator, 100 square. They can all contribute to being able to understand what is happening. Children are likely to be reaching for relevant mathematical understanding as they seek to articulate their understanding. Evaluate these answers for their relevance:

Child A: 'Not all the digits change when you add 200 because 200 is a round number.'
Child B: 'The other digits don't change because say its hundreds added … well … the other columns aren't hundreds.'
Child C: 'If you add 200 to another number, say 164. There will be two more in the 100s column but nothing to add in the tens or ones. If the number had been 864 and not 164 then the thousands column would change too because you now have enough hundreds to make a group of 1000.'

Big idea

As you evaluate these comments you are also realising the difference between subject knowledge and teaching or content knowledge as it is sometimes referred to (Shulman, 1986). These concepts were introduced in Chapter 2.

It isn't so much the answer, it is the reasoning, asking the right question, that allows children to understand at a deeper level rather than gaining procedural understanding only. This is what the Singaporean Maths Mastery approach currently being taught in many academy schools seeks to develop.

Success criteria linked to place value

Alongside learning objectives, or intentions, it is important to have success criteria to ensure we have some way of assessing the learning that has taken place. There is sometimes very little difference between learning objectives and success criteria. However, some objectives can be rather broad. For example: 'To develop an understanding of place value'. Others can be almost as precise as success criteria or assessment indicators. For example: 'Through careful removal of concrete resources including Dienes blocks, Numicon and the 100 square children use visualisation to deepen their understanding of place value involving last-digit values'. This is a complex but specific success criterion. Both statements assist us in processing the purpose of having a clear understanding of what you want the children to learn.

Big idea

Clearly thought-through learning objectives, or learning intentions, allow you to evaluate whether you are helping children to understand, as you teach.

Here are some examples of success criteria related to teaching and learning about place value:

a   Children learn to group in bundles of some kind and interpret visual and physical representations of these with objects such as cubes, pencils or sweets.

b   Children learn to partition or recombine 2-digit and 3-digit numbers, for example, $24 = 20 + 4$ or $20 + 4 = 24$.

c   Children understand that 10 in one column is worth 1 in the column to the left.

d   Children understand our counting system has 9 symbols 1–9 and a placeholder – zero.

e   Children can use Numicon and Dienes blocks to see how only the tens digit changes when you add ten on. (This could be extended to adding multiples of ten and could also include subtraction and bridging forward and back through 100.)

f   Children identify the effect of multiplying and dividing by powers of ten, for example, $\times 10$, $\times 100$, $\times 1000$, $\times 0.1$, $\div 10$, $\div 100$, $\div 1000$, $\div 0.1$.

g   Children can understand and explain how, and why, 3×2 and 3×20 are connected.

h   Children use known facts to deduce others connected by place value. This is closely linked to representing multiplication as 2D rectangles, for example, using 3×2 to solve 3×20 because one of the dimensions is ten times bigger.

i   Children understand $\times$ and $\div$ as inverse operations with place value, for example, $20 \times 4 = 2 \times 40$ or 0.2×400.

Sometimes it isn't until we teach that we realise some of the complexities involved in understanding place value ideas, and this is a point that can apply to any other aspect of learning, maths or otherwise. This is absolutely fine, so long as we use our realisation to adjust our focus and our teaching, either in the same lesson or later. The reason objectives and success criteria are separated here is to distinguish between what you are trying to teach and indicators that learning has taken place.

Dienes equipment and place value

Dienes equipment is a versatile classroom resource. A 1000 block can be used as representing ten hundreds. It can also be used as a single unit to show 1/10ths and 1/100ths (Figure 3.4).

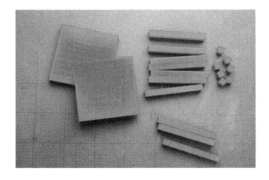

Figure 3.4

The BIG IDEA, already referenced, that ten in one column is worth the same as one in the next column to the left cannot effectively just be told to children. They have to engage in ways to take the information in. Place value overlay cards assist this, and so do physical representations. Children can see that a tube of 10 single cubes is the same as 10 single ones. They have or can see similar physical links through Numicon and Dienes rods.

In this instance the 10 rod shows the link with the 10 ones. It is as though a bar of chocolate has 10 squares. What if the Dienes cube (10^3 or $10 \times 10 \times 10$)

showing 1000 small cubes is used as the whole, say a massive cubic solid chocolate object. Then there are many powerful connections that children readily and willingly take on.

Each layer of the cube has 100 squares (100/1000 = 1/10).

Therefore, the layer (or 100 square) is 1/10 or 0.1 of the cube. One single row of 10 cubes is 1/100, a hundredth of the 1000 cube. As a decimal this is 0.01 of the cube. Finally each single cube is 1/1000, a thousandth of the whole cube or 0.001.

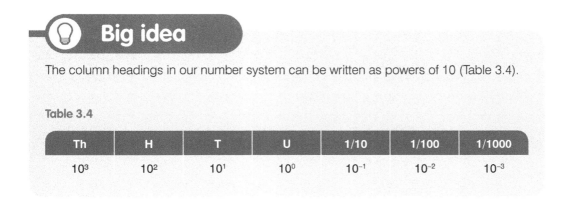

Big idea

The column headings in our number system can be written as powers of 10 (Table 3.4).

Table 3.4

Th	H	T	U	1/10	1/100	1/1000
10^3	10^2	10^1	10^0	10^{-1}	10^{-2}	10^{-3}

Thus the columns and their relative values take on a real meaning that children are both able and motivated to make some sense of. The use of analogies like this and some of the discussion and interest they create mean that deeper areas of discussion and misconceptions can be accessed and tackled.

Applying knowledge of place value

If children have used a healthy amount of manipulatives they are likely to be comfortable with deducing facts from known ones. Let us see if we can capture some BIG IDEAS around this theme. Good experiences linked to repeated digits and the concept of grouping mean that children can apply knowledge of small calculations with single digits when they are used to calculate different sized groups. 'Two lots of three' will still make 'six' whether we are talking about ones, tens, millions or hundredths.

- 2 groups of 3 ones makes 6 (ones)
- 2 groups of 3 tens makes 6 (tens)
- 2 groups of 3 millions makes 6 (millions)
- 2 groups of 3 hundredths makes 6 (hundredths).

 **Activity: Extending tables**

Learning intention: The statements below actually are learning intentions related to understanding tables. They supplement the process of trying to remember them

Rote learning is only one of the strategies that should be used (see also Chapter 5 on multiplication and division). Others include deducing unknown facts from known ones in some of the ways described below.

- Knowing that 9×4 is 4 less than 10×4 (well supported by 100 square patterns and Numicon).
- Knowing that 'even times even is even' so 8×6 can't be 49 (well supported by Numicon).
- Knowing that the last-digit pattern for the 8 times table is 8, 6, 4, 2, 0, 8. So 8×6 must be 48.
- Understanding that 8×7 will be double 4×7. The Maths Mastery approach to tables explores the links with 2, 4 and 8 times tables involving doubling, followed by the 3 and 6 times tables, which are also linked in a similar way. With the 5 times and 10 times tables following obvious patterns this only leaves the 7 and 9 times tables.

In time this should include 3-digit multiples of 10. Where answers can be deduced in similar fashion, For example:

$$5 \times 3 = 15$$
$$50 \times 3 = 150$$
$$5 \times 30 = 150$$
$$50 \times 30 = 1500$$

Big idea

If one factor is made ten times bigger then the product becomes ten times bigger. If both factors are ten times bigger the product will become 100 times bigger.

This activity can be extended further to set problems where the multiplication facts in the first column can help you to find factors for the products in the second column.

Column A	Column B	
6 × 7 = 42	□ × □ = 360	(40 × 9 or 4 × 90)
4 × 9 = 36	□ × □ = 720	(80 × 9 or 8 × 90)
8 × 9 = 72	□ × □ = 480	(40 × 12 or 4 × 120)
4 × 12 = 48	□ × □ = 420	(6 × 70 or 60 × 7)

Column B might have had other numbers linked to these four products by place value. Such as:

a   3.6, 4.8, 7.2, 4.2
b   3600, 4800, 4200, 7200

The original facts given need not have been given. Children could simply be asked to find factors or as many factors as they can for 2-, 3- or 4-figure numbers that can be derived from basic table facts. For example:

$$360 = 6 \times 60 = 60 \times 6 = 9 \times 40 = 40 \times 9 = 3 \times 120 =$$
$$30 \times 12 = 8 \times 45 = 45 \times 8$$

These patterns can be extended into decimals:

$$360 = 4 \times 90 = 0.4 \times 900 = 0.9 \times 400 \text{ and so on.}$$

This task allows connections to be made, strategies to be investigated. Calculators can support this work well as a scaffold, if the learning intention underpinning the activity is clear. Children are expected to be able to answer questions related to applying knowledge of tables linked to place value. The extent to which they understand why those links are there will determine how much they are able to apply the knowledge in later areas of work.

Misconceptions with place value

There are number misunderstandings about decimals and place value that no version of the curriculum has been able to identify; although the writers of the curriculum would undoubtedly happily welcome children being assisted to make sense of them. The effective primary teacher seeks to get a handle on why, or how, children may fail to be able to understand mathematical concepts successfully. Children pick up information naturally, regardless of whether it is accurate or serves them well. Here are a few of them:

- *A longer decimal means a smaller value.* A child may well see a decimal such as 0.821579 and assumes it has less value than 0.4 because it has lots of decimal places and they have understood that these are only tiny little pieces. They are unaware that the value of the earlier digits remain the same even if other digits are added on.
- *Applying whole number logic to decimal numbers.* For example, a child may think that 0.0975 has a greater value than 0.7 because 975 has a greater value than 7.
- *Prototyping.* This is concept explored in greater depth by Ryan and Williams (2007). When related to place value it can lead to oversimplified usage of the first decimal place so that, for example, £3 and 2 pence may be recorded as £3.2 or even £3.2p because several key points have been superficially understood or misunderstood. The same child may be able to tell you that £3.02 is in fact 3 pounds and 2 pence but hasn't made the connection. Behind this misunderstanding lies the idea that the value of the first decimal place is determined by the unit measurement in question (this has links to Chapter 11 on measurement).

Hansen (2014, citing Moloney and Stacey, 1997) notes that: 'Errors in the use of decimals are likely to have two sources of misunderstanding: place value and fractions'. Clearly it is preferable to teach decimals with some working understanding of fractions in mind. The 'chocolate cube' analogy that we introduced in our discussion of Dienes blocks is one way of contextualising the link with tenths, hundredths and thousandths.

Decimals as rational numbers

All rational numbers are a result of division of one integer by another. Thus a decimal number has to be rational because it can be expressed through a fractional division. For example:

$$2/5 = 2 \div 5, 0.7 = 7 \div 10, 0.135 = 135 \div 1000, 2.4 = 24 \div 10$$

A decimal number equates to a proper or improper fraction and can thus be expressed through division using a divisor which is a multiple of ten. A chocolate analogy works well here too (Figure 3.5).

With this kind of referencing of the part wholes in a known context, children often start to see interconnections between 1/10th bars and 1/100th bars. The analogy

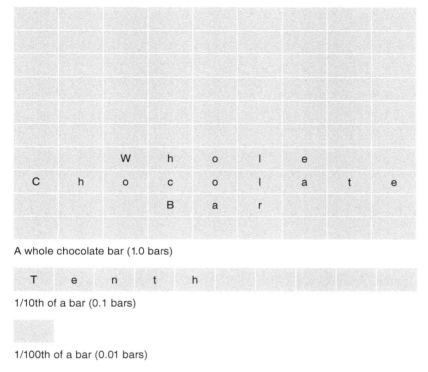

A whole chocolate bar (1.0 bars)

1/10th of a bar (0.1 bars)

1/100th of a bar (0.01 bars)

Figure 3.5 Using a chocolate bar analogy to explore decimals

can be continued to include 1/1000th bars and 1/10,000th pieces. The aim is to realise that each decimal place indicates a value (as in whole numbers) and that the later decimal places are of less value. It does depend partly on how big the whole is, insofar that 0.001 of a grain of sand is pretty tiny. 0.001 of a football pitch would still be about 6 square metres! You can also follow this theme in Chapter 8 on fractions as it references a similar idea that a small part of something large can be worth more than a large part of something small.

Big ideas

- Decimals can be expressed as fractions with a denominator that is a power of 10.
- The value of a fraction is dependent on the relationship between the numerator and the denominator.
- If the numerators are the same the larger denominator will determine the smaller fraction.

These are not ideas to run away from. They are a goal. They represent a rich area for experience and discussion if your understanding can include these ideas. It is something to strive for. It is sound practice to encourage activities which strengthen the understanding of how decimals and equivalent fractions are linked. For example:

- Write 7/10 as a decimal (answer: 0.7).
- Write 0.25 as a fraction (answer: 25/100).
- Record 3/100 as a decimal (answer: 0.03).

This last one is harder, as a child has to interpret that this decimal possesses no tenths. The discerning teacher may promote a discussion among the class about whether or not the answer should be 3/10 or 3/100. This deepens the understanding about zero as a placeholder.

Big idea

The use of the counter example can be the point at which the child's understanding shifts.

For example, if a child records 4/100 as 0.4 the follow-up question could be: 'So what will 4/10 be?'. They can't both be 0.4 and the child is more ready for the discussion or scaffolding that can follow. We have hinted at a lot of connections in teaching and understanding related to place value. To end this chapter let us explore one of these areas a little further.

Division and multiplication by powers of ten

The division and multiplication of and by powers of ten has particular significance for us because 10 is our counting base, the amount we count to group in; thus being able to multiply any number (Y) by ten completes Y groups of ten. We could record this as $Y0$ (in the way that $4 \times 10 = 40$). The same would be true in, say, base 6. If a given number (Y) was multiplied by 6 then, again the answer would also be $Y0$, because *it is the group size* that is being multiplied. For example, in our standard base 10 number system 3 lots of 10 make 30. In *base 6* … 3 lots of 6 make 30. Thus the multiples of 10 as factors or divisors are significant.

If we look into this further we can see that powers are linked through subtraction and addition.

$$\frac{10 \times 10 \times 10 \ (10^3)}{10 \times 10 \ (10^2)} = \frac{1000}{100}$$

Essentially $10^3 \div 10^2 = 10^1$. To multiply or divide with powers the indices are added for multiplication and subtracted for division. Thus $10^2 \times 10^2 = 10^4$ (10 to the power 4).

In short, the key to understanding place value is grouping. The digits move across the columns when we multiply and divide by the base number (the number we group in) for the reasons stated above. That is why the manipulatives that bring the connections to life are important. In essence we return to the guiding BIG IDEA that 'Ten in one column is worth one in the next' because 10 is our base system. It is what we group in.

Conclusion

An understanding of place value is linked to the idea of needing symbol values up to 1 less than the base being used to group in. In our base 10 number system we need symbols up to the value of 9. We also need a placeholder. The chapter is aimed at emphasising experiences, discussions and tasks that will assist understanding. In doing so we should emphasise key features of place value to children so that they *understand* them, rather than simply try to remember them.

The chapter has emphasised that understanding the BIG IDEAS about how our number system works will allow children to develop a sound basis for tackling mental calculation and making written methods efficient. We have chosen base 10. It operates within these rules. The discussion and ideas here aim to bring this to life.

Addition and subtraction

Learning objectives

By the end of this chapter you should:

- Be aware that understanding must accompany procedural learning in addition and subtraction, building on a process that begins in the early years.
- Understand how confidence in mental calculation needs to underpin horizontal and vertical written methods.
- Be aware of how common misconceptions and misunderstandings in children can and have to be confronted to deepen understanding.
- Understand what curriculum strands and goals may look like in practice.

 ## What does the National Curriculum say?

In addition and subtraction the curriculum builds on early years guidance, which emphasises children learning both to count and to understand what counting is for. In the early years children should have learnt sequences of numbers that can be used to signify an increase or a decrease in quantity. They have started to use this knowledge in a range of real situations.

Now they start to use this knowledge, learning to recognise numbers as symbols as well as in writing. This is extended through the idea of place value where symbols are repeated in different columns to denote different sized groups of tens, 100s and 1000s. They start to memorise key number facts and to realise the patterns that exist around this. The National Curriculum in England (DfE, 2014) specifies levels of age-related competence that mean children can deal with numbers of increasing size and decimals. These can be used for developing strategies for writing calculations that are, in turn, relevant for developing both standard formal calculation and efficient mental confidence.

The aim of this chapter is to emphasise the possibilities for making the links, interconnections and relevance of this process by stressing the interrelatedness of how closely the two operations of addition and subtraction are linked.

Introducing addition and subtraction

In focusing on addition and subtraction this chapter builds on the BIG IDEAS discussed in Chapter 2 exploring how early number understanding is developed in young children. Essentially, children need to have a feel for number, gradually learn early counting skills and, crucially, be encouraged to make connections between their everyday world and the one being referenced in their maths lessons. This matches the philosophy behind the Maths Mastery approach, currently a feature of a growing number of schools in England. This approach involves children experiencing real world word problems that are represented using manipulatives – physical objects that can be manipulated to explore mathematical concepts. The manipulative representation is transferred to a mathematical model, probably involving symbols and numbers. A bar model method may be used. Finally this model is related back to the real world problem.

Teaching addition and subtraction as inverse operations

Addition and subtraction can be described as inverse operations, as the effect of one reverses the other, and this link should be taught at every possible opportunity once children are familiar with the counting sequence forward and backwards, which should start to emerge as they sing and hear counting songs and rhymes in the early years foundation stage. There are many resources that clearly support the teaching of both operations in an interconnected way. In this chapter we discuss Numicon, cubes, beads, numberlines and hundred squares, all of which lend themselves to growing an understanding of how the two operations link.

There is now an increased emphasis on mental calculation and mental strategies in the National Curriculum, although traditional formal written methods are still relevant. However, without the ability to understand, use and adapt number knowledge, children and adults struggle to know when and how to apply the written procedures they know. In addition to this they can be held back further by an inability to choose efficient strategies to solve calculations. This has been articulated well by people like Ian Thompson and also Anita Straker, who was part of the original team who put the National Numeracy Strategy together, which was published and used from 1999 onwards and adapted into the Primary Framework 2005. One of the main differences between teaching number calculation now and a generation ago is the willingness to encourage procedures through methods that children fully understand. The concept of the empty numberline as a tool for children to demonstrate their mental strategies gives a much higher currency to thinking mentally when solving addition and subtraction. This makes understanding more likely as children are taking responsibility for how a problem is solved.

Experience shows me that many anxious student teachers are far more able to teach effectively than they initially believe. By learning that the way in which our counting system works is logical and intelligible it is possible to address any feelings of insecurity about teaching this topic and to understand the rationale behind our counting system. If you feel this way yourself, this chapter will show you how it is perfectly possible to change.

Standard progression of understanding and use of manipulatives

Very young children tend to deal solely with real objects in a physical world. In time they can start to use fingers or cubes to represent other real world situations. In mathematics any object that can be used by a learner in order for them to understand a mathematical concept is known as a 'manipulative'. The physical representation and manipulation forms a link between the real world familiar to the child and the abstract world we seek to help them make sense of.

Big idea

It is a *huge* step for children to move from counting and subtracting with real world objects to symbolic representations of them such as cubes or fingers.

It is a massive step for children to represent a real world object by using something else in its place. It is a cause for celebration when children start to do this. This contrasts with some shameful teaching cultures from yesteryear which actively and publicly criticised children for representing amounts on fingers when they couldn't remember the number fact.

So, children are gradually freed from needing actual representations of objects in context and begin to use representative ones such as fingers, cubes, counters amongst other things. They are encouraged to use standard resources such as base 10 equipment, numberlines, 100 squares and more. This in turn often leads to the development of the empty numberline, which will be discussed in detail later in this chapter. The idea of children beginning to take control of solving calculations themselves requires them to interpret the calculation. Hopefully, children will make mistakes; these can guide us as teachers towards good questions and discussion that can unpick and clarify any misunderstandings and misconceptions.

What are manipulatives for?

This question is sometimes asked by students and new teachers; is there mathematical knowledge outside of using real objects? Well, there are patterns that are generally accepted as being true: 3 cats and 2 cats make 5 cats, just as 3 sweets and 2 sweets make 5 sweets. So the move towards abstracted understanding is a powerful important idea. Also, being able to work out problems without real world representations is clearly more efficient. The best teaching often takes place with teachers who understand what is in a child's world and mind as well as having *some* mathematical understanding themselves. The word 'some' is carefully chosen. A key skill is helping children use manipulatives to help them see links and patterns. Wherever possible links should be made with real world situations that are familiar to them.

Big idea

Children must always be helped to understand what they are doing and why. We have all failed to ensure this at times but it should always be in our minds as we plan and teach.

Child development

We have seen in Chapter 2 how children learn at a deeper level when they can relate number to their own world and their natural curiosity and understanding can be nurtured and galvanised. The early stages of number acquisition, counting (for a fuller discussion see Gelman and Gallistel (1978) on counting principles) and mark making (Hughes, 1986) harmonise their natural abilities to make sense of number and symbolic representation leading to a stage where children are ready to apply knowledge to explore connections and efficiency in our particular counting system, base 10. Thankfully, this system has many features that can become our friends, serve us well and allow pattern and logic to lead the way.

Teachers' own learning at school

You may feel that the ethos of understanding our counting system didn't underpin the teaching you received at school; if this was the case you can take pride in ensuring the children you teach receive support that was sometimes denied to you. You may have heard arguments debating whether children should rote learn number bonds or whether they should be allowed time to work them out. There is a history of children and adults struggling to recall key facts and therefore being hindered in the effective use of such information. This is partly offset by the use of calculators in the world of work. However, much of everyday life has a mathematical nature to it. Children need understanding of how numbers join, and systems for deducing as quickly as possible the information they are seeking; if they struggle repeatedly to recall number facts and bonds they will need other strategies.

Memorising number facts

The efficiency we are seeking in children was captured in the National Numeracy Strategy (DfES, 1999), the Primary Framework (DfES, 2006), and the recent revisions of the curriculum have also named and captured different features of our counting system that can make its usage more efficient. The latest version of the National Curriculum (DfE, 2014) is less explicit about such features; not wishing to prescribe what teachers should do. However, much of the listed curriculum should still involve children taking control of their work. This determines what should accompany the need to learn number facts, number bonds and tables, and makes the learning relevant.

Developing efficiency in early addition

Once children are able to count out small groups successfully they are ready to add or join groups to create a bigger one (Figure 4.1). Having counted two separate groups, young children often start the count all over again when they combine the groups. They can stay in this 'count all' phase (Carpenter and Moser, 1984) unless provoked into greater efficiency.

Figure 4.1

 **Big idea**

Children's ability to visualise as a means to learning to count on from a number can be grown if the context is clear.

 Activity: Developing 'counting on' addition

Learning intention: We are trying to provide a means to grow the ability to visualise; to begin to move away from unnecessary inefficient counting of objects and start the process of using experience to abstract; to connect prior knowledge

This can be a teacher-led activity initially, or an independent activity if the children are secure with the task. In Reception, or Year 1, children might be presented with two separate, defined sets of sweets on a whiteboard. For example, 2 sweets in one set and 5 in the other. If children see both sets together they are likely to use the count all method by default. So they need to see each set separately, either on different flipchart pages or a rotating tray with one group on each side of a wall. Children are shown each set separately and asked to count them. They can go back to one set but not see them both together.

In Reception, or Year 1, the numbers 2 and 5 are significant. They are large enough to require calculating with one larger and one smaller. Children are beginning to be able to visualise the 2 in particular, as they watch the group of 5. They can hold the 5 in their head as they look at the 2 still to be counted. In the end they could have the process of 'counting on' modelled to them and then be invited to do the same thing with two other numbers provided (Figure 4.2).

Would some children call out the answer? They might, but decent classroom management can usually prevent this. Teachers often praise those who don't call out or ask children how they feel when they have waited or put their hand up and someone else calls out. Also, working with

Figure 4.2 Sets of 2 and 5

a partner often provides an outlet for mouths desperate to speak or show their thinking. Thinking time is a procedure often established by teachers even with very young children. Clearly the grade or difficulty of question that you set will provide challenge, using the numbers 3 and 9 would provide a small/large combination; 7 and 2 offers a chance to think about which number to count on from. You can adjust this activity as appropriate.

A follow-up idea could be to then allow children to make two different sets of real objects, such as pencils, toys or coins, or representative objects such as counters or cubes. Find out if the children can make the two sets separately. One child could cover up one of the sets and work out the algorithm for addition involving the two numbers by only viewing one set. They could then check if they were correct or how near they were to the right answer. They could be assisted by a numberline. The rationale for this is to grow the idea of counting on through visualisation. The visual representation of the known counting sequence could scaffold this task. More confident children could be challenged and extended by tackling larger numbers or possibly by tackling the work without the numberline as a scaffold. In the main children enjoy challenges that they understand and where the outcome is clear.

As a reflective task for your own lesson planning you may want to list any additional issues you can think of that you would want to address. Also, consider possible assessment indicators that would indicate that children have or haven't understood the task. This would greatly assist you as you teach.

Big ideas

There are several BIG IDEAS associated with this activity:

* When you teach you can realise what children find hard or easy in a way that isn't necessarily clear beforehand.
* Well-chosen examples can be very useful if they draw out appropriate issues with the right degree of challenge. Examples can, and probably should, be chosen to exemplify or confront an issue directly relevant to securing understanding or moving thinking on.
* Challenge can be provided both by increasing number sizes or adjusting the level of support. Both have relevance and don't need to happen simultaneously.

Opportunities for children to apply this knowledge

Children of all ages love the freedom to apply what they have learnt, especially if they know their work might be used as part of class discussion or for other children. The purpose can stimulate their motivation. Children who show understanding could be allowed to create tasks. For example:

- Working in pairs children take it in turns to select a group of cubes, counters or teddies or other items, up to nine or so. They then show the number symbol to show the total.
- They then split the total into two groups and cover one group up. Their partner has to find out how many are under the covered pile.
- They take it in turns to try to work out how many have been hidden under the sheet, book or cup.

Activity: Counting on through visualisation

Learning intention: Using visualisation to help understand 'counting on' and 'counting back'

This task focuses on moving from 'counting everything' to 'counting on' through visualisation. The constituent parts are two sets, known as the addenda, which are aggregated to make a total. This can been done through visual representation and visualisation. In algebraic terms children have been developing the ability to add *a* and *b* to get *c*.

At a very fundamental level they have also seen, first-hand, that *a* and *b* make *c*. They can see that to get from *a* to *c* there is a bit that needs to be added on. Haylock (2014: 89) would

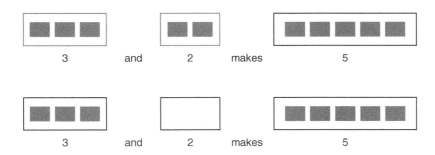

Figure 4.3   Adding two addenda with visual representation

Figure 4.4 Working out the missing addend

describe this as augmentation. In the first part of Figure 4.3 both addends are visible showing that 3 and 2 makes 5, in the second part the 2 has been removed, requiring children to visualise the missing addend in this sum.

Children are then invited to work out what is missing from a further addition (Figure 4.4) now that they are familiar with the process. The structure of finding what has been added to make the new total is being scaffolded and reinforced.

There are other ways to represent this concept visually in class. For example, working in pairs to support and provoke thinking, children could be shown a set of 3 counters on a flipchart. They are told that the other set on the next flipchart page is hidden but that the result of combining both sets makes 5 counters, which they can see on the third page. With their partner they need to agree how many are in the missing group. This could be supported by cubes or counters, which the children could have ready. Some of the children's own choices of numbers could be used, particularly if you are teaching children with more secure mathematical understanding.

The debate here creates three likely results. One, they will understand and work out the missing addend to reach the total. Two, they will get confused and think that 5 needs to be added to 3 and might get 8, confusing the addend with the total. Three, they will simply not be clear on the task in some way. It would be useful to model what number sum has occurred, for example: 'We had 3 … and to reach 5 we counted on … 1, 2 … 3 and 2 makes 5.

Whatever category they fall into, and there could be more, we are into the field of two very BIG IDEAS that can greatly affect primary maths teaching for all of us.

Big idea

It is fine that not all children understand the task or know how to access it. The ideas of their peers and the discussion may well trigger a response in them that is illuminating. As teachers we don't always know when significant learning has taken place.

Teaching with misconceptions in mind

Hansen (2014) and Ryan and Williams (2007) are useful sources of thinking in this area of using children's likely misconceptions to inform our teaching. Trust me, any responsible and reflective teacher soon becomes familiar with what children struggle to understand even if the reasons why aren't so immediately apparent. Let us return to the sum on our flipchart:

$$3 + \square = 5 \text{ or } 5 = 3 + \square$$

The experienced teacher may well draw out discussion. He or she may well ask if anyone had the answer 8, which would be the total if the two sets had been added, before asking for other answers. If 8 was not forthcoming they may well outline it as a possible, but flawed answer, to deepen the overall understanding of the problem. Young children are often taught solely with a view to getting an answer. This is a missed opportunity.

A Maths Mastery approach to linking addition and subtraction

We have looked at important structures in early addition. This includes adding two sets to make a third, larger one. We also explored the question: 'How much has been added to a smaller group to make a larger one?'. The logical progression here would include the process of taking away from a larger one to get a smaller one. A more complex question but one that is still logical to use with visual representation would be 'How much did we begin with if we took some away and were left with this?'. This progression in thinking can be shown through the following series of equations.

$$3 + 2 = \square$$
$$3 + \square = 5$$
$$5 = \square + 2$$
$$\square - 2 = 3$$

 Big idea

Keep the structure the same as you vary the numbers to deepen the understanding of each different structure.

This is key to growing understanding, it links to Maths Mastery approaches and it should follow the pattern of physical and visual representations that are discussed, practised and understood. This is not complex maths; it is, however, deep analysis of fundamental maths.

'Difference' – the natural link between addition and subtraction

The concept of 'difference' has always appeared early in the National Curriculum around about Year 1. It references the idea of comparing two different amounts. This can be a challenge for two reasons. Children often experience the concept of difference first as the idea of things or people being different in some way. In maths it refers to the actual amount by which two numbers or amounts differ. Also number difference can be described with regard to the smaller or larger number. 2 and 5 have a difference of 3. This means that 2 is 3 smaller than 5 and 5 is 3 bigger than 2.

Big idea

Difference is related to the need to teach addition and subtraction simultaneously wherever possible.

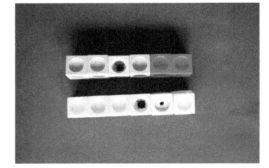

Figure 4.5

It is crucial to understanding that addition and subtraction are taught as inverse operations as much as possible and as early as possible.

$$2 + 4 + 6$$
$$6 - 4 = 2$$

The modelling and discussion of how these algorithms can be reversed is empowering and needs to be prioritised in teaching. It can be modelled through cubes, Numicon, Cuisenaire rods and also by the use of numberlines (Figure 4.5). Adding two numbers to make a larger one is logical. Taking one of them away takes you back to the other. This is also logical if explored through physical resources, visual representations and then with numbers. It matches child development with mathematical thinking. The variety of resources will deepen children's ability to remove the maths from the concrete experience.

Deepening understanding through applying knowledge, tasks and removing scaffolds

Big idea

Just as it is a skill to match resources to learning and understanding, it is also a skill to support children to move away from scaffolds and manipulatives.

Teachers can play a big part in removing the scaffolds that support children in their understanding. Physical resources and manipulatives will continue to be necessary to assist understanding with number calculations for longer with some children. Trainees and new teachers will often question how having the chance to use objects to represent a problem is teaching children to think mathematically in an independent way. Others will say that children should be allowed manipulatives and resources to assist them at any stage and it is the understanding that matters. These are big questions; you may welcome clarification of what the reflective primary maths teacher should, realistically, be seeking to achieve.

The world of young children does not revolve around written algorithms, symbols, formulae and mathematical procedures that are taught, learnt and hopefully applied. Their world involves real, everyday experiences of number amounts and space, with a growing realisation that the relationships within their real world can be captured and expressed in words and symbols in a way that is universally accepted. The use of resources assists this understanding. However, the world of brightly coloured Numicon and cubes is still arbitrary without meaningful contexts to relate to. Unless linking takes place then real world and procedural school maths remain unrelated. Julia Anghileri (2006) references the relevance of counting songs, rhymes, games and daily procedures that all give meaning to number situations by providing a context for agreeing what is happening. Similarly, resources such as numberlines, 100 squares, cubes and fingers all provide assistance in visualising our number sequences and how this is linked to the world of counting, adding and subtracting.

Using resources: Best practice

In the end manipulatives are a means to an end. It probably shows more secure understanding if physical resources are not needed, as it would suggest that the patterns, links and interconnections have begun to be understood. The teacher's role is twofold: to match up the resource with the child and to match the child with the activity to allow the task to be completed and understood with assistance. For example, using a numberline to 'count on': 'If you have 7 sweets and I give you 4 more, how many will you have?'.

It will not be the teacher who makes the boldest choices who will necessarily generate the most learning; it is likely to be the teacher who is trying to work out what their children are able to do, at quite a detailed level. Why? Because if they are looking carefully at the resources they are using, what the resources are helping to achieve, and whether or not the child is being assisted in deepening their understanding, they will make good decisions.

Big idea

If the child can use a resource effectively it is time to begin to think how the need for that resource can be removed.

Whether it be a numberline, 100 square, Dienes block or Numicon, if the resource is fundamental to children continuing to make connections it stays in use, but as teachers we need to know how to move the child on so that the knowledge is in the child, not the resource. So, alongside using the numberline would go supplementary activities about securing the count forwards and backwards. Alongside using the Dienes blocks to represent number calculations would go independent work on paper about partitioning numbers and recombining. The same thinking can apply for all learning resources.

Table 4.1 Progression of development and suggested support resources

Activity	Support resources
Child learns to count number amounts up to ten, then a bit higher.	Cubes, Numicon or real world objects.
They can match a spoken tag name, for example, twelve, to a symbolic one, 12.	Cubes, Numicon or real world objects.
They can aggregate two groups of objects whether they count all of both groups again or count on from the cardinal number for one group.	Cubes, Numicon or real world objects.
They can use a numberline to represent both groups in an addition.	Numberline (potentially linked to other concrete resources).
They can subtract or take away a part of a group they have made to establish the number of those that remain.	Cubes or real world objects.
They understand how a numberline is capturing or representing the real world situation of having a certain number of something and removing some to find out the remainder.	They can use the numberline to achieve this goal.
They then start to begin to remember and deduce addition and subtraction facts that can be used around a growing understanding of place value to interpret the meaning of 2-digit numbers and beyond.	Place value cards, Numicon, Dienes blocks, base 10, place value discs.
Deduction of number facts through addition and subtraction is linked up with ideas and understanding connected to work about grouping and place value.*	100 squares, empty numberlines, Dienes blocks, Numicon.

* Children by this stage, which will probably be at the end of Key Stage 1 if not further, will have ideas that they are secure about and some that they are less secure about. This gives you plenty of choice to focus in on.

 **Big idea**

Children adore being creative, applying what they have learnt, particularly when there will be a real purpose to what they are doing.

When children begin to deepen their experience of what they know, they are ready to move from the physical to abstract understanding. They understand that connections they make in one situation also apply elsewhere. For example:

* I have 7 apples, I get 3 more so I have 10 apples.
* I have 7p. Someone gives me some money and I end up with 10p. They must have given me 3p.

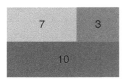

Figure 4.6 Representing 7 + 3 = 10 using the bar method

There is a subtle difference in the focus of each question around the theme of difference. It also relates clearly to the Singaporean 'bar method' often used in Maths Mastery approaches, where children interpret real world problems, use resources to represent the problem and then transfer back to the original question (Figure 4.6).

Cubes or Cuisenaire rods could support this process. In time a representation on paper is to be encouraged as the impact of using physical resources is internalised.

Big idea

These scaffolds of Dienes, Numicon, 100 squares are with a view to children taking control of key connections such as the effect of adding 10, or multiples of 10. Just as Anghileri (2006) specified, the visualisation of early number groups helps to grow links in children's minds. We should look to remove the scaffold of the 100 square once the key features of it are understood.

The application of 100 square knowledge is able to be used in a subsequent scaffold to understanding and taking control, when using the empty numberline.

The journey towards formal written methods: Allowing children to take control of their understanding

As a precursor to formal written mathematical methods children can use informal written structures that assist their development. These are beneficial if they relate to improving and adapting mental calculation skills. Children need to continue to adapt informal methods as they near the time when they could choose to use formal ones because they understand them.

Empty numberline

A useful resource to use at this stage is the empty numberline. This allows children to apply the skills learnt through Dienes blocks, 100 squares and other place value resources. It can allow them to acquire efficiency that will allow them to choose whether formal methods or informal ones will suit their purpose better. Unlike formal recorded methods it is a resource they cannot use independently without having secure understanding.

 **Big idea**

The empty numberline supports understanding grouping in tens and ones, as well as adding and subtracting in ones, tens and 100s. It allows this knowledge to be applied in situations that allow children to take control and show their understanding. It links directly to trios and to complementary addition linked to subtraction. It is a powerful, visual scaffold.

Empty numberline example: 24 + 32

This is a standard use of an empty numberline showing strategies involved in adding together two numbers, in this example 24 and 32 (Figure 4.7).

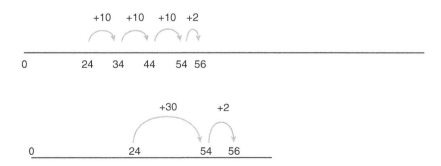

Figure 4.7   An empty numberline calculating 24 + 32

Empty numberlines give children the opportunity to show the connections they can make to solve problems. Children can start to take control of algorithms by thinking and applying what they know. Tasks related to using them can vary enormously, for example:

- Adding two numbers together (as above 24 + 32).
- Subtraction (such as 72 – 58 = 14). Figure 4.8 subtracts 58 from 72.

Figure 4.8   An empty numberline calculating 72 – 58

Having already explored how subtraction and addition are inverse operations the child has a choice of using addition to solve a subtraction sum. For example, 72 – 58 = □ is closely connected to 58 + □ = 72. It should have been through the earlier use of resources where the child internalised this knowledge that the algorithms are inextricably linked. Now it can be transferred to symbolic form. Ultimately it can become a mental calculation.

When we model solutions and allow children to do the same we are deepening the connections between one strategy and another. We are giving children the chance to match up their own ideas, successful or otherwise, with other relevant thinking or solutions. The children begin to internalise thinking and thus take over the understanding that the scaffold and manipulatives provides.

Taking control, estimation and changing from an algorithm you don't like to one that you do

Linked to the way that the empty numberline can both generate and indicate confidence in children it can also be part of their development towards taking control of solutions to questions they are being asked. In fact, one way of capturing this might be as follows.

Big idea

If you don't like the question you've been asked, can you choose a different one to get to the answer or solution?

Given that we can see how manipulatives, real world experience, guided discussion and time can increase children's ability to make connections, we can also help them to adapt what they know to solve different calculations. Carpenter and Moser (1984) termed this 'deducing' or 'deriving' facts and answers from other known facts. To do so the mind has to be opened to such possibilities and, again, using scaffolds to support learning can be very illuminating. Figure 4.9 gives examples of adapting known facts to solve unknown ones.

Add 9 by adding 10 then subtracting 1

Start	7	9	23	64
Add 10	17	19	33	74
Subtract 1	16	18	32	73

add 98 by adding 100 then subtracting 2

Start	13	27	93
Add 100	113	127	193
Subtract 2	111	125	191

Subtract 9 by subtracting 10 then adding 1 back on (compensating)

Start	14	23	42	71
Subtract 10	4	13	32	61
Add 1	5	14	33	62

Figure 4.9 Adapting known facts to solve unknown ones

They can also be represented on the empty numberline, Figure 4.10 is an example of adding 134 + 98, which is solved by calculated as 134 + (100 – 2).

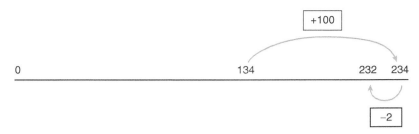

Figure 4.10 An empty numberline calculating 134 + 98

It is for this reason that a lot of time is invested in getting children comfortable with adding and subtracting multiples of 10, 1 and 100 from all numbers, not just those that end in zero. Other common adaptations would include changing 49 + 23 to 50 + 22. One number has one more, the other one less, and so on. There are many variations that you can make. Take control. Switch to a calculation you are more comfortable with.

Choosing examples

A well-chosen example can be very illuminating whereas a thoughtless one can cause problems that are unnecessary for that moment.

The examples above and the discussion of the empty numberline have all been selected with some kind of rationale guiding the choices. The tables of patterns attempt to define the patterns forward and backwards. They begin to cross over the 100 barrier, for example, 78, 88, 98, 108, which children find hard when matching understanding of pattern and place value. In short, the examples have been chosen to try to match the nature of the discussion and points being made.

In your time in school to date you may have found that teachers' lessons flow effortlessly or reach sticky moments; some of these sticky moments may be intentional. You don't learn anything unless there is a problem to solve or overcome. Some sticky moments may be unplanned and some may be avoidable. The aim of the teacher shouldn't be to avoid awkward or challenging moments but, as far as possible, to choose examples that may provoke, challenge or confuse, deliberately rather than by accident.

Rowland et al. (2009) identify four key areas that good primary maths lessons should address. Two of these, 'transformation' and 'connections', link directly to choices of examples. Good examples should be designed to provide relevant challenge. For example, if the learning intention behind an activity is to secure understanding about trios, that two numbers add together to make a third, this can be achieved by teaching that this process has an inverse mechanism that allows one of the original numbers to be subtracted from the total to leave you with the other original number, so: 3 + 4 = 7 and also 7 − 4 = 3. This would satisfy the teaching point. To use another example, 4 + 4 = 8 and also 8 − 4 = 4 would also satisfy it but the presence of the two fours may well cause unnecessary confusion for some children. Rowland et al. talk about the opportunity the teacher has to transform their lesson and children's learning through carefully chosen examples and resources.

When exploring difference on the empty numberline by counting up from the lower number it makes sense, initially, to choose two numbers that are close together but also where there is some challenge to overcome. So, for example, 80 − 68 may allow the concept to be understood in a way that 125 − 79 may make unnecessarily complicated (Figure 4.11).

Figure 4.11   An empty numberline calculating 80 − 68

Developing formal written methods

We will now look at the progression to formal written methods for larger and more complex algorithms using addition and subtraction. Given that children are now expected to be able to use formal column method by Year 4 for numbers up to and over 100, it is essential that their ability to calculate mentally is developed and extended and that they go through the stages of acknowledging digit values. Let us take the sum 138 + 598 and show how this can be written using the formal column method. There are two examples of this below. The left hand example shows an expanded column method which includes how the sum can be broken down into smaller calculations, using a similar approach to that used on the empty number-lines in the previous section. The right hand example shows the formal column method for the same calculation.

Expanded column method	Formal column method
138	138
+ 598	+ 598
16 (8 + 8)	736
120 (90 + 30)	1 1
600 (100 + 500)	
736	

You will notice that the formal column method is clearly quicker and takes up less space. However, the empty numberline and sustained mental calculation work through the horizontal informal layout creates deep understanding. The reality is that using an empty numberline might lead to solving the problem as in Figure 4.12.

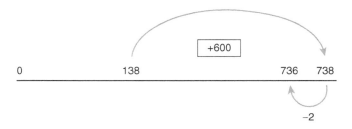

Figure 4.12   An empty numberline calculating 138 + 598

The approach (138 + 600) – 2 is probably more efficient still and I would want many upper Key Stage 2 children to be able to calculate this mentally without the formal method. They need to know formal methods for when calculations are genuinely more challenging, but active thinking and efficiency should always be at the heart of addition and subtraction work.

Let's take another example, the calculation 341 – 279. An informal horizontal layout, drawing on our empty numberline work could be as follows:

$$341 = 300 + 40 + 1 \qquad\qquad 200 + 130 + 11$$
$$279 = 200 + 70 + 9 \qquad\qquad \underline{200 + \ \ 70 + \ \ 9}$$
$$\qquad\qquad\qquad\qquad\qquad\quad 0 + \ \ 60 + \ \ 2 = 62$$

Formal column subtraction would need to be shown like this:

$$
\begin{array}{r}
{\scriptstyle 2\ 3\ 11} \\
341 \\
-\ 279 \\
\hline
62 \\
\hline
\end{array}
$$

The exchange of a ten for ten ones and a hundred for ten tens means this is quite a complex technique that needs to be understood not simply followed as a procedure.

Building on the mental method with empty numberlines and using what we know about subtraction being the inverse of addition, there are possibilities to find other ways of solving this problem. $341 - 279$ can be turned into $279 + \square = 341$. Our numberline work can tell us that the answer is $21 + 41 = 62$ (Figure 4.13).

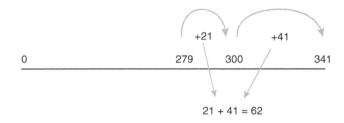

Figure 4.13   An empty numberline calculating $341 - 279$

Big ideas

- Efficiency has to relate to understanding. Children need formal methods and understanding. The discerning teacher is looking to provide both. The empty numberline has real relevance as children work with decimals. Similarly, children also need exposure to formal methods and mental calculation involving decimals (see Chapter 8 on fractions).
- Calculating addition and subtraction with decimals involves extending the idea that 10 in one column is worth 1 in the column to the left.

Applying knowledge with subtraction and addition

Children need opportunities to apply knowledge in all aspects of maths. Above all they need experience at deciding which of the different bits of knowledge they need to use. This process can be hindered in school textbooks when themes are set out by chapter, and where the problem solving section of the addition and subtraction chapter is likely to be about addition and subtraction only, without links to related topics. Children will, in time, need such guidance removed.

Further activities

The following are examples of activities that aim to develop understanding in key skills needed to add and subtract efficiently with a feel for understanding. These ideas also build on understanding at a fundamental level through resources and manipulatives at which point the scaffold can be removed.

Target number (age suitability: Year 2 to Year 5)

Learning intention: To use place value with addition
and subtraction in context

A number is selected between 100 and 200. All players start at zero. Before a child rolls the dice they have to decide if they will count on the number they roll in tens or ones. Each player keeps a record of their new total. It should be agreed by another player. The winner is the player to reach the target number first. If a child's score goes past the total the new score is recorded and the child can move backwards towards the target next go. Dienes or other base 10 equipment could be used as a scaffold, 100 squares serve this purpose well too. Rules can be adapted to include smaller totals or the use of target numbers with decimals. Working in pairs could assist discussion and understanding.

Closest to 500 (age suitability: Year 2 to Year 5)

Learning intention: To use multi steps when problem
solving with addition, subtraction and place value

Use 1–6 or 1–9 sided dice (virtual dice exist online if you have none to hand). Children are allocated a starting 2-digit number, for example by rolling dice. They then take turns to roll a dice once. They choose where to add the value to in terms of units, tens, hundreds or even fractions, with the aim of being the closest to 500.

For example, taking 24 as a starting number, if a child then rolls a 5 there is a choice to take the score on 5, 50, 500 or even 0.5. 5 units takes the new total to 29, 5 tens takes it to 74, and so on. After three turns each, the nearest to the total of 500 wins. Different totals can be chosen. This game can be played with hundreds, tens and units and/or decimals. To find whose total is nearer, empty numberline calculations to explore difference can be used.

Children can play in pairs to assist discussion. In developing this activity further children could both interpret and make 1-, 2- and 3-step problems for each other and the class.

For example,

Q: How could you get from 57 to 102 in 2 throws?
A: If you roll a 4, adding 4 tens takes us to 97. If you then roll a 5, adding on 5 units takes us to 107.

Estimation challenge (age suitability: Year 2 to Year 6)

Learning intention: Children apply knowledge of number value to visual estimation. Children learn to discuss and reason

This activity requires having two piles of cards, one contains cards numbered 0–20 the other contains cards numbered 0–100. Children will also need a page with a series of numberlines on it with different scales (see Figure 4.14).

Working in pairs children take it in turns to pick a card from each pile and record the number on a numberline. When they have placed 10 numbers they should discuss their answers with another pair. The value in this discussion is the justification that children will make; why they chose to place a given number in a specific position. Marks can be placed on the number scales to show halfway points and other possible clues to aid calculation and estimation. The game aims to develop effective use of the empty numberline, where estimating numbers and distance can be very useful.

0		20
0		50
0		100
0		500
0		1000
0		1
0		3

Figure 4.14 Possible numberlines for the estimation challenge

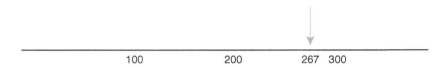

Figure 4.15   Estimating using an empty numberline

In estimating where 267 should sit on an empty numberline (see Figure 4.15) a typical response might be: 'I put it here because it is more than 200 but it is nearer to 300'. It is often useful to let children play in pairs as a class activity so that here each pair fills in the sheet together. Questions concerning placement and estimation can then be discussed using a visualiser, with teacher or children taking the lead in the discussion.

Variations to this activity can include part numberlines that don't start at zero; short numberlines up to 1, or 2, or 5 that include decimals involving one decimal place or more. Some kind of resolution is advisable, either a pre-prepared sheet or ideally a group or class discussion. An additional benefit of this exercise is that it really helps children with the concept of scale interpretation they need to do in measuring objects. This is a constant feature of standardised tests.

Estimating to calculate: Rounding off and last digit values (age suitability: Year 4 to Year 6)

Learning intention: Learning to use estimation to predict addition and subtraction calculations

In this exercise children work in pairs to agree estimates to addition and subtraction problems. They use a 2-, or possibly 3-step, preparation. One relates to rounding, the other to last digits.

For example, let us take the calculation 37 + 48.

Step 1: Firstly, round the numbers off to the nearest 10. This becomes 40 + 50 = 90.

Step 2: Indicate the value of the last digit (of the original calculation). In this example 7 and 8 make 15, so the last digit will be 5.

Step 3: Indicate whether the estimate generated in the second step will be higher or lower than the actual answer. In this case the rounded numbers (40 + 50) are both higher than the original pair (37 + 48) meaning the estimated answer will be too high.

Marking schemes can take into account the relative proximity of the estimate. Variations to this activity will clearly involve changing the size of numbers. Decimals can be used, and calculators could be used to check accuracy. With some calculations you could set multiple-choice answers so that children can eliminate some answers through discussion and reasoning.

For example: 97 + 98 = ?

Possible answers:

a) 205 b) 195 c) 197 d) 185

Opportunities to develop mathematical reasoning to solve this would focus on things such as 100 + 100 = 200 so the total has to be less than that, or that the last digit must be a 5 because 7 + 8 make 15, which ends in a 5. These are sound skills to develop. Children strongly benefit from discussion and reasoning. An important teaching skill is to try to generate a purpose for applying reasoning. Here, it would be accuracy and ensuring the challenge involved was appropriate. Children of slightly different levels working together can benefit from such work. Preliminary or supplementary work on this theme could include time spent investigating patterns with last digits. For example, any two whole numbers ending in 6 will always end in a 2 when added.

Work is often carried out on estimating first before calculating and children may spend less time evaluating whether or not the estimation is likely to be too high or too low.

97 + 98 can be rounded to 100 + 100, giving an estimated total of 200. This will be too high because both numbers have been rounded up. This is rich ground to develop a feel for number and confidence.

'Breakthrough' (age suitability: Year 2 and Year 3)

Learning intention: To count on and back in tens

This activity will require a physical resource such as Dienes blocks or a 100 square, Numicon can also work, and a pack of cards numbered 20–80 (these could be drawn from the same cards used in the Estimation challenge above).

Working in pairs, children select a card from a pack, which will give them a 2-digit number between 20 and 80. They make the number with Dienes (or Numicon). They place a coloured cube on their hundred square showing the number. They then remove a 10 from the Dienes to establish the new total. They place a similar colour cube on the 100 square. They agree the answers with their partner and carry on. They do this three or four times and then repeat the game with counting on by 10.

In time the game can be extended. They can roll a dice with values on it that include -10, -20, $+10$, $+20$ and work out the new totals with or without Dienes or the 100 square. Someone else needs to be on hand to check. This could be another child, or they could play in pairs or check on a calculator. Children can find crossing the 100-point hard in patterns so developing understanding of how to do this is worthwhile. In time the scaffolds of physical resources can all be removed as children visualise as a result of developing their mental calculation skills.

Conclusion

In exploring a range of concepts and strategies relating to addition and subtraction this chapter has sought to engage you in an important dialogue about how this topic can be taught. It is currently thought that specific addition and subtraction procedures are to be taught. That is to be respected. However, the significant advances in mental dexterity and efficiency that have characterised teaching and learning in the primary maths classroom in the last 15 years must be maintained and extended. Informal methods and horizontal layouts for working out calculations are how children show they are in control of what they are doing. It is this active thinking we must all aspire to promote in our classrooms. Once again I am indebted to any teachers who, in teaching for understanding, can surpass the experience they personally received in their own primary school years.

Multiplication and division

Learning objectives

By the end of this chapter you should be able to:

- Understand how these operations emerge from knowledge and understanding related to addition and subtraction.
- Be familiar with how they are inverse operations and that teaching models and methods should naturally stress this.
- Have greater understanding of learning foci that can ensure children develop understanding as well as procedural knowledge.
- Have greater familiarity with how relevant resources can assist deep understanding.
- Be familiar with common misconceptions and how they can be used as a basis to confront barriers to learning.
- Link all of these threads around the content and guidance of the National Curriculum.

 ## What does the National Curriculum say?

Prior to Key Stage 1 young children are making sense of how number tags match up to objects that exist in the real world. They are learning that the number order applies consistently regardless of which object or context is being used and that the symbols and names equate to an exact amount. Although they do experience counting and recognise groups of objects this is in a very visual, concrete way. In Key Stage 1, through being taught specific language and vocabulary development, they learn to both represent and interpret situations where same size groupings exist, such as doubling, halving and multiple groups of a similar size. They explore sequences and patterns and are expected to begin to be able to recall and deduce groupings of 2, 5 and 10 fairly quickly. They are introduced to multiplication and division as inverse operations through, among other things, the use of numberline groupings and arrays.

In Key Stage 2 they are expected to access multiplication and division work involving multiples of single figure groupings and 10. As their fundamental understanding of the operations increases they are strongly encouraged to develop mental strategies that enable them to move away from concrete representations of problems. They are expected to be able to remember table facts related to multiplication and division. They are also encouraged to be able to deduce unknown facts from ones they already know, including multiples of 10 and 100. They are expected to know tables up to 12 × 12 by 9 years old. They learn techniques for multiplication and division involving larger numbers. In multiplication this includes 4-figure numbers multiplied by 2-figure numbers. Division would involve up to 4-figure numbers divided by 1-figure numbers. They are expected to understand prime numbers, and rules that affect strategies that they can use to break down larger numbers to calculate. The curriculum is structured but essentially content led.

Background context and theory

Of the significant number of children leaving school with insecure knowledge of how to multiply effectively, two issues predominate: one is that many were taught procedures that although they could follow them, to an extent, they didn't understand and therefore forgot or misapplied the information; the second is that they struggled to retain key factual information, particularly knowledge of tables and didn't secure enough grasp of how they could deduce information they couldn't remember. The structure and content of this chapter aims to address both of these issues to allow greater focus on understanding so that fewer adults in the future have to hide behind the nagging feeling of insecurity when needing to use such knowledge.

Early concepts and activities related to multiplication and division

Young children's early experiences with multiplication

The theory that young children need to add and subtract before they can multiply and divide is an interesting one; clearly it has relevance but (thankfully) young children's development is not necessarily linear. It is accepted that children need to be able to tally and count to be able to find answers to multiplication sums. However, their world is full of objects and known experiences that include multiples, groupings and divisions.

They can soon tell you if a shoe is missing, they quite happily pair up the socks or know if the teams are unfair when the sides have three in them and one only has two, especially when they are in the team with two! Their visual, and increasingly technological, world allows them to experience groupings and divisions in a way that is impossible to avoid. Cakes being cut, packaged groups of items; small babies, a few months old, watch moving patterns of objects being formed and partitioned to the backdrop of classical music or some other accompaniment. All this means that our job as teachers is to begin to formalise what they have already begun to experience.

If we accept children's experiences of the real world they access in their everyday life the following activities take on relevance:

- Matching socks, shoes, gloves and other items and finding which ones have no partner.
- Using moulds and other objects to make impressions of repeated groupings. This can include Numicon pieces in sand or plasticine, potato prints, and software that can create repeated patterns. (The electronic 'repeat' or 'copy and paste' modes make this visual group patterning much more accessible.)
- Showing children pictures of bikes, tricycles, cars, chairs, egg boxes, apple packets. These all give repeated groupings that link to the way multiplication is represented and used in higher order maths. For example, 5 tricycles can be interpreted as 3 wheels × 5. Or it can be interpreted as 5 lots of 3 wheels.
- Piecing together groups of Unifix or Multilink cubes. For example, if all the green groups are grouped in twos and all the red groups are grouped in threes. It is important to repeat such activities with variations so that these colours are not always linked with one number. This is unlike Numicon pieces where the colour is initially part of the number recognition.

Understanding inverse operations: Scaling and repeated addition

Multiplication grouping can be viewed as one of two related but slightly different forms. The same is true with division. But before any misunderstandings occur, it can be confirmed that the outcome, answer or total will be the same. It is the interpretation and representation that differs.

If I say to you that for every sweet I eat I will give 3 to you then we would create what Haylock has described as a 'scaling up' form of multiplying (2014: 91).

	Me		You
	1	►	3
	2	►	6
	3	►	9
	4	►	12

Figure 5.1 Scaling up with sweets

For every one there will be three, so three times as many for you as for me (Figure 5.1). This then becomes a mapping exercise. It also relates to ratio; a ratio of 1:3.

If I say I would like 3 boxes of eggs we are looking at a 'repeated addition' representation of multiplication, such as 6 + 6 + 6 = 3 × 6. Is this significant? I think that it is. Children often struggle to decide which operation to use in word problems. One of the reasons they struggle is because problems can be represented using either of these two different interpretations, even though the answer is the same.

'Shared between' or 'shared into groups of'?

The same is true for division. The commonly taught interpretation of division has referenced a division sum sharing an amount (called the dividend) into several different groups (the divisor) and resulting in an equal amount in each group (the quotient).

For example,

$$12 \div 3 = 4$$

12 (dividend) shared among 3 people (divisor) gives 4 each (quotient)

This has come to be known as a 'share between' or 'share among' interpretation of division. The alternative interpretation sees the calculation slightly differently. Sharing into 'groups of' would mean we interpret the problem as: 12 shared into 'groups of' 3 will mean there are 4 of them. Two word problems related to the two styles of interpreting the division problem could look like this.

a   Share 12 creme eggs between 4 people to see how many they get each. (Answer: 4)

b   If you share 12 creme eggs into groups of 3 how many groups will there be? (Answer: 4)

The answer is the same but the representation and interpretation of the problem is different. The second representation is the one that lends itself most easily to division into fractional amounts.

Another example is the calculation: $6 \div \frac{1}{3}$, this is often misinterpreted as $\frac{1}{3}$ of 6 whereas it is actually asking us to find how many thirds there are in 6, which would in fact be 18.

The role of the teacher in multiplication and division

A number of trainee teachers are simply looking for a general way to talk about multiplication fairly loosely, possibly focusing on 'lots of' and, in division, the 'share between' models. That is understandable. However, if we as teachers can be aware of the two interpretations of both multiplication and division then we can model and provide examples that encourage children to interpret the different ways that the two operations can appear.

 **Big ideas**

- Try to ensure children become familiar with interpreting and using two different methods for multiplication and division.
- Too much modelling and discussion is confusing for children. Too little is likely to mean they are shown a rule they can't use independently and can't relate to.

Arrays: A resource to connect two inverse operations

The array is a commonly used representation linked to multiplication and division (Figure 5.2). From this array we can see the four operations, two relating to multiplication and two to division.

$$6 \times 4 = 24$$
$$4 \times 6 = 24$$
$$24 \div 4 = 6$$
$$24 \div 6 = 4$$

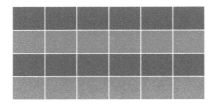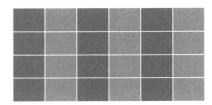

Figure 5.2   An example of an array

Intriguingly each of these four algorithms can be interpreted in each of the two ways just outlined for that operation.

- 4 × 6 can be seen as 4 lots of 6 (repeated addition).
- It can also be seen as 4 (6×).
- 24 ÷ 4 = 6 can be seen as 24 divided into 4 groups with 6 in each (rows) or 24 divided into groups of 4 (columns).

The skill of interpreting and representing number problems (an aspect currently emphasised in the influential Singapore Maths Mastery approach) is fundamental to developing as a teacher, to try to make the mathematical modelling of a given problem as clear as possible with appropriate discussion as to which methods are relevant and which are not.

The array becomes a relevant model to use when children are first able to interpret same-sized groups of objects. The rectangular representation shows quite clearly the *commutativity* of multiplication; that the order the operation is carried out in makes no difference.

Rectangular arrays as visual proof for primes and factors

Rectangles using squared paper represent multiplication sums and inverse division algorithms. They show commutativity. Thus 12 can be made using two rectangles. One shows 3 × 4 and 4 × 3. The other shows 2 × 6 and 6 × 2 (Figure 5.3).

This is in addition to the single line representation that even prime numbers have (Figure 5.4).

So if the only array that can be made for a number has only one line then it must be a prime number. This ability to create links between what is being discussed and visual representations is necessary to help the majority of children stay in the moment. They can see these links and gradually relate these to their understanding without visual cues over a period of time. The concept of the rectangle gets

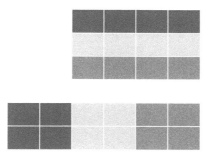

Figure 5.3   A series of rectangular arrays

12 represented as a single line

1 × 7 or 7 × 1

Figure 5.4   Single line representations

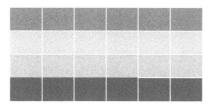

Figure 5.5   A rectangular array with 4 rows of 6

developed further in area work as children explore why the array concept doesn't relate to compound or non-rectangular shapes.

Area is a useful way to explore factors and products. Factors and areas of rectangles are linked. All rectangles have a length and width, even if this measure is the same (as for a square). The length and the width of any rectangle represent the factors. The area number represents the product. This is because multiplication is a repeated form of addition creating a row repeated a certain number of times. The parallel continues as with both factors and area inverse operations apply. As we can see in Figures 5.5 and 5.6, if we double one number and halve the other the area or product number is maintained.

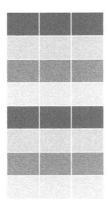

Figure 5.6   A rectangular array with 8 rows of 3

The new rectangle is twice as long but half as wide, giving the same number of squares.

Factual knowledge, mental calculation and deducing answers

One big debate continues, should children have to learn their tables? The answer, to my mind, remains the same: they should. However, there are two additional issues. Firstly, short-, medium- and long-term memory issues mean that learning and retention of information are much harder for some children and adults. Secondly, if the table facts have been learnt without good quality discussion and understanding to accompany the process there will be a problem. The information may be used in straightforward situations with reasonable accuracy. If it isn't accompanied by understanding or the ability to interpret situations, the child or adult will be unsure of when to use or adapt the knowledge they possess. So, children need to learn multiplication facts.

Why is it necessary for children to learn up to 12×12 by Year 4? This is because our old counting system had variations on the base 10 grouping that underpins our number system. 12 old pence made a shilling, 12 inches were in a foot. We tend not to use these very often now. Therefore the requirement to learn up to $12\times$ is obscure. The need to be able to deduce tables up to 10×10 fairly easily is irrefutable. These facts underpin all our number connections, algorithms, and struggling to deduce them is a serious inconvenience, with or without a calculator. Therefore a broad progression to ensure understanding might look something like this.

Focus on multiplication

- Real objects, such as cubes, Numicon pieces, sweets and so on being grouped, described and used to solve and create number and real world problems.
- Simple patterns in 2s, 5s and 10s have links to pair work, rhymes, fingers on hands and feet, and are commonly repeated, used and referenced in our culture.
- Numberlines (which can be laminated to make a sturdy reusable resource) support linking physical resources through looping that denotes the multiples through evenly sized jumps.
- Deducing multiplication facts through going through rehearsed or derived sequences and patterns, for example, 6×3 is 3, 6, 9, ?, 15, 18. This may or not be based on memory.
- Understanding the links between different multiples. For example, knowing that 6×4 will be 4 more than 5×4 if that is already a known fact.
- Knowing that 4×5 could be used to derive 6×4. Commutativity means that 6×4 would give the same answer as 4×6. This knowledge of understanding what multiplication is allows a range of unknown multiplication facts to be worked out in an efficient way. For example, 99×3 can be calculated in a number of ways, including:

$$(100 \times 3) - (1 \times 3)$$

$$(90 \times 3) + (9 \times 3)$$

The distributive law

The interpretation of multiplication as repeated addition means that the multiples of any table can be partitioned into more manageable amounts and then recombined through addition. Many of us have picked up and used this information almost without realising; sometimes struggling to apply it with any confidence outside learnt procedures.

For example, we learnt that 23×4 would be the same as 3×4 added to 2×4 with a nought at the end (this is in fact 20×4). We probably also learnt the digits had to be in a particular column.

$$
\begin{array}{l}
23 \\
\underline{4 \times} \\
12 \ (3 \times 4) \\
\underline{80} \ (0 \text{ recorded first then } 2 \times 4) \\
92
\end{array}
$$

Securing knowledge of the distributive law (Figure 5.7)

Figure 5.7   Visualising the distributive law

The distributive law states that when two numbers are multiplied together either or
both numbers may be split up into parts, multiplied and then recombined through
addition. Often this is visited through partitioning. After tables have been secured
or partially secured, children are then encouraged to break larger numbers down
and multiply in parts before recombining. Looking at the examples in Figure 5.7 we
can see that $6 \times 2 = (5 \times 2) + (1 \times 2)$ and also $(4 \times 2) + (2 \times 2) = 6 \times 2$. If this can
be experienced by young children, for example in Year 2 and Year 3, with physical
resources and discussion with smaller numbers then the multiplication methods
with larger numbers have some real meaning and are less of a leap of faith in carrying
out a procedure.

Concrete resources such as Numicon or Dienes may be needed to secure the
understanding that our place value system links, for example, 3×2 with 3×20.
Some understanding that 3 lots of 2 units or 3 lots of 2 tens or hundreds are going to
be connected allows place value to be understood and used. This gives more control
to children than inviting them to put a '0' down before multiplying by a single digit,

as shown above. Calculators programmed to multiply or divide by 10, 100, 0.1 can greatly assist children's understanding here. They both trust and learn from a calculator in a way that is different to being told by a teacher or even a peer.

Variations on partitioning, including grid multiplication and horizontal or vertical layout, move children towards formal written methods. Children should use a longer written method, that helps them to develop their understanding, unless they had a more efficient and reliable one that would work.

Grid multiplication as an extension of the distributive law

Once the idea of partitioning numbers to multiply in parts has been secured, your teaching can move on to the idea of multiplying larger numbers. Clearly multiplication with larger numbers is underpinned by knowledge of times tables. Children who struggle with tables will be compromised at this stage. This can be offset if they have methods to deduce them (see support for table development below). Grid multiplication is a system for multiplying that children feel in control of.

Big idea

Each part of one number must be multiplied by each other part of the other one.
For example, 45 × 23

$$45 = 40 + 5$$
$$23 = 20 + 3$$

Thus, the grid method reflects each part of one factor being multiplied by each part of the other factor.

45 × 23

×	20	3
40	800	120
5	100	15

900 + 135 = 1035

(Continued)

(Continued)

We could have partitioned differently

$$45 = 20 + 20 + 5$$

$$23 = 20 + 3$$

×	20	3
20	400	60
20	400	60
5	100	15

$$900 + 135 = 1035$$

Children can become very attached to the grid method shown above. That is good so long as they understand the distributive law that lies behind it, rather than learning a procedure that they don't fully comprehend. This model will also work with decimals (see Chapter 3 on place value).

 **Big idea**

The inverse nature of multiplication and division means that reference to one operation or the other should never be far away. This relates to estimating and checking answers, considering how to solve word problems. The confidence to interpret and represent a problem correctly is one that needs to be grown through experience and discussion.

Focus on division

The emphasis wherever possible should be on both 'shared between' and 'shared into' models of division. Initially this would involve sharing with real objects, often linked to real world context: sweets, fairness, pencils, a plate of biscuits.

Big idea

The 'shared into' interpretation of division allows a clearer understanding of dividing by 'part wholes'. It also creates the image that the smaller the group size being formed by dividing then the larger the outcome (quotient). For example:

$$12 \div 2 = 6$$
$$12 \div 4 = 3$$

This concept is illustrated so beautifully in Pat Hutchins's book *The Doorbell Rang* (1989) where a dozen scrumptious biscuits are being continuously reallocated as more and more friends arrive. 12 to yourself becomes 12 among 2 and finally 12 among 12. The more you share between then the fewer you actually get. Or, the smaller the group sizes that you make then the more groups you can create.

Laminated numberlines can be used to encourage the 'shared into groups of' model and can be accessed by counting up or back, $20 \div 4$ can mean 'count back 4 each time to zero' (5 steps) or 'count up from 0 to 20 in 4s' (5 steps). Under the 'shared between' model it would mean 20 shared into 4 groups means 5 in each group. The numberline also works very well for modelling that there are remainders or numbers that do not divide into groups with a whole number size (quotient). This works whether counting up or back in a given number to a total (dividend). Gradually children need to experience division that results in remainders. This can be described as grouping sizes that aren't exact.

There is a need to start to draw on known facts in order to move beyond the concrete objects. The empty numberline can be a natural move on from the actual numberline.

$28 \div 7 = 4$ can be represented as:

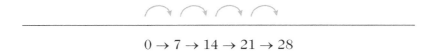

$$0 \rightarrow 7 \rightarrow 14 \rightarrow 21 \rightarrow 28$$

As the size of the calculations increase children need to learn how to carry out division of larger numbers either by grouping or understanding a formal method that partitions the number. Teachers should consider teaching the chunking method before moving to a formal one. The aim here is to allow children to take control of the sum. Just as the multiplication process allowed numbers to be partitioned and recombined (12×3 was separated into 10×3 and 2×3, or an equivalent) the same can be true for division.

Instead of dividing a large number into a particular group size it is possible to chunk the total into smaller pieces and do these calculations; then total the different quotients to achieve the answer that solved the original problem.

The following example shows three different ways of chunking $378 \div 3$ into smaller calculations.

Partition method 1

$$378 = 300 + 60 + 18$$
$$= (\mathbf{100} \times 3) + (\mathbf{20} \times 3) + (\mathbf{6} \times 3)$$
$$= 126 \times 3$$
$$\text{Answer} = 126$$

Partition method 2

$$378 = 150 + 150 + 60 + 18$$
$$= (\mathbf{50} \times 3) + (\mathbf{50} \times 3) + (\mathbf{20} \times 3) + (\mathbf{6} \times 3)$$
$$= 126 \times 3$$
$$\text{Answer} = 126$$

Partition method 3

$$378 = 360 + 18$$
$$= (\mathbf{120} \times 3) + (\mathbf{6} \times 3)$$
$$= 126 \times 3$$
$$\text{Answer} = 126$$

The number used in this example, 378, could have been partitioned in a different way to suit the child. The outcome will be the same if they carry out both their chosen partitioning and the resulting calculations correctly.

Removing the scaffold of physical resources

The process by which the scaffolds of support that create links for children are removed is subtle but distinct. Children should aim to progress from calculations using real world objects to representational ones such as cubes, beads or Numicon. Once comfortable with solving problems with physical objects it is likely that a crossover point has been reached. Often teachers will try to engage children in recording based on number symbols but choose small enough numbers for children to understand how the physical objects and representational written methods connect. The empty numberline in particular bridges this gap and Dienes equipment and Numicon can support this too. Alongside this, the effective teacher is trying to maintain the links between the two operations to secure and deepen understanding. A typical teaching interaction could be as follows:

Teacher: 'Yes. That could well be right. You have $39 \div 3 = 13$. If I wanted to check through multiplication that this was correct how could I do that?'

Child: $(10 \times 3) + (3 \times 3) = 13 \times 3$
$30 + 9 = 39$

This is an understanding that can be built up from the early array work and rectangle model showing that: $3 \times 13 = 39$, $13 \times 3 = 39$, $39 \div 3 = 13$ and $39 \div 13 = 3$ (Figure 5.8).

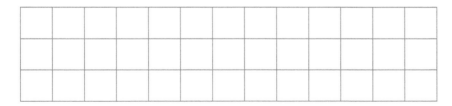

Figure 5.8 An array of 3×13

Variations in learning intentions

When thinking about which resource to use and how to establish the learning intention for a lesson, a key consideration is to think about the knowledge, skill or understanding you are actually trying to develop. For example, with the use of the numberline it could be: 'to transfer groupings of cubes onto a numberline with loops' or 'to equate the equal sized cube groups with the loops on the numberline'.

Later, children might be making groups of three from different amounts of cubes and finding out what this will look like on their numberlines, leading to an intention for your lesson such as: 'children begin to predict the effect of grouping with cubes on how their numberline will look'.

For example:

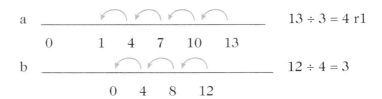

a $13 \div 3 = 4 \ r1$

0   1   4   7   10   13

b $12 \div 4 = 3$

0   4   8   12

Carefully worded learning intentions help to give you a feel for exactly what new development you are trying to secure. They can give you a real focus as you teach, giving you a point to refer to as you consider if children are understanding a concept or what you can do to help. The tightness and effectiveness of such teaching is something we can all aspire to improve. It is shaped by how much we stop to think what small steps and ideas underpin the longer term success we are trying to help children achieve.

The relevance of real world problems

Here are some examples of real world multiplication and division problems that can encourage children to understand the relevance of multiplication and division to everyday life.

1. My cat eats 2 small tins of cat food every day. How many has she eaten after 7 days? Young children would probably use a 'repeated addition' approach to the problem, such as: $2 + 2 + 2 + 2 + 2 + 2 + 2 = 14$ which at some point could be captured as 7×2 or '7 lots of 2'. A 'scaling' approach to the problem would see them reasoning that 'for every day there are 2 tins. So for 7 days there will be 7 lots of 2 tins'.

2. If the question was 'how many days would it take the cat to eat 20 tins?' it would be necessary to understand the key features of the problem. The question is asking either 'how many 2s in 20?' or 'if there are 2 tins for 1 day then there will be 20 tins for how many days?'. Division by 'grouping' will be needed rather than a 'share between' model.

3. If I had 24 eggs and needed to put 3 eggs in each cake. How many cakes could I make? This division problem is really inviting a 'divided into groups' method interpretation of division leading to $24 \div 3 = 8$. Or it can be seen as a multiplication sum that is say represented as $8 \times 3 = 24$.

4. If there are 24 cakes and I want to deliver the same amount of cakes to 3 different shops how many will each shop receive? In answering this I am also looking at the sum $24 \div 3 = 8$. However, this time I will be dealing with a 'shared between' approach to division to achieve the answer. Represented as a multiplication problem again this would be $8 \times 3 = 24$.

A key point in these examples is that any discussion deepens connections and understanding. In order to do this it needs to ensure that a representation of a problem matches the maths in the problem. Also, the 'scaling' approach in multiplication lends itself well to later work in ratio. For example:

- If a class has a ratio of 2:3 for boys to girls how many boys will be in a class of 20 (dream class size!)?

The interpretation would be that in every 5 children there are 2 boys. So in every 20 children there will be 4 times as many boys ($4 \times 2 = 8$).

Big idea

Give children the chance to discuss and represent real world problems. Listen to different representations. Discuss whether the child's model fits the question.

The depth to which you can respond quickly may vary because it can be a challenge to process and respond at speed. Your response time will increase and any meaningful discussion is exactly what the children need. This strongly relates to the notion of 'teacher contingency' explored by Rowland et al. (2009).

Activities

The following activities and ideas are to assist you in developing understanding around the themes of multiplication and division. These include specific games and active tasks. There are references to relevant learning intentions.

 Activity: Table patterns

Learning intention: To understand multiplication patterns related to odd and even

Multiplications with odd and even numbers produce very significant patterns. For example:

- Odd × Odd = Odd
- Even × Even = Even
- Even × Odd = Even
- Odd × Even = Even

Big idea

Any multiplication sum involving an even number will produce an even number. This is because all even tables only have even products. We can demonstrate this by looking at the 4 times table: 4, 8, 12, 16, 20, 24, 28, 32, 36, 40.

Also half of the products in the odd tables are even too, which we can see in the 3 times table: 3, **6**, 9, **12**, 15, **18**, 21, **24**, 27, **30**.

The Numicon pieces demonstrate these patterns beautifully, emphasising another key point.

Big idea

Two odd numbers make an even number. Therefore every second multiple in an odd table is even

$$3 = 3$$
$$6 = (3 + 3)$$
$$9 = (3 + 3) + 3$$
$$12 = (3 + 3) + (3 + 3)$$
$$15 = (3 + 3) + (3 + 3) + 3$$
$$18 = (3 + 3) + (3 + 3) + (3 + 3)$$

Activity: Counting out table multiples

Learning intention: Internalising tables as a continuous visual and numerical pattern

This can be done with a calculator on repeat mode (pressing 3 + + = 0 will programme most calculators to count in 3s) or by using a 100 square or numberline to see the pattern with continuous, equal sized jumps. It can be done by taking turns or by children working in pairs and could use an interactive whiteboard (IWB) 100 square as scaffold if necessary.

Big idea

Mnemonics can be a valuable tool to assist memory recall and retrieval. This would include understanding patterns and musical cues to assist retention of table facts.

Activity: Mnemonics

Learning intention: To allow the pattern of the familiar tune to assist the mental recall of the number facts

Sometimes table recital is done to music. The idea behind this is that children take in multiplication facts at different speeds and in different ways. Some children and adults find it very difficult to retain information over a longer period. The idea of devising mnemonics, systems that will allow retention or retrieval of information can be useful. The music isn't a background pleasure; it is a tune. Sometimes people and children remember lyrics through knowing the tune to a song. It can be so with tables. For most children it is only a few tables or table facts they struggle to retrieve as time goes by. Other children need more mnemonics; more neural pathways grown to assist memory recall.

For a task that you can carry out by yourself, look at a copy of the table that challenges you most. Try singing the table facts to three different familiar tunes to see which one scans the best. If none of them work then Google 'maths multiplication table songs' and select your chosen style of music. Rap beats can act as a good rhythmic backdrop to multiplication facts.

Ultimately, understanding how tables are derived impacts heavily on children being able to apply and use their knowledge. In the mix somewhere is the need for them to know or retrieve the key facts, now up to 12×, as quickly as possible when they reach Key Stage 2.

Big idea

There are two key skills when it comes to basic multiplication. One is knowing the basic facts concerning multiplication, the other is understanding how to deduce them. Children, ideally, need to make progress in both areas. Understanding how tables are derived allows application of knowledge much more easily.

Some teachers find that looking at finger systems used in the past can be instructive for children; admittedly, in some cases it is children with secure understanding who make sense of historical methods, such as the finger methods used by the Victorians. However, for children searching for a system to deduce unknown facts it can be worth trying.

 # Activity: Bingo

Learning intention: To consolidate, deduce and use table knowledge

To start children select five numbers, although more could be used for a longer game. For example: 12, 16, 21, 13, 20. These are the products. The teacher (or another child) chooses some table facts, such as single-digit multiplication sums, to read out one by one. These are recorded for reference. Children cross through their number if it relates to the multiplication fact read out.

So, with the above group the table facts '7 × 2' and '3 × 5' would not score because those products (14 and 15) aren't on the list. '5 × 4' and '7 × 3' would score because those totals (20 and 21) are on the child's list. The winner is the first child to cross through all five numbers (products) from the multiplication sums that are read out.

There are several learning benefits here. The game encourages closer listening and thinking skills. It can be played in pairs to assist discussion and focus. Discussion can take place about whether some numbers have more factors and are more likely to be crossed off a child's list.

For example,

$$12 = 4 \times 3 = 3 \times 4 = 6 \times 2 = 2 \times 6$$

$$24 = 12 \times 2 = 2 \times 12 = 4 \times 6 = 6 \times 4 = 3 \times 8 = 8 \times 3$$

Whereas some have no factors except themselves and 1, for example, $13 = 1 \times 13$. This can lead to discussion about factors products and primes. In general, it would appear that multiples of 12 are rich in factors and number patterns and connections; 2 is the only even prime number. Even numbers tend to have more factors, although some odd numbers can have several factors for example, $81 = 9 \times 9 = 27 \times 3$.

It is possible to agree that the chosen numbers may or may not be in the 1 times table.

 # Activity: Programming calculators to count in patterns

Learning intention: To use calculators as feedback as multiplication patterns are investigated, explored and understood

Most calculators can be easily programmed: typing 3 + + = 0 will programme a calculator to count in threes. Accompanied by a numberline or 100 square this can be used to develop an understanding of constant-sized jumps. Equally as useful is to see even-sized jumps from different starting points. For example, 3, 6, 9, 12, 15, 18, or 1, 4, 7, 10, 13, 16, 19, or 2, 5, 8, 11, 14, 17, 20.

Activity: Factor investigations

Learning intention: To use inverse knowledge to investigate factors

Building on the earlier point it is worth stressing that multiples of 12 are rich with multiplication links. Thus when focusing on factors there are active connections to allow children to see. This is partly because 2×6 and 4×3 and 1×12 all multiply to make 12, whereas it is only 1×10 and 2×5 that do so to make 10.

 Big idea

Multiplication and division are inverse links. Therefore multiplying a number will be counterbalanced by an equivalent division operation.

This is shown by the following two algorithms.

$$12 \times 2 = 24$$
$$6 \times 4 = 24$$

The 12 has been halved and the 2 has been doubled, meaning the product remains the same (24). With larger numbers this can be explored further.

$$72 = 1 \times 72 = 2 \times 36 = 4 \times 18 = 8 \times 9$$

In addition to doubling and halving to maintain parity other reciprocal inverse operation patterns work too.

For example, multiplying and dividing by three.

$$1 \times 72 = 72$$
$$3 \times 24 = 72$$
$$9 \times 8 = 72$$

We maintain the same total through using inverse operations on the factor partners.

 # Activity: Fizz buzz

Learning intention: To secure, apply and enjoy growing knowledge of tables

This is a traditional game where children take turns to say the numbers in the counting sequence. The words 'fizz' and 'buzz' are used to denote particular multiplication tables. For example, if 'fizz' were said for numbers in the 3 times table and 'buzz' for numbers in the 5 times table the alternating children would say the following things, if carrying out the game correctly.

A: 1
B: 2

A: fizz (instead of 3)
B: 4

A: buzz (instead of 5)
B: fizz (instead of 6)

A: 7
B: 8

A: fizz (instead of 9)
B: buzz (instead of 10)

You would say 'fizzbuzz' when the multiple was in both tables, so this would apply for 15 (5 × 3) and 30 (3 × 10 = 5 × 6).

The game can be played with one single table focus if a lesser challenge is more appropriate. Here is what the 4 times table would look like:

1, 2, 3, fizz (instead of 4), 5, 6, 7, fizz (instead of 8), 9, 10, 11, fizz (instead of 12)

When playing with two multiplication tables: two odd numbers go together well such as 3× and 5× or 5× and 7×. Alternatively consider using an odd and an even (3× and 4×).

An extreme challenge can include 'fizz', 'whizz', 'buzz' played with three different multiplication tables, for example, 3, 6 and 7 times tables. Ouch!

Fizz buzz can be played with two or more children. You can either play that they are out of the game when they make a mistake or you keep a count of the number of mistakes. There needs to be someone overseeing the game who is secure in their tables. This is usually the teacher but could be another child. A lot of children enjoy this kind of game. Some don't; but those children can learn and make connections through listening and watching. They are usually happy to play with a friend they trust or with a partner to support.

 Activity: Last digit patterns

Learning intention: To secure and deepen table knowledge and patterns. To understand same size multiples in context

Patterns involving last digits can also be instructive. Even table multiples always generate the same last 5 digits in different orders. Odd tables generate all 10 digits but in different orders (Table 5.1). Again, it is the opportunity to explore the same information from a different perspective. For some children the experience will be curiosity to add to their knowledge; for others it may be a breakthrough to securing understanding.

Table 5.1 Last digit patterns

Table	Multiples	Last digit patterns
2×	2, 4, 6, 8, 10,12, 14, 16, 18, 20	2, 4, 6, 8, 0, 2, 4, 6, 8, 0
3×	3, 6, 9, 12, 15, 18, 21, 24, 27, 30	3, 6, 9, 2, 5, 8, 1, 4, 7, 0
4×	4, 8, 12, 16, 20, 24, 28, 32, 36, 40	4, 8, 2, 6, 0, 4, 8, 2, 6, 0

 **Big idea**

Last digit patterns are *very* useful when predicting or checking multiplication calculations with larger numbers.

$$6 \times 4 = 24$$
$$16 \times 4 = 64$$
$$6 \times 14 = 84$$
$$36 \times 24 = 864$$

This pattern and link exists because when multiplying whole numbers through standard partitioning it is only when the unit digits are multiplied together that there can be a different digit to zero at the end, for example, 23 × 42 (Figure 5.9).

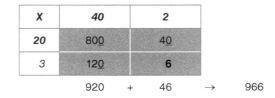

X	40	2
20	800	4<u>0</u>
3	12<u>0</u>	**6**

920   +   46   →   966

Figure 5.9 Last digit patterns

This example shows that it is the last digits in each number being multiplied that determines the last digit in the answer.

$$2 \times 3 = \underline{6}$$

Therefore 23×42 will also end in a 6.

$$23 \times 42 = 96\underline{6}$$

Mental calculation techniques using place value knowledge with multiplication

In base 10 the multiplication facts work whatever the value of the column in which the digit is in. Learning this point functions as an appropriate learning intention for this activity.

Table 5.2 sets out this principle using the sum 3×2, across values of 100s, tens, units and tenths.

This idea often needs manipulatives such as Dienes or groups of straws or cubes to model and interpret. I would favour children exploring how this information is linked by verbally representing this as:

- 3 lots of a group of 2 will always make 6 lots of that same group.
- 3 lots of 2 units will make 6 units.
- 3 lots of 2 tens will make 6 tens.
- 3 lots of 2 million will make 6 million.
- 3 lots of 2 tenths will make 6 tenths.

Table 5.2   Exploring the sum 3 × 2 across values of 100s, tens, units and tenths

	H	T	U	1/10	Value
3×	2	0	0 •	0	= 600
3×		2	0 •	0	= 60
3×			2 •	0	= 6
3×			0 •	2	= 0.6

Starting with a single multiplication sum we would want children to be able to combine two BIG IDEAS.

Big ideas

a   3 × 2 of any group size will always make 6 of that group size. This applies to any two numbers multiplied.

b   Multiplication and division are inverse operations; so dividing by 10 will reverse an operation of multiplying by 10. Therefore 6 × 10 = 60 and 60 ÷ 10 = 6.

So...

2 × 4 = 8	also...	20 × 0.4 = 8	0.2 × 40 = 8
20 × 4 = 80	also...	2 × 40 = 80	200 × 0. 4 = 80
200 × 4 = 800	also...	20 × 40 = 800	2 × 400 = 800

Conclusion

Many of the features of multiplication and division generate misunderstandings and create misconceptions. It is why throughout this chapter the value of digits has been kept clear; also, the approaches to multiplying and dividing by larger numbers have been chosen to demonstrate understanding. Ultimately, they tend to lead onto formal recording of these operations. This should mean that when children reach this point they will understand why such methods work and how to adapt them.

Children will have to learn to formalise their understanding of grouping numbers, multiples and strategies for calculating grouping, sharing, scaling and repeated addition. The BIG IDEAS in this chapter are to assist you as you seek to emphasise key points that link to understanding as well as answers.

There are real connections between both multiplication and division linking them to work covered in many other chapters, particularly fractions, algebra, and addition and subtraction. There is also a place value link to units of measure.

6

Time

Learning objectives

By the end of this chapter you should be able to:

- Understand how time is both linked to and different from other aspects of measure.
- Be aware of the subtleties of both teaching and understanding time as a concept.
- Identify progression in understanding both the passing of time and being able to tell the time.
- Utilise ideas and activities that will support both understanding the maths curriculum and focus on active learning.

What does the National Curriculum say?

The National Curriculum in England contains the following requirements relating to the concept of time:

- Tell the time to the hour and half past the hour and draw the hands on a clock face to show these times (Year 1).
- Tell and write the time to five minutes, including quarter past/to the hour and draw the hands on a clock face to show these times (Year 2).
- Tell and write the time from an analogue clock, including using Roman numerals from I to XII, and 12-hour and 24-hour clocks (Year 3).
- Estimate and read time with increasing accuracy to the nearest minute (Year 3).

- Record and compare time in terms of seconds, minutes and hours; use vocabulary such as o'clock, am/pm, morning, afternoon, noon and midnight (Year 3).
- Know the number of seconds in a minute and the number of days in each month, year and leap year (Year 3).
- Solve problems involving converting between units of time (Year 5).

These statements and requirements are significant; and yet, without some analysis of what concepts underpin these skills, understanding and the ability to apply knowledge may be compromised.

Teaching time

Time is a fundamental part of everyday life and the ability to manage time effectively is often cited as a key requirement for a successful working and personal life. Time is a finite resource that many of us are inspired by when we see examples of it being used effectively. Children from a young age aspire to tell the time. Given the chance, they thrive on understanding how it works and then being able to use this knowledge. We need to teach for understanding and allow natural mistakes and misconceptions to occur. Many teachers have realised the problems teaching about time can present and have wrestled with ideas to avoid making the process so confusing.

Teachers are effective when they are clear on how the activities and discussions with children about time help them to understand how we measure it. A practical strategy is for teachers to focus on encouraging familiarity with key ideas rather than developing isolated knowledge and skills such as recognising 'o'clock', 'quarter past' and 'half past', without understanding what they mean or how they interconnect. This may require putting some traditional time-related activities to one side, but may prove more a manageable teaching approach in the long run.

The ways in which time has been understood

Time has been elapsing for, well, a long time! There are many ways in which it has been referenced and captured to assist everyday life. For example, the daily passage of the sun from sunrise, through to high sun, sunset, dawn, daybreak has been used as a method of tracking time for centuries. Such time-keeping is less reliable than modern means due to variations in the amount of daylight at different times of the day in different parts of the world or where the path of the sun was blocked by mist or cloud or rain. Short intervals now captured as seconds or minutes are harder to measure.

The developed understanding of time in our world today is underpinned by two features: measuring time and how to apply the concept of time. In modern times most of the world uses a common way of measuring time: days, hours, minutes, seconds. Most, though not all, countries use a standardised time system where there are variations linked to time zones and daylight hours. They are shown and referenced in reasonably standard form using a combination of digital and analogue time references, a mixture of the visual and the numerical, or symbolic. So, our children need to be inducted into the time system that we use, its nuances and its interconnections. It is a world that, in time they may contribute to adapting, as life and society change. However, for now we need to consider how to develop a feel for how time exists, its features, its interconnections and its units of measure and also the skill and knowledge of how to tell the time and make it fit for use in their world and the world around them that they are part of. This will include understanding of both digital and analogue clocks.

Big ideas

- Focus on understanding more than on memorising.
- Use young children's life experiences and feelings to help them understand the need for some kind of accuracy in measuring time.

Time is a theme that can be confusing because of its subtleties, yet empowering if you feel you have taken control of how it works. Teachers down the years have varied in their approaches and their levels of success with teaching children time. Unless its features are understood rather than learnt then complete control, understanding and the ability to apply knowledge will be elusive. The progression of the chapter from here will include ideas and discussion related to two features: one is the passing of time; the other is the skill of learning to tell the time.

Child development and nurturing a sense of connectedness with time

Young children have no formal sense of time in the numerical sense. They would certainly have instincts that would tell them that they have been doing something for too long or that they would rather be doing something else. This may link both to their curiosity and, initially, an inability to use standard language to represent their feelings, which can be a frustration. If they are loved, nurtured, fed and engaged, their curiosity starts to allow them to process how the world has connections and physical attributes that they can explore and start to understand. Into this space come the physical objects such as clocks, sundials, sand-timers and others linked to measuring time, though to a young child this may not be apparent. Also, there are a variety of repeating patterns that have to be understood.

Progression using familiar contexts with very young primary children

It seems vital to make experiences and understanding tie in with the curiosity young children have. If we are to keep understanding at the centre of teaching and learning we must focus on the world that children know and are coming to know. This includes concepts such as 'more than', 'less than', 'longer than', 'shorter than'.

Although pre-school and Early Years Foundation Stage children are learning rapidly how to communicate verbally, their world is very visual and much of their understanding has a visual aspect to it. They can see and talk quite quickly about whether there is more of something or less. For example, if you ask a 3-year-old child who likes sweets which plate they would like, the one with 3 sweets or the one with 5 sweets on it, they will, in all probability choose the latter option. Asking the same child whether 3 is more than 5, or 5 is more than 3 may not be so successful.

From the visual contextual understanding about length and whether something is more than, less than, shorter than or longer than something else, it is a relatively small jump to discuss whether we spent more time on one thing or on something else. This is a fascinating area because our perception of time can depend on how interested, engaged and motivated we are by what we are doing. Time often appears to be passing quickly or slowly, if (as in the very young child) we had yet to develop any way of realising time exists at all. Young children respond in very interesting ways to questions such as:

- 'Can you think of something that lasts a long time?'
- 'Which of these lasts a long time … assembly, morning play, taking the register?'
- 'Can you remember something that seemed to last for a long time?'
- 'Can you remember something that lasted for a short time?'
- 'What things in school last a short or long time?'

The responses of all children, and adults for that matter, to these questions can be fascinating, particularly with young children where you can get an insight into the very active ways their minds work; only sometimes do we as teachers tap deeply into this. Some examples of young children's responses to such questions include:

- 'It took ever such a long time to get to Grandma's because there was a traffic jam.'
- 'Playtime is usually short but when I had an argument with Chloe and played by myself it went on for ages.'

- 'When it was just before dad's birthday suddenly it was his birthday … but when I waited for my birthday it took a long, long time.'
- 'Mum said we would each get 5 minutes on the swing and she would time it but mine went quicker.'
- 'I brush my teeth quickly but when Dad is around he makes me brush them for ages.'

These anecdotal references to time are full of honest expressions of how time feels. They are an example of how the real world impacts on the feelings of young children. It may mean such opportunities to share, alongside hearing the tales of classmates, prepare them for the idea that perceptions of time passing are personal and are probably shaped by experience and life's journey. Some children have to make their own amusement more than others and may get used to creating ways of making time pass more quickly, or pleasantly, for themselves. Alongside this comes the concept of finding out how long something takes and not just how long it *seems* to take. For example:

Teacher: 'I have loved hearing you talk about things that seem to last a long time and which ones don't. I wonder whether the things we like seem to last a short time when really it has been a long time. I also wonder whether we could find a way to work out whether some things do last for longer than others.'

There is normally some response at this point about clocks and timers. Telling the time with clocks is a much more meaningful experience for children if they can match specific experiences with how much time has passed. To deepen their feel for what analogue and digital clocks actually measure they need to experience what the units signify.

Resources to help children evaluate and compare lengths of activity

Many everyday classroom items can be used to help children evaluate and compare the length of time taken for different activities, including:

- sand-timers;
- plastic water containers with small holes, with marks calibrated – the small holes will let the water out and the calibrations indicate how much time there is to go until the container is empty;
- number counters;
- stopwatches;
- candles.

Problems

A typical way of setting a time-related problem in class could be: 'How can we tell if it's quicker when we get changed for PE or quicker to take the register or quicker when we eat our fruit or quicker to tidy up the classroom?'. Let's face it, there can't be any harm in trying to provide some interest and engagement in the process of tidying the classroom! Young children are quick to respond when engaged in a real world situation with relevant resources that motivate and support their understanding and fuel their imagination and ability to make connections.

They may say things like:

- 'We could let someone keep count with the 100 square and put a mark every time they reach 100 and we count how many times that happened and so on...'
- 'I don't think the candle will work for the register time ... or the others really.'
- 'Look it's burning slowly. We won't be able to see which thing that we did burnt for longer.'
- 'But if the sand has finished before the register finishes or before we're changed for PE then how will we know which was quicker?'

Or they may start thinking through the props you are using.

Don't be fooled by children who can't or don't say much. Children's thinking is often well ahead of their vocabulary. Give them the chance to share ideas and thinking in twos and then to the class as it lets them rehearse their thinking and speech. This concept is based on Vygotskian thinking (Vygotsky, 1978) and should be welcomed by any teacher whose instincts favour children taking control of their learning. Foundation Stage children may need some initial structure when talking an idea through with a partner and some kind of thinking space or overt process may work for them. Following this mixture of thoughts, understanding, ideas and discussion there needs to emerge some real world 'doing'. Young children learn, in the main, through being active and then reflecting afterwards. Certainly, physical experience often alters their thoughts.

Before the sand disappears ...

A sand-timer can be used for time-related challenges, such as:

- 'How many skips can you do?' 'Why were there different answers?'
- 'How many verses of "One man went to mow" can you sing?' ('Could we try it slightly faster, slightly slower to see what difference this makes?')
- 'How far through the alphabet can you write, or say?'
- 'How far have you got getting dressed?' (It might be a good idea to agree the order a child will put clothes on.) This could be repeated after PE lessons where getting changed can be a very long, drawn-out business.

Other visual clues that begin to reference number

- Class events can be timed using stopwatches, and the times (measured in seconds) can then be visually displayed on the 100 square. 37 could be described as 3 rows and 1, 2, 3, 4, 5, 6, 7. A good online version can be found by Googling 'Splat 100 square'.

All of these experiences help children to identify the challenge of measuring time as well as some solutions. Comparing events or the time of repeated events as quicker or slower is instructive to understanding time passing. Ultimately, non-standard units, such as claps, are impractical because they are either inaccurate or not accurate enough or not able to be commonly understood by people who aren't present at the time. Initially though they are of real personal significance to young children in their world. Sand-timers begin to bridge that gap.

Numbers

As children's understanding of the stable order count, 1, 2, 3, 4, 5, extends, numbers can start to be more of a discussion point and to be understood and used by children and teachers. Interactive whiteboards (IWBs) have timers that can be used both to count up and down that assist this process. You could ask if it is possible to show time passing on the IWB stopwatch, using questions such as:

- 'What number does it reach before going back to 0?' (As the counter changes from 59 to 60 seconds it returns to zero to begin a new minute or hour. Moving from 11 to 12 also starts a new cycle of hours.)
- 'Why have we now got two different numbers, one still and one changing?' For example, 1:08, 1:09, 1:10?

Young children really benefit from watching a digital timer count the seconds up to a minute. They can begin to chant and be guided to the rhythm and pace of the change. All kinds of games can be played about opening their eyes when they think 10, 30 or 60 seconds has passed.

For some Year 1 children expressions of time such as 2:30, 2:51 and 3:02 will be understood. Others will communicate a partial understanding recognising that 2:51 is, say, two whole ones and a part of another. This multi-sensory immersion of children is not to be underestimated. Writers who have critiqued Piaget's assessment of children's developmental stages stress that the cognitive development process is accelerated through children accessing thinking on the edge of, or just beyond, their current level of understanding through support and stimulation from peers and adults. If they are interested and can make connections they can thrive (Hughes, 1986; Donaldson, 1978; Vygotsky, 1978).

We will now look at some relevant mathematical activities that are suitable for using with young children. They greatly assist a child's readiness to interact with more formal ways of capturing time through agreed units of measure and number patterns and groupings.

Routines, sequences of events and timelines

By making children's early experiences of time involve referencing activities and events that are familiar and repeat themselves as routines and regular occurrences, we can ground children in understanding what our time system is useful for. The Development Matters Document (Early Education, 2012) and P Scale steps are in keeping with the idea of children experiencing first-hand situations where it would be useful to measure the duration of an event or compare two events to see which is longer or shorter. From such comparisons comes the idea of a standardised referencing of time and the analogue and digital systems we rely on to keep time across the world. The first direct reference to time in the National Curriculum states that children in Year 1 need to be able to 'Tell the time to the hour and half past the hour and draw the hands on a clock face to show these times' (DfE, 2014).

Big idea

In order for children to be able to achieve the Year 1 targets in time through understanding, they need to have both understood and participated in events which involve the passing of time. They also need to have experienced and discussed that some things appear to happen quickly and slowly, partly depending on whether we are enjoying them.

If they understand why time is needed and some of the limitations of non-standard measures such as water-clocks, sand-timers and candles then there is a real basis for teaching how to tell the time through number-based units of measure. Part of this process is building up a feel for the passing of time in context linked to units of measure such as seconds, minutes and hours.

Activities that encourage understanding about how to tell the time

Children from early years through Key Stage 1 will benefit from a range of the following:

- How many times they can perform certain tasks in a certain amount of measured time – sand-timers, filling up a bowl of water. Activities such as writing their name, doing step ups on a bench, standing up and sitting down.
- Keeping their eyes shut for 10 seconds, 30 seconds, a minute. Being able to see how near or far out they were. For example, if they guessed 10 seconds at about 6 seconds to be able to see their guess at 6 on a numberline alongside where 10 appears.
- Listening to some music or a dog barking and trying to work out how long it is.
- Listening to people counting from 1 to 20 slowly and quickly and establishing that seconds are a form of counting that happens at a steady, agreed speed.
- Watching seconds elapse on digital and analogue clocks.
- How many bricks they can build in the tower in a minute.
- Trying to count seconds by putting something in between each number as you say it. For example: '1–pudding–2–pudding–3–pudding–4'. It should really be a two-syllable or three-syllable word such as *el-e-phant*, which is a harder word to rush. Young children often keep a rhythm initially and then speed up.

As you can see the emphasis is on meaning and immersing children in activities that develop a feel for time intervals. This is also supported by matching with regular, familiar school and home routines that they may have only interacted with informally. It greatly assists them to put their short lives in context alongside wider sweeps of history that they can relate to.

Activities involving routines and timelines

Relevant activities include:

- Ordering events in the school day: morning play (fruit play), assembly, lunch play, hometime, PE, news time, story (photos of the events will support the associations and ordering).
- Ordering events in their full day including school.
- Ordering events in their everyday life when not at school. Understanding is clearer for young children when concepts covered in school have some real meaning in their world outside.
- Creating time pictures, books and time lines. This can include picture drawing, photography and family tree work.
- Displays and projects about 'a long time ago' can add to connections children can make, along with questions such as 'How do we know this happened a long time ago?'. There are real possibilities to make cross-curricular links with history work. Again, it is fascinating to hear the active thinking, flawed or otherwise, as children make sense of historical accuracy from valid knowledge

accrued in and out of school and by intelligent guesses. It all adds up to being ready to understand and make sense of the digital and analogue systems we use to tell the time.

- Timelines with references to 'now', 'the past' and 'a long time ago' are instructive. They can cover different periods, for example, this week, this school year, a child's life or family tree.

Linear representations of time passing are probably better examples to use when comparing recent time with time further back. They provide clear opportunities to understand the passing of time and the child's place in that development. Above all they provide visual information at a time when children are slowly developing an understanding and motivation to access writing. Circular representations can be good to show repeating routines as well as cycles of time involving 12 or 24 hours, the seasons and yearly cycles.

Big idea

Teaching young children how to gain a feel for the passing of time and some relevance to understanding shorter or longer periods of time is, I believe, a question of understanding child development.

Primary children learn by doing, by building up concrete experiences that give them the opportunity to make connections and begin to understand the world.

There is 'no point in a child being able to read off a digital display or even off a clock face if they are still asking questions such as "Have I had my dinner yet"' (Merttens, 1997: 95).

If children are supported to make sense of events they are familiar with they become more receptive to understanding how to read and interpret analogue and digital clocks.

Telling the time

So now a decent grounding has taken place developing an understanding of why time is needed and what it can achieve, we come to the *potentially* tricky aspect of teaching children to tell the time. I say 'potentially' because although this area has caused teachers and children some problems down the years it doesn't need to be this way. There are so many big ideas regarding telling the time, and if attention is placed on these this may allow children to gain an understanding of key concepts rather than simply memorising information. Once this understanding starts to kick in much of the stress related to this topic for both children and teachers can disappear. So where to begin?

Below are a range of interconnections linked to time that demonstrate that an understanding of our place value is of only limited use when telling the time. In reading the following section consider the following questions:

- What units of measure do we use to record, understand and communicate what the time is?
- How well developed is our understanding of the length of each of the units of time?
- In what ways are they interconnected given that the units of measure are varied?

Dealing with units of measure in telling the time that don't conform to place value

There are so many different units of measuring time and no real common group size. For example:

- 60 seconds make a minute although part seconds tend to get split into tenths, hundredths and thousandths as the columns in our base system reflect. So formal written column addition can take place around this.

$$12.42 \text{ seconds} - \text{Runner A}$$

$$10.95 \text{ seconds} - \text{Runner B}$$

$$\overline{}$$

$$1.47 \text{ seconds}$$

This can be used for calculating the difference between two times for running 100 metres. However, once minutes become involved, we are not able to use standard written methods to record calculations. We would need to have 100 seconds in a minute to do this.

- 3 minutes and 12 seconds cannot be written as 3.12 minutes. The standard representation is to use a colon rather than a decimal point to distinguish between one unit of measure and the next, particularly when referencing hours and minutes.
- 60 minutes make an hour but 24 hours make a day.
- 7 days make a week although the number of days in a month varies from 28 to 31.

- 12 months make a year although every fourth year an extra day is added on. This is because the year as a unit of measurement captures a period of time that elapses to measure the time it takes the earth to rotate one complete cycle around the sun. Given that this period totals 365 $\frac{1}{4}$ days it necessitates an extra day when the four quarters are totalled.
- History is often defined in countries by the rulers of the period or by significant events or by decades, centuries, millennia or longer depending on the context of study or conversation.
- Koshy et al. (2000) discuss the Babylonian theory (from whom many of our units of time stem) that there might have been 360 earth rotations in one passage around the sun: certainly this number might link with the numbers 12, 24 and 60 that key to the other units of time.

Haylock and Cockburn (2008) also reference the distinction between informal and recorded time. We will say 'ten past three' but would not expect to record that as a way of expressing the time formally. At some point the linking up of colloquial references and formal ones ought to be addressed, to avoid or overcome misconceptions. My belief is that it is a much easier issue to deal with from a secure understanding of formal descriptions referencing hours and minutes passed.

Telling the time

Hours and minutes – The hour hand and the minute hand

The following resources are needed for the suggested activities relating to telling the time (Figure 6.1):

- Cog clocks with simultaneously moving hands.
- Electronic teaching programmes, or an IWB that can reference and show both analogue and digital time changes and progression.
- Two analogue clocks with only one hand – one with an hour hand and one with a minute hand.

Figure 6.1 Telling the time

- Clocks that show fractions – divided into quarters.
- $\frac{1}{4}$ circle measures that can show other orientations of $\frac{1}{4}$ hour. For example, from 1 to 4 on the clock or 5 to 8.

Issues that cause confusion and how to face them

Two clock hands

It is a big debate as to when and how to introduce and use both hour and minute hands when learning to understand and use the analogue clock (Figure 6.2).

Figure 6.2   An analogue clock face

Children really struggle with two hands that move simultaneously at different speeds, measuring different units, so it is important that they are guided through this process with some clear thinking.

Related activities: Moving clock hands

Learning intention: Developing an understanding that both hands are moving but at different speeds

Go through with children in Years 1, 2 or 3 showing them analogue clocks with *simultaneously* moving hands, electronic IWB clocks and cog clocks with simultaneously moving hands. It is crucial that children see both hands moving together. Ask them to work out which hand is moving faster (it is the longer hand). Draw out that the longer hand rotates one complete turn in the time that the shorter hand moves from one number to the next. I believe children make healthy inter-connections around the idea that telling the time, initially, should be taught and understood through 'how many hours have passed and how far towards the next hour it is'.

Big idea

Use cog clocks to demonstrate time passing. They show the correct relationship between the two hands that travel at different speeds. Manually moved clock hands create confusion for children.

How many hours have passed?

Rona Catterall (2008) likens children's ability to understand the process of hours passing to a child's awareness and description of their age. They will happily accept that they aren't 7, for example until they actually are 7 (on their birthday). Until that day they are '6 and a bit' and later '6 and quite a lot'. This would also tie in with the quite radical, but logical idea that we could simply focus on the hour hand for a while to understand the passing of hours (Barmby et al., 2009). If you had two analogue clocks and could remove the minute hand from one and the hour hand from the other the interconnections between two hands travelling at different speeds might be easier to take on board. A 'junior' clock might operate with two clock faces in that way.

Developing an understanding of the passing of time

The following activities can all help to develop an understanding of the passing of time:

- Activities with just the hour hand visible on the clock. Asking 'How many hours have gone' could generate discussion about whether the hand has reached halfway towards the next hour or not, or what part of the next hour has elapsed.
- Activities where children look at clock faces with both hands but the sole purpose is to decide how many hours have gone and therefore record the hour digit correctly. 'To be able to decide how many hours have passed' is a very valid learning intention.

- Clock faces showing 'o'clock' with the hour hand on a number indicating the hours that have passed and the long hand (minute hand) covering the 12 or the 'o'clock' position.
- Clock faces showing the hour hand having gone past the hour with the minute hand somewhere else (Figure 6.3). This would work well with the minute hand covered up or not – children probably need to experience both variations.

Figure 6.3   This example has the hour hand roughly half way between the 4 and the 5

 **Big idea**

The numbers on the clock only relate to the hours, not the minutes. (Some clocks will reference the minute marks in multiples of 5 in small digits, but in the main not.)

Children discuss and answer questions with answers such as '5 hours and a bit', '5 and quite a lot', '5 and ever such a lot'. Some children may actually see that when the long (minute) hand is on the 6 it is halfway towards the next hour. It would be very good to begin this stage of identifying the hours and simply asking the children 'How many hours have passed and is it … exactly … a bit past … a lot past or ever such a lot?'.

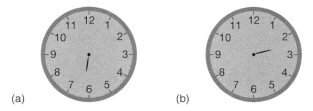

(a)   (b)

Figure 6.4   Understanding the hour hand

In Figure 6.4a we can see that it is 6 hours and only a little bit of the next hour, whereas in Figure 6.4b the next hour has nearly been reached. Teachers would want to try to allow discussion about how many minutes might have elapsed, bearing in mind 60 minutes, rather than 100 represents the full turn.

Clock times could be chosen on cog clocks to allow half the clockface to be covered so that only the hour hand can be seen until discussion and choices have been made.

These clock faces, when the minute hands are revealed, would look something like Figure 6.5.

(a)   (b)

Figure 6.5   The minute hand revealed

Building on from this children can respond to questions such as 'Show me what your clock will look like when 4 and a bit hours have passed' or 'when it is 4 and a bit hours' or 'when 8 and quite a lot hours have passed'. For these activities children *can* use clocks with manually manipulated hands. They are capturing a particular time as opposed to understanding time passing. Children can work in pairs to discuss and support each other. They could then hold their clocks up simultaneously for you as the teacher to see. This allows evaluation of learning. It also gives you the chance to show different variations that represent the same idea. For example, 4:35 and 4:45 would both be relevant for '4 and quite a lot'.

There is a whole hour between each 'o'clock'. It can be a very good idea to create activity charts showing all the things that happen within each hour in school. 'From 9 o'clock until 10 o'clock we …', 'from 10 until 11 o'clock we …'. This could be an hourly update through the day to generate an understanding of both the passing of each hour, what happens within it and the need for more precision. It is also an activity that children could complete for homework: either with a pre-prepared timeline to record activities and events or as a greater challenge for older children to compile their own one.

Understanding hours and minutes

A colon is usually used to separate the hours and minutes. It serves a different purpose from the decimal point.

Following on from these activities, which have focused on identifying whole hours, we have created the idea that these loose terms such as 'and a bit', 'and a lot' and 'ever such a lot' will need a more precise description. Why? Good understanding can be developed through lots of different examples. For instance, it would cause confusion to say school starts at '9 and a bit' hours. Is that 9:05, 9:01, 9:10 and so on? The same point applies with train departure and arrival times, and TV programmes. These are real, meaningful events that necessitate more precise time telling. Most teachers at this point will probably want to use cog clocks to illustrate the hour hand moving from one number to the next as the minute hand rotates completely.

 Big ideas

- The minute (long) hand is measuring the parts of an hour we call minutes.
- 60 minutes make the whole hour and so place value does not apply. 3.5 hours doesn't equate to 3 hours and 5 minutes.
- We should always reference the hours first when discussing time at this stage: 09:20 *or* 9:20am. 9 hours and 20 minutes.

Activities relating to dealing with hours and minutes together

The clock numbers multiply by 5 to indicate the number of minutes that have passed. On a clock face, real or electronic, children count through each minute agreeing the hour numbers show where the multiples of 5 are. This can be supported by clocks that actually show the minute numbers next to the hour numbers.

For example:

- 1 (5);
- 2 (10);
- 3 (15);
- 4 (20).

There could be time spent with the minute numbers covered up. For example, in pairs children could be asked to work out how many minutes are indicated when the minute hand reaches the 4 on the clock face. Then the number can be revealed and it can be agreed that 20 minutes is the minute count at this point. This can of course be extended to include the minute indicators between the numbers.

At this point it is the idea that there are two hands (pointers) measuring two different things (hours and minutes) that is now being stressed. Ask children why the hands of the clock are different lengths. (Was it that they didn't have two the same size when the clock was made?!) Children stay engaged with humour and will hopefully make connections. It also shows you whether they understand the two different clock hands.

Further activities that can be set to reinforce these concepts include:

- Use a clock face with only the minute hand showing to work out how many minutes have passed. Initially this would be in multiples of 5 and they would calculate how many minutes had gone.
- Watching the simultaneous movement through a whole rotation (an hour), for example, 9 o'clock until 10 o'clock. This would be best done alongside other work in class.
- Agreeing a sequence of events for a day with your class, including events within the school day. Make sure some events occur within the same hour. For example:
  - Wake up.
  - Leave for school.
  - School starts.
  - Assembly starts.
  - Assembly finishes.
  - Morning play starts.
  - Morning play finishes.

Other notable known events can be included. Children can be presented with handouts of these events. Together they can be given the time on the analogue clock and have to agree how to record the time in hours and minutes. This would support a learning intention of deepening an awareness of how time elapses.

Other ideas linked to understanding hours and minutes

The following ideas can support learning intentions relating to applying knowledge about measuring start and finish time durations.

- TV schedule lists. Luckily these are referenced in hours and minutes anyway and usually fairly motivating for children. Variations on using this can include:
  - Children making the start times of programmes on their clocks.
  - Being shown analogue programme start times and recording these in hours and minutes.

Gradually these can become more challenging and children can begin to take on the length of periods between different times. For example, you could work up to questions such as:

- 'How long did a show or journey last that started at 08:15 and finished at 08:50?'
- 'At what time did the 40-minute journey begin that ended at 15:25?'

Big idea

Check examples through first before using them, as some time lapses go across the hour and add complexity.

Children can initially find crossing the hour barrier a challenge, seeing as there are not 100 minutes to an hour. Therefore a time such as 02:70 can't exist. Ryan and Williams (2007) identify that passages of time crossing the hour are a constant source of misunderstanding. Discussions around key features of TV schedules can deepen children's understanding as strategies are discussed. For example:

- 'So, if the news was on for 20 minutes and began at 8:55pm how did you solve the problem? Ah! I see, you drew a line and calculated from 8:55pm to 9pm (5 minutes) and added 15 minutes onto that. Well done. If I told you that a child had recorded 8:75 as the answer, could you discuss in twos where this answer may have come from?'

Fractions of an hour and digital time

Within the framework of this development, non-standard, visual time references and experiences, following the hours and minutes approach, come fractions of an hour. Logically, if children are comfortable interpreting and linking hours and minutes then they are already able to interpret digital time referencing. There are one or two tricky connections, which we will cover below, but the approach is the same in terms of understanding how many hours and how many minutes.

To understand fractions of an hour a child should be able to have a meaningful understanding of part wholes. Part whole sections of the clock can assist seeing the journey of the minute hand as a fraction of an hour. Children are only able to reference 'quarter past', or 'half past' with any understanding when they can do this. Part whole segments ($\frac{1}{2}$ circle and $\frac{1}{4}$ circle) can do two things: firstly,

Figure 6.6

they can indicate the journey from the whole hour (o'clock) towards the next mark, 6:00 to 6:15 or 6:30. This can support a learning intention concerning applying knowledge of fractions to parts of an hour (Figure 6.6). Also they can be used to link that particular passage of time ($\frac{1}{4}$ hour and $\frac{1}{2}$ hour) to other time differences and time passages that have a different orientation. As in work with shapes and fractions, children often have a very underdeveloped sense of the orientation of part wholes. The part whole clock segments can be used to grow different neural pathways; that the $\frac{1}{4}$ hour segment (15 minutes) and the $\frac{1}{2}$ segment (30 minutes) can be represented in many orientations, for example with the minute hands between 11 and 2, for $\frac{1}{4}$ hour or between 2 and 8 for $\frac{1}{2}$ hour, and so on.

 **Big idea**

Half an hour is half of 60 minutes. ¼ hour is 15 minutes because four lots of this make an hour. The passing of an hour doesn't have to begin at 'o'clock'. These sorts of discussions, visual experiences and related activities will help children to understand quarter past, half past, and three quarters past (or 'a quarter to'). Many children have been taught to recognise a hand pointing at 3, 6 or 9 and connect it to a term without understanding what it means, consequently it has not been knowledge that they could use and apply.

There is the option at this point for the teacher to introduce colloquial language, for example, 'ten to', 'twenty to' or 'ten past the hour'.

Understanding the term 'ten past six' would involve children in working out what the numbers referred to: ten minutes and 6 o'clock or 6 hours. Until now they have learnt hours and minutes referenced in that order.

Train or bus timetables are very good for showing how much information can be shown in table form. Maps can also be included. Children enjoy both known places and fictitious ones. I have compiled timetables and maps linked to children's names in class. For example, Samstone, Kelly-on-Sea, Hollyville, St Katherine's Port. They are a valid way of referencing the 24-hour clock in context. For some reason 11pm is often mistakenly associated with 21:00, possibly because each number is one more than a multiple of ten.

The responsible primary maths teacher is keen to teach for understanding. Issues such as the above form part of a series of potential misunderstandings and confusion that a knowing teacher will seek to clarify and explain. I would strongly argue that if these potential misunderstandings can be confronted head-on as clearly as possible they can be part of the way in which children deepen their understanding. We will now have a look at a number of these and how you might introduce them in your classroom.

Possible misconceptions

Confusing the hour and minute hand

For example, mixing up 7:10 with 10:7. This is partly overcome by encouraging hour:minute recording. Also use the key questions 'Why aren't the hands the same length?' 'Why does one hand travel faster than the other?'. These secure the idea that the shorter, slower moving hand indicates the hours and the minutes build on to this. A way of confronting this head on could be to actually put times on an analogue clock with common mistakes and correct answers to choose from to discuss.

Figure 6.7   An analogue clock showing 01:50

For example, 'Does this clock show 2:10 or 10:02 or 01:50'. In fact ten minutes to the hour is the one time when the numbers are accidentally correct. The long hand is on the 10 when it is ten to … but at no other point do the numbers signify the minutes (Figure 6.7).

Thinking the hour will be the number the pointer is closest to rather than the one it has reached

Figure 6.8 An analogue clock showing 06:50

For example, thinking 6:50 must be 7:something because the hour hand is close to the 7 even though it hasn't reached it (Figure 6.8).

Somewhere along the way you would want to develop the idea that when the time is just past 'o'clock' there will be only a few minutes of the new hour gone; when the minute hand is on 11 it is indicating that another whole hour has not quite been reached. This links nicely to Rona Catterall's idea about age, for example, 6:55 is not quite 7 o'clock in the way that a 6 year old whose birthday is next week is 6 and ever such a lot but not quite 7 years old yet. It would also be supported by a lesson focus on the BIG IDEA that 'the numbers on the clock only indicate the hours'.

Thinking that 20 minutes after 3:55 will be 3:75

This can emerge from the misconception that there may be 100 minutes in an hour. Specific work around the change over to the new hour can be very useful. Visual representation, initially, can greatly assist children.

How far to the new hour (o'clock) and how far beyond?

__3:55 _____ 4:00 _____ 4:15 _____

5 mins   15 mins

Why are there two hands?

The answer to this is really that the minute hand gives a more exact idea of what part of the next hour has passed. On an analogue clock if you tried covering up the minute hand the position of the hour hand would still allow you to estimate the time fairly well. The same could not be said with the minute hand.

Not understanding how to tell the time using a 24-hour clock

Converting from a 12-hour to a 24-hour clock means counting on from 12 and not 10. So 3pm is derived by counting on 3 from 12 to get 15.

Why do we need to put a 0 in when we write 7 hours and 5 minutes (07:05)?

This can be a tricky point to convey but digital clocks that reference hours and minutes are still looking to put the first digit after the colon as multiples of 10 minutes even though there aren't 100 minutes in an hour.

Not understanding that it is one quarter of an hour from 4:10 to 4:25

Often this can be attributed to an underdeveloped sense of the time intervals. Children are sometimes only engaged in $^1/_4$ hour time passages from $^1/_4$ past to $^1/_2$ past or $^1/_4$ to until o'clock. The solution is a sound one: they need to make other connections. If they can create and use $^1/_4$, $^1/_2$ and $^3/_4$ clock face templates they can identify from a list of times which ones do and don't represent such passages of time. They may also like to create their own questions for friends and indeed the class. These can include:

Which of the following is not a time difference of $^1/_4$ hour?

- 3:30pm until 3:45pm ✓
- 4:55pm until 5:10pm ✓
- 7.15am until 7:30pm ✗
- 8:50pm until 9:10pm ✗
- 4:00am until 4:15pm ✓

Problem solving with time

Children should be exposed to problem solving at all ages. The ideas covered in this chapter about teaching the topic of time to young children provide opportunities for problem solving; as do the ideas about timetables, TV listings and part whole templates. The ideas about using one hand only relate to applying knowledge. Children really enjoy setting their own questions to show their understanding, as in the BIG IDEA on the next page.

Children need to apply knowledge. When you can see they are grasping what you are teaching get them to take control by creating their own problems. For example:

- Children will need to learn the days in each month. Rhymes can help this. They also need opportunities to test out the different number groupings through problems to solve.
- 'How many days, seconds, weeks or months have I been alive?'
- 'How many minutes until my birthday?'
- 'I am 7. I was born on 07-08-2008. Today's date is 21-02-16. How many days until I am 10?'

These kinds of problem can be well served by using a calculator. Why? Because the thrust of the thinking is about interpreting what the question is asking and thinking what calculation to put in the calculator; not so much the calculation. NRICH (nrich.maths. org) and other websites have a range of ideas that can be used to support teaching for understanding.

Conclusion

Keep your nerve when you teach time. Be determined to teach for understanding. Hopefully a number of the points raised here will resonate. The two which I really feel strongly about are: the numbers on the clock relate to the hours; and try not to teach the passing of time without a cog clock with simultaneously moving hands. Comedian Dave Allen's stand-up routine about 'Teaching Your Kid Time' (available on YouTube) covers most common misconceptions about time in a very amusing form. The idea that the numbers show the hours only on most clocks could be emphasised through radical ways of stressing this as the chapter has illustrated; above all ensure that children have experience of or can relate to the features of time you are teaching.

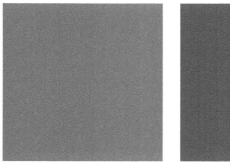

Algebra

 Learning objectives

By the end of this chapter you should be able to:

- Understand and identify key terminology of variables and constants within patterns and algebra related visual and written sequences.
- Have a wider understanding of algebraic reasoning through examples discussed.
- Know how resources, particularly Cuisenaire rods and function machines, can support the bridging of understanding from the concrete to the abstract.
- Understand the relevance of balance in how equations, algorithms and problems are expressed and solved.
- Begin to know how to get children to articulate understanding related to patterns and sequences of events.
- Understand some common misconceptions that can prevent deeper understanding, such as the fruit salad approach to unknown items.

 What does the National Curriculum say?

The process of identifying patterns and being able to identify and express them using symbols relating to relationships that will hold for variable inputs alongside constants is, understandably, not specified in detail in the early stages of the National Curriculum. The use of formulae to calculate area and volume of two-dimensional and three-dimensional shapes and representation is related to algebra. There are identified suggestions related to area and volume formulae in Years 4 and 5. These relate to knowing the perimeter of rectangles as $P = 2(L + w)$ as opposed to doubling the length, doubling the width and adding them together. By implication there is an algebraic link in as much as the perimeter, width and length of certain shapes are linked; as in the radius, diameter, perimeter (circumference) and area of a circle.

By Year 6 the expectation is explicit and the requirements are clear. They build on the use of simple formulae, which I will argue, strongly, needs to be understood if it is to be used. It is expected that children will be able to generate and describe 'linear number sequences'. They are required to represent 'missing number' problems algebraically. This will require addressing problems around this issue in ways children can understand. There are clear ideas on how to do that in this chapter.

Children are also expected to tackle equations that include two unknowns and to explore combinations of two variables. These skills will need to have relevant and effective pre-steps with younger primary children to allow this work to have both meaning and a relevance to later understanding in secondary school. These issues will also be addressed in this chapter.

The other earlier, though not explicit link to algebra appears in Year 2 where children are expected to know and begin to use commutativity. This relates to addition in particular and also multiplication. If approached at a sound fundamental level this will link well to later requirements in upper Key Stage 2.

Let us now clarify what algebraic reasoning, thinking and doing can look like with primary children and how it can be developed.

Algebraic reasoning

Algebraic thinking and reasoning relates to thinking that is simply different to coming up with a single answer to a problem. It relates to looking for links between different parts of a pattern or some numbers or sequences. It involves being able to explain what the pattern that explains these situations actually is. Although words can be useful, it includes representing relationships numerically or symbolically.

Curriculum guidance in England quite rightly continues to reference the importance of applying knowledge. Upfront this includes the process of problem solving, supported by the need to articulate and reason and for fluency in how mathematical work is carried out. Algebra, particularly focuses on the first two of these. Problems need to be solved. Algebraic problems involve understanding, explaining and representing the thinking behind problems. They can and do involve numbers but also symbols to represent groups of numbers that are defined.

Example

Two siblings, Alex and Billy, are aged 5 and 7. That is to say, Billy is 2 years older than Alex. That is a fairly straightforward calculation related to difference. Within the same model it could also be said that Alex is 2 years younger than Billy.

Algebraic reasoning and thinking would and could explore the link between the two siblings not just now, but at any point in their lives. This gives rise to multiple, linked sums, involving the two *variables*, Child A and Child B and how they are linked.

Symbolic representations of the pattern linking the two would include showing how the two ages are linked.

$$X = \text{younger sibling}. \quad Y = \text{older sibling}$$

$$X = Y - 2$$

$$Y = X + 2$$

The pattern of the relationship between the two ages at any point can be represented by these statements. We have captured the link between the two siblings at any point in their lives, not just one. This difference between the specific calculation and the representation of how the two ages are linked in multiple ways is the essence of algebraic thinking and it underpins the way that more complex equations are expressed, unpicked and used in algebra in later school or post school.

Links with commutativity and the associative laws

You will remember the discussion in Chapter 4 on addition and subtraction, about how addition and subtraction are inverse operations; a reversal of the operation allows a return to the starting point.

$$2 + 4 = 6 \text{ therefore } 6 = 2 + 4 \text{ and } 6 - 2 = 4$$

These calculations can be demonstrated visually using the coloured blocks in Figure 7.1.

Figure 7.1

It is not such a large leap from this to the commutative law identifying operations of addition and subtraction.

$$a + b = c$$

$$c - b = a$$

With addition and multiplication the order in which the algorithm is carried out makes no difference.

Caleb Gattegno (1988) states that 'You can't learn arithmetic without learning algebra'. It has certainly been the case that in the past arithmetic has taken place in isolation from algebraic reasoning. More recently these connections underpin much more modelling and mental calculation development. It can be fine-tuned further to develop algebraic reasoning.

💡 Big ideas

- The associative law invites us to teach both addition and subtraction through visual resources. This grows the pathways for applying the knowledge, algebraically in equations.
- Children deepen their understanding when they are encouraged to explore at the upper end of their understanding.

Here are some ways they might visit algebraic thinking in commutativity in the primary years.

Holly is 3 years younger than her brother Raj. Cahal is 3 years older than Kayleigh, who is a year older than Emil. Complete Tables 7.1 and 7.2 showing how old each child will be at various points in their life.

Table 7.1

Holly	Raj
3	–
	7
7	
	14

The ages of family members makes a very sound basis for exploring algebraic relationships. Children are often knowledgeable and motivated to explore thinking around the ages of their family. A typical activity exploring this could be as follows:

a   Record the ages of your family.

b   How much older is your cousin than you?

c   What age will you be when your cousin is twice as old?

d   Why do you double your cousin's age to find how old they will be when you are half their age?

Table 7.2

Cahal	Kayleigh	Emil
2		
	7	
		14
	14.5	
18		

e   Will you ever be older than your cousin?

f   Write an equation that would allow us to work out your age if we know the age of your cousin.

g   Can we use this equation to find your age if we know your cousin's or does it need to be changed?

Algebraic thinking

This involves reasoning and making sense of how problems often have key features to them that can be understood. It is these connections that define the work as a problem. Otherwise we would be talking about several problems. If children are to be able to look at multiple problems that are connected by and through common features then they need to invest time early in their primary school lives to explore this understanding that is built on progressively. This means they will become confident in looking for patterns, understanding how connections are present through the variables involved, even though the numbers involved are different. This is what Gattegno meant by the link between arithmetic and algebra. Cahal is 3 years older than Kayleigh; not just now, next year or in a decade. The sums that calculate their ages now are specific. The ones needed for a few years' time are different. Crucially, the difference is predictable. Understanding this connection is almost more important than the answer.

Big idea

In algebraic thinking it is more important to understand the pattern and the connection than it is to be able to work the answer out.

Clearly the answer is important, but without the understanding the ability to work out the answer is meaningless. So how are these thought processes developed in ways that focus on deepening understanding and not just on rules that need to be learnt, remembered and, in all probability, misapplied? Here is an example of a problem involving algebraic thinking and reasoning that is appropriate for children in later primary school who are operating with some confidence.

Activity: Paving slab problem

Learning intention: To use (visual) pictorial sequences as a basis for understanding sequences links that are not visual

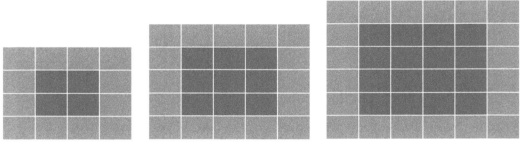

Figure 7.2   **Figure 7.3**   **Figure 7.4**

Figures 7.2–7.4 represent different sizes of gardens with a central lawn surrounded by a perimeter of paving slabs. There is a link between the amount of squares of lawn and the amount of similar width paving slabs needed to make the path acting as a perimeter to the lawn. The shape of the lawn inside the paving slabs is also a square shape. The task is to work out an explanation or a formula or equation that would allow us to be able to tell the amount of paving slabs or squares of lawn needed if we are in possession of only one of these amounts.

Possible and common strategies

Counting the number of squares is an extremely sound initial strategy and is very likely to be illuminating in some way, particularly if the counting is accurate. It may not lead to further thinking initially. Possible teacher prompts here could include:

- 'How do you know there are that many slabs?'
- 'There are 4 sides to that perimeter. Each side has got 3 slabs. So why isn't your total 12? 4 lots of 3 make 12' (This is a slight risk but possibly one worth taking. You are trying to provoke mathematical thinking and algebraic reasoning. It may or may not prompt a response.)
- 'Oh yes, it is 4 less than what we might have expected. Is that always the case or just on this one?'

Clearly the art of judgement determines when to keep quiet and when to speak. On other occasions a discussion can be initiated for children to share ideas. Encouraging a classroom culture where all children are thinking and evaluating each others' ideas is vital. The teacher's role is to know possible options to prompt and to encourage debate and deepen justification, rigour and understanding as best as they are able.

Listed below are other interpretations that children can suggest. The goal is to provoke deeper thinking and understanding of the variables involved and their connections. In this case, the number of paving slabs, or the side of one square and either the number of squares of lawn or the length of the side of the lawn.

- $(4 \times$ length of side of path$) - 4$ (double counting).
- $4 \times$ length of the lawn $+ 4$ (add on 4 corners).

Length of side of lawn and length of side of path differ by 2:

- $4 \times$ length of a side half way between lawn length and path length.

Cuisenaire rods are perfect to represent and grow this way of thinking. The four repeated lengths dovetail to allow this interpretation of the problem.

- 2 longer sides and 2 shorter sides:

$$((2 \times n) + (2(n - 2))) \text{ where } n \text{ is the path side length}$$

$$((2n + 2) + 2(n - 2)) \text{ where } n \text{ is the lawn side length}$$

- The path and the lawn can be seen as 2 squares. If we see the paving slab square as n^2 and the lawn square as $(n - 2)^2$, we could find the number of paving slabs by subtracting the number of squares for the lawn from the number of squares for the whole space. This could be expressed as:

$$n^2 \text{ (whole space)} - (n - 2)^2 \text{ (lawn space)} = \text{number of paving slabs}$$
$$\text{in the perimeter of the space}$$

Please take time to examine the different interpretations of the problem. It is a rich problem that demonstrates clearly that time spent with young children getting behind problems at a fundamental level with illuminating, manipulable resources can create deep thinking. This thinking can be captured in words, symbols and figures to a greater or lesser degree.

Big ideas

- Clarity of the problem matched with relevant resources to represent it provide rich potential for children to notice connections and to speculate.
- As with problem solving maths pedagogy, it is important to let ideas, flawed or otherwise, emerge. It is the journey that is important. Even if children were all able to come up with a solution that was similar there would still be real merit in opening the discussion and interest up to consider other ideas and solutions.
- The answer isn't everything. A BIG IDEA for the teacher is to keep asking 'What else can you see?'.

Balance and the question of the = sign

As you may be aware, one of the things children can struggle with later in secondary school is the idea of balanced equations. This is a concept that can be explored and developed in an age-appropriate manner in primary mathematics.

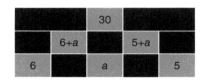

Figure 7.5

In Figure 7.5, if we are adding two numbers together to find the number in the top row we see that in the middle row we end up with:

$$6 + a + 5 + a$$

which added up will make 30 altogether.

This can be changed to:

$$11 + a + a = 30$$

This equation can also be expressed as:

$$11 + 2a = 30$$

If we then subtract 11 from both sides of the equation we have:

$$30 - 11 = 2a$$

Thus

$$19 = 2a$$

If we halve each side of the equation we can find out that a has a value of 9.5.

It is here that we can see that it is very much to children's advantage to understand equals (=) in the context of balancing. Then we can say that $6 + 5 = 11$ but also that $11 = 6 + 5$.

It depends which side of the seesaw you are sitting. We could also use 'does not equal' ($\neq$), for example, in expressing that $6 + 4 \neq 11$ and $11 \neq 6 + 4$.

Seeing the equals sign (=) as meaning balanced

There are several things that you can do to develop this understanding about seeing 'equal' as balanced. Numicon resources are useful here. The Numicon pieces have been weighted so that a 5 and a 2 would indeed balance with a 6 and a 1. Or an 8 would balance with a 6 and a 2 (Figure 7.6). The scales that accompany the

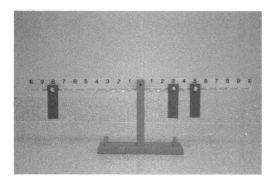

Figure 7.6

resource ensure that the weight distribution reinforces the concept of balance and there are various tasks, experiences and discussions that can take place.

Activity: Can you find ways to make the scales balance?

Learning intention: Developing a deeper understanding of equals; to know that the equal sign (=) can be placed anywhere between two equivalent representations. (The unbalanced concept also works for establishing concepts of 'greater than' (>) and 'less than' (<)

Record the number(s) on the left hand arm of the balance. Record the number(s) on the right hand arm on the right. Use an equal sign in the middle to show they are balanced.

For example, $8 = 3 + 5$

The idea of 'balanced' can be expanded to include 'has the same value', and a range of balanced algorithms can emerge showing = as a reference to balance rather than 'makes'.

5 and $2 = 7$

$6 = 4 + 2$

4 and $3 = 5$ and 2

If you take some off the left hand arm what will you need to do to the right hand arm?

This demonstrates very clearly that if an adjustment is made to one side of the 'equation' or 'algorithm' then a similar adjustment needs to be made to ensure that the overall balance and equality is maintained. Children are then able to adapt and record calculations in the following ways:

i $5 + 4 = 9$

ii $5 + 4 - 4 = 9 - 4$

iii $7 = 3 + 4$

iv $7 + 2 = 3 + 4 + 2$

In a practical and visually rich context children can become comfortable with such adaptations and amendments to algorithms that they have made or followed. In doing so they are learning the early stages of balancing equations.

Balanced equations and the equals sign in primary maths – multiplication and division

At some point children will be able to apply the same principles to multiplication and division, although this really requires them to accept the premise that these operations require the same interconnected adaptations. Multiplication and division have inverse links, a topic we explored in detail in Chapter 5.

Commutativity activities that grow early confidence

Commutativity is a fundamental principle of early calculation as children begin to see that there is a logic to our counting system. There are links and connections. It is not solely about memorisation. Consider the following ways that cubes, Cuisenaire rods or square paper and colouring pencils can be used to cement this understanding. Figures 7.7 and 7.8 are made up of different sized groups of squares, or cubes that have been colour-coded into 1s, 2s, 3s and 4s.

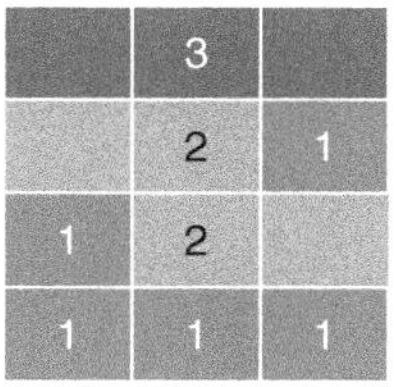

Figure 7.7

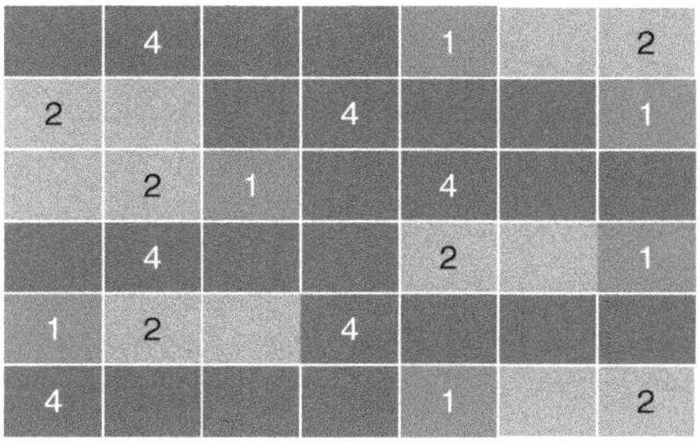

Figure 7.8

Tasks like this and those that follow can serve children's understanding well, as the ability to understand cognitively is supported and developed initially through the visual, concrete experience.

Activity: Commutativity with cubes

Learning intention: To deduce different but equivalent algorithms in the context of rearrangement and the ability to articulate what has happened

Use Figures 7.7 and 7.8 to see how many ways you can make 3 (or 6 or 7):

i   Choose three small numbers to put together in different ways.
ii What is similar and what is different?

Can you find a different way to use these three colours that hasn't been used yet?
    This ties in closely with the problem solving pedagogy of children being encouraged to find all possible solutions and to know when they have finished, a topic explored in greater depth in Chapter 6. Furthermore, although there are specific patterns to the multiple arrangements of different numbers, above all it reinforces a key early algebraic idea.

Big idea

Physical arrangements of numbers prove commutativity of addition and its relevance to algebraic thinking.

Activity: Making 12 using 1, 2 or 3 only

Learning intention: To establish and refine understanding of patterns in the context of game play; and to be able to use other children's thinking alongside your own

Versions of the 21 game (see Chapter 1 for a fuller explanation of how to play) also give children the opportunity to understand, either consciously or subconsciously, how algebraic thinking can be used. Here the target of 12 or a number less allows algebraic thinking to emerge naturally.
    Played in pairs the above game, played with 1, 2 or 3 blocks (Figure 7.9) and with the goal of reaching a total of 12, references key strategies such as 'the winning number' and numbers that allow you to control the outcome. It also uses knowledge of interpreting the variable of the

Figure 7.9

Figure 7.10

number your opponent says. These features can be developed with very young children, for example, the first one to reach 6, taking it in turns with 1 and 2 blocks (Figure 7.10). It is even possible to reference the variables algebraically. The 2 variables here are the total that is 1 more than the number required to reach the desired total (y). We can say that the target number (y) equals y minus multiples of x between 0 and y.

Reception children playing 'first to 5', and taking it in turns, are still able to use algebraic reasoning to establish that some numbers work and others don't, depending on whether you go first or second.

Multiplication and division

Building on this, it is also possible to use concrete resources such as cubes, Cuisenaire and Numicon to show commutativity and balance regarding multiplication and division.

Again the balance scales with Numicon and the Cuisenaire rods greatly assist this understanding. They can also be used to introduce the concept that acting equally on either side of a balanced equation will maintain the balance.

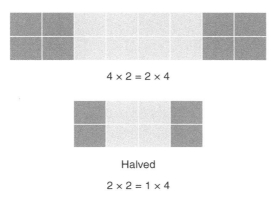

$4 \times 2 = 2 \times 4$

Halved

$2 \times 2 = 1 \times 4$

Figure 7.11

Therefore, $3 \times 4 = 12$ will have links with other multiplication facts (Figure 7.11):

$2(3 \times 4) = 2 (12)$ where we have multiplied both sides by 2.

$(3 \times 4) \div 2 = 12 \div 2$ where we have divided both sides by 2.

Distributive law

Figures 7.12 and 7.13 show how larger multiplication sums can be broken down into smaller parts.

The distributive law, mentioned in Chapter 5 is stated as $a(b + c) = ab + ac$.

As shown above this is allowing a break up of numbers being multiplied into smaller parts, so long as all the parts of one number multiply by all the parts of the other. The recombining through addition is vital to understanding this concept. It

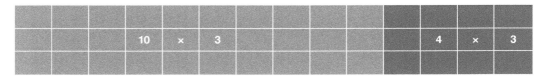

Figure 7.12 14×3

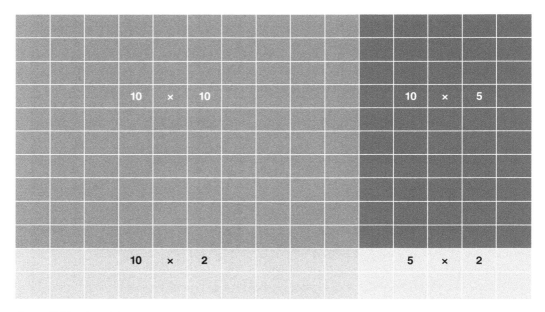

Figure 7.13 15×12

Figure 7.14 $6 \times 2 = (5 \times 2) + (1 \times 2)$

can be emphasised clearly through the use of Numicon. When also represented by Cuisenaire rods this rule is not only modelled but its meaning becomes clear.

The choices made in solving a problem such as 6×2 by drawing on knowledge of 5×2 and adding on 2 is clear evidence of understanding balanced equations in algebraic thinking (Figure 7.14).

When children first encounter multiplication they should be encouraged to partition multiplication sums to develop this understanding.

Symbols as 'explicit' or 'variable' references

The relevance of algebra is that non-numerical symbols can allow relationships between different variables to be explained, meaning that for a particular set of circumstances the relationship between these features will hold. It is a fallacy to suppose that primary children cannot understand this.

So, in the 6 times table, the number of groups of 6 eggs (described here as x, although it could also relate to boxes) has a link to the total altogether (known as y but here relating to eggs). If x equals the number of boxes and y equals the number of eggs then $y = 6x$ is explaining the idea that for every 6 eggs there is 1 box. If there are y eggs in x boxes we can say that $y = 6x$. This is because every box contains 6 eggs, thus you need to divide the number of eggs by 6 to derive the number of full boxes.

In numerical quantity if we are comparing the same number of full boxes as eggs (say 5 boxes full of eggs as opposed to simply 5 eggs), we would have 6 times as many eggs in the boxes. However, if we are simply comparing the numerical value of x and y then they would be the same. For the relationship of a balanced equation involving eggs (y) and boxes (x) we would say that $y = 6x$ and not the other way around. In other words, there are 6 times as many eggs as boxes, even though the equivalent amount of boxes as eggs would suggest the relationship is the other way around. So, in the 6 times table we could say that x was the number of groups of 6 and y was the total once the groups had been put together. Then y would equal 6 times the value of whatever x is. So if $x = 4$ then y will equal 4 lots of 6.

Haylock (2014) suggests that when working with older primary children on the use of letters to demonstrate general statements it is made clear that 'a letter in algebra stands for whatever number is chosen'. Thus it is a variable and not the item itself. The general thinking is that the 'fruit salad' approach of referencing a = apples, b = bananas and c = cherries is confusing for children, suggesting it is the specific object or fruit that is being represented rather than the variable value.

 Big idea

When encouraging older primary children to represent variables emphasise the symbol is standing for whatever value is being used in this relationship.

If x boxes of eggs equal 30, then the value of y is 30.

With 6 eggs in a box the value of x would be 5.

$(6 + 6 + 6 + 6 + 6) = 30$.

Finding relationships from familiar contexts to emphasise variables

Although we have used eggs in the example above many everyday items can be used to emphasise the concept of variables. Other examples might include: bicycles, cars, shoes, 5-a-side teams, cards in a pack, stumps in a wicket, strings on a violin, strings on a guitar. Presented with this list I am fairly certain that children throughout the primary age range would add relevant contexts where a certain number of items form a known group size, such as football stickers, sweets in a packet, squares in a chocolate bar, how many matchsticks make a triangle and so on.

 ## Activity: Using everyday items to emphasise variables

Learning intention: to emphasise the concept of variables using everyday items

Define the symbols of the connected items (taking care to avoid the 'a = apple' fruit salad approach). Express them in terms of one another.

For example,

a   *h* is the number of guitars, *x* is the number of strings. Therefore $x = 6h$ and $h = x/6$ or $x \div 6$. If the guitars are strung then the number of strings will be 6 times the number of guitars.

b   *s* is the number of players needed, *b* is the number of teams. Therefore $s = 5b$ or $b = s/5$. In this example 5 teams would obviously include more than just 5 players.

c   Jasvinder is 2 years older than Carly. *F* represents Jasvinder's age, *C* shows Carly's age

$$F = C + 2 \text{ or } C = F - 2$$

 Big idea

There is a difference between numbers that the variables reference as opposed to the group sizes involved. 6 guitars and 6 strings have an equal value in 6. However, there are clearly more than 6 strings on 6 guitars.

Multiplication or a missing number?

Consider the following: C is the number of groups of 3, P is the total when the groups are put together, so we can say: $P = 3C$ or $C = P/3$. It is important to distinguish between $3C$ meaning 3 lots of the value of C in algebra as opposed to $23 + 8 = 3C$ where it is being used as a missing digit. That point may need some focus for a while.

Rules as a concept to explain how variables are linked

There are two big ways that primary children can really start to make sense of variables that are connected by rules or actions. One is to try to make sense of what the rule is numerically. The other is to look at visual representations of problems that show the impact of what is happening through what is staying the same and what is changing. Let us look at them both.

A number of teachers report both success and complexity through encouraging children to look at variables that are linked and trying to work out in what way: it can be a successful way of developing their understanding, it can also be a

Machine 1		
IN (x)	Action	OUT (y)
1		4
2		8
3		12
4		16
10		40
n		4n

Rule $y = 4x$

Machine 2		
IN (x)	Action	OUT (y)
1		10
2		20
3		30
10		100
25		250
n		10n

Rule $y = 10x$

Machine 3		
IN (x)	Action	OUT (y)
0		7
1		17
2		27
3		37
10		107
n		10n + 7

Rule $y = 10x + 7$

Figure 7.15 Function machines

complicated process. In Figure 7.15, sometimes referenced as a function machine, the focus is on what is happening to the number going into the machine to create the number coming out.

In Machine 1 the action or rule connecting the initial number with the one emerging is that it is being multiplied by 4. The evidence for this is that for each additional number added to the number going into the machine the number coming out grows by 4. This is in fact a BIG IDEA.

Big idea

The amount that the input variable increases by to produce the output variable is an indicator of the multiple involved, if there is one.

Thus, when we look at the following rule or function in Machine 2 we again see the output increasing by a steady amount, 10, each time. The rule is that the starting number is being multiplied by 10, effectively giving us the 10 times table. In the third machine we see that the output is increasing by 10 although the outcome is not the 10 times table: there has been an addition.

In short the equations that govern Machines 2 and 3 are connected. $y = 10x$ *and* $y = 10x + 7$

If we look at how the equations look as graphs we can see that the gradient is the same (10) and therefore the graphs are parallel. The point at which the equation

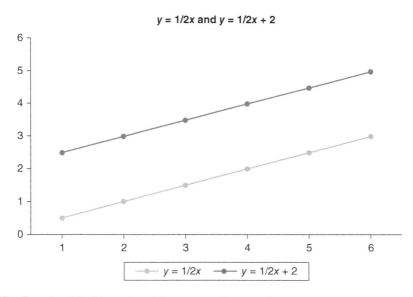

Machine 4

In (x)	Action	Out (y)
0		0
1		½
2		1
3		1½
4		2
10		5
n		½ n

Rule $y = \frac{1}{2}x$

Machine 5

In (x)	Action	Out (y)
0		2
1		2½
2		3
3		3½
4		4
10		7
n		½ n + 2

Rule $y = \frac{1}{2}x + 2$

Figure 7.16   Two more function machines

Figure 7.17   Function Machines 4 and 5 expressed as graphs

crosses the *x* axis will tell us the *constant*. There are related patterns for functions that involve division. We will explore this use of graphs with two more function machines (Figures 7.16 and 7.17).

Sequential and global generalising

Trying to establish rules that connect independent variables is hard. The discussion above is an attempt to break down some of the mystique for children, and for you with regard to 'global generalisations', that is to say, the rule connecting the whole way in which the two variables are connected.

Machines 4 and 5 both show a gradient of $\frac{1}{2}$ although the adjustment of 2 in Machine 5 is shown clearly when 0 is inputted. Therefore, we could easily give a global generalisation of the rule connecting any sequence of integers inputted that increase by a regular amount, be it $\frac{1}{2}$, 5 or 1000. These are potentially powerful ideas for you and the children you teach. Children find what is termed the 'sequential generalisation' much easier to identify and name (Table 7.3). That is to say they follow a sequence from one term to the next.

Table 7.3 Generalisations for Function Machines 4 and 5

	Machine 4	Machine 5
Sequential generalisation	It goes up by ½ each time	It goes up by ½ each time
Global generalisation	Rule $y = \frac{1}{2}x$	Rule $y = \frac{1}{2}x + 2$

They both go up by $\frac{1}{2}$ but there is a difference that the sequential globalisation misses.

Progression

We should be delighted to hear that young children spot patterns to do with common difference. We seek it when we fill in 100 squares or show even or odd number pieces of Numicon where we can show a visual pattern of jumps of 3 but using numbers not in the 3 times table such as 1, 4, 7 rather than 3, 6, 9. All of this learning is to be welcomed.

It may well be that global generalising is not secure for some children by the end of primary school. We should strive to make it secure in situations where there is only a one operation rule or function in place, as in eggs in the box, shoes for a child, wheels on the car and so on. Children being able to use a symbol to represent two different variables and being able to link them effectively is huge. Being able to understand that: $m(\text{wheels}) = 4n(\text{cars})$ or $n(\text{cars}) = \frac{1}{4}m(\text{wheels})$ is very significant.

This understanding can be enhanced considerably through visual data rather than purely numeric, so the line graphs in Figure 7.17 showing the equations $y = \frac{1}{2}x$ and $y = \frac{1}{2}x + 2$ assist discussion. Linear graphs show the progression and relationship of how two variables, often called x and y, develop as the values change. The fact that they are in a line indicates that the increase is by a consistent, continuous amount. This will be in the form of a ratio. This can be 1:1 or something different.

Children can benefit from both interpreting and creating straight line graphs. Tables, costs of items, conversion rates, euros or kilometres and miles – these ideas all relate to straight line graphs. They can be used to show the consistency of the relationship between two variables in a visual way.

Explore Figure 7.18 to establish what function each machine has performed.

Machine A		Machine B		Machine C		Machine D		Machine E	
Input	Output	Input	Output	Input	Output	Input	Output	Input	Output
1	4	1	7	1	12	1	5½	1	1
2	5	2	10	2	14	2	6	2	5
3	6	3	13	3	16	3	6½	3	9
4	7	4	16	4	18	4	7	4	13
10	13	10	34	10	22	10	10	10	37
	100		100		100		100		97
n	$= 2x + 3$	n		n		n	$= \frac{1}{2}x + 5$	n	

Figure 7.18   Function Machines A–E

Using numberlines to develop understanding

The algebraic problem $x + 5 = 8$ is hard for young children, unless they have had a lot of experience early on about balancing scales and the way sums and algorithms are structured around the equals sign. However, they are sharp about processing and adapting information when they are able to understand the task. As a prelude to 'mapping' exercises involving a rule or function acting on an input to produce an output, children can be encouraged to develop an awareness of preparatory steps required for this skill. Games such as 'Guess my jump' will awaken their curiosity and flexible mental thinking in a way that the inaccessible missing number statement may fail to do.

Activity: Guess my jump (Figure 7.19)

Learning intention: To be able to use visual stimulus to deduce addition and subtraction as inverse operations

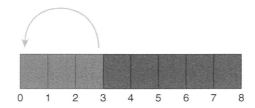

Figure 7.19 A 'Guess my jump' numberline

A teacher (with a numberline in view) could say: 'Rachel made 2 jumps to reach the number 8. We know the second one was a 5. She won't tell us what her first one was.' Or, 'Carol says that her second jump back from 8 took her from 3 to zero. She won't say what the first one was.'

Similar games that use inverse knowledge in a natural, intelligible way serve to deepen children's understanding of structure in algorithms and the necessary focus on them balancing regardless of where the equals sign is. Numicon or Cuisenaire rods might also support the children as they work through these kinds of problem. A typical teaching interaction could go:

Teacher: 'How do you know Carol's first jump was 5?'
Tom: 'Well, I knew she was at 3 for the second jump … so I kept trying numbers to see how far from 8 to 3.'
Teacher: 'That sounds good. Did anyone do it a different way?'

The explanations can be matched with written algorithms and in time children can be encouraged to record a written sum in words or numbers to explain what they did. The Maths Mastery approach to developing number highlights a similar approach. The calculator version of this game works well too. One player puts a number into the calculator and then presses 'add 4'. The second player then gets to see the calculator and presses equals and the number 10 appears.

Now the second player has to work out what the first number was. Essentially they are working out $x + 4 = 10$, although they may not choose to record their calculation as such. Their way may be different but appropriate, for example $10 - 4 = x$ or even something else. Either way the seeds for understanding balanced equations are being sown.

Big idea

Visually assisted problems initially support algebraic thinking to establish how the variables are connected.

These are very good for children to look at, discuss and begin to establish what variables and connections the problems present. A number of standard connections have been put into different contexts. Some are familiar, others less so.

The handshake problem

This problem is beautiful in as much as it lends itself to children and adults finding different ways to represent it. Essentially it is seeking to find all the different pairings that exist and a rule that connects how many people or objects are involved and how many different pairs can be made. In the context of handshakes (two people) children or adults can physically carry out the handshakes as well as discuss and represent them on paper or a computer.

Looking at the two models shown in Figures 7.20 and 7.21 there can be different ways of representing the problem and of misinterpreting it initially. Therefore, clarifying the thinking is the key role for the teacher and asking the right questions to allow the child to spot the flaw in their approach. This is a BIG IDEA.

Big idea

Finding questions to allow children to self-correct their thinking is a key purpose to such work. It supports children discussing and articulating their thinking.

Crossing out and flawed representations of problems are to be encouraged. Figures 7.20 and 7.21 represent possible thinking. Logically, if a group of people (n) shake hands with each other this will mean they shake hands with everyone else except

	A	B	C	D	E
A		AB	AC	AD	AE
B	BA		BC	BD	BE
C	CA	CB		CD	CE
D	DA	DB	DC		DE
E	EA	EB	EC	ED	

A	AB	AC	AD	AE
B	BC	BD	BE	
C	CD	CE		
D	DE			
E				

Figures 7.20 & 7.21   Ways of representing the handshake game

for themselves $(n - 1)$. Thus, the rule connecting the number of people with the number of handshakes should be: $n(n - 1)$.

However, this would double-count the handshakes as the handshake AB will in fact be the same as the handshake BA. Thus, this total would need to be halved, giving a formula or rule of: $n(n - 1) \div 2$.

This builds on the model in Figure 7.20. An alternative approach is Figure 7.21, which looks at the idea that if A shakes hands with everybody else then when B's handshakes are recorded they should omit the handshake with A, which means there will be one less. This continues down to E by which time there are no new handshakes left to record. This way of thinking lends itself, one way or another, to a total involving two variables:

L = the number of people involved (in this case 5).

M = the total of all the numbers from 1 up to 1 less than L (in this case 4).

This would make $1 + 2 + 3 + 4 = 10$.

Mathematically this would be captured as $N!$ or $\overset{(L-1)}{\underset{1}{\sum}}$, although this use of algebraic symbols will be too sophisticated for primary age children.

Remember, children will have their own ideas. It is very important that they are heard. Choice of pairs or groups can have a positive influence on children's willingness to think, risk ideas, match thinking to their peers and access what is going on. They may draw arrows or write. They should be encouraged both to do so and to evaluate different ways of working. Matchsticks, cubes and Cuisenaire rods make great visual concrete patterns which children can be supported in using to pick out variables, relationships and generalisations.

Conclusion

Algebraic thinking is a part of a deeper understanding of fundamental mathematics in primary school. It draws on the idea that our number calculations are linked to creating balanced equations. All primary teachers should seek to emphasise this. Balancing scales used in number operations and variations around the = sign in algorithm work assist this development. In addition to this, children need opportunities to both use, interpret and understand symbols used to represent variables that capture relationships between related features of problems. This opens up the idea that it is not just one algorithm but a range of them that are underpinned by the algebraic equation. Children need experience in understanding these equations and describing them. In the main this will need to be underpinned by visual representations as a basis for generalising ideas. Children find sequential links easier to see than generic links between multiple mappings. The referenced problems and activities attempt to scaffold how teachers can assist children's development. Pattern problems are found in a range of books and websites including Nrich (nrich.maths.org).

One final thought which, to my mind is a BIG IDEA: the mathematical ideas covered in this chapter do involve harder reasoning than other topics covered in the book; however, it is worth developing your own understanding of the basic principles of algebra as best you can in order to give children a foundation from which they can access algebraic thinking through secondary school. If you are struggling with any of the concepts discussed, this is one area of the book where it may be worth finding a friend as a 'more knowledgeable other' (Vygotsky, 1978). It is much better to engage children tentatively or slightly nervously, in work involving algebraic thinking than to shy away from it. Of course it will make you question your knowledge at times. If you reach that point, then I thank you.

8

Fractions

Learning objectives

By the end of this chapter you should be able to:

- Understand why children's early experiences of interpreting simple fractions need to be varied so that the fundamental principles are grasped fully.
- Know how this work can and should include variations in size, shape and orientation.
- Understand fractions as amounts on a numberline.
- Know how fractions relate to division, ratio and proportion.
- Use the BIG IDEAS in this chapter as a guide to teaching fractions with a focus on developing manageable, relevant understanding.
- Understand that it is the relationship between the numerator and denominator that determines the size of the fraction.
- Understand how to divide by part fractional amounts.

What does the National Curriculum say?

Early years children will experience opportunities to play with part whole objects. Through their play and discussion they may describe and make connections with equivalent amounts, such as squares of a chocolate bar or the wheels on a bus. No formal teaching or evaluation as such will take place at this stage. However, the reflective and insightful early years teacher will know that informal discussion with young children about more, size, fairness in meaningful contexts increases children's readiness to engage in meaningful discussion and activity in Key Stage 1 in fraction work. This is a visual, logical area of study which underpins later powerful mathematical knowledge in algebra.

In Key Stage 1 children are expected to identify ½ and ¼ of a range of shapes and begin to apply the idea of these fractions to groups of objects that can be shared equally. Towards the end of this key stage they are expected to recognise versions of other fractions such as ⅓ and common fractions where the numerator isn't 1, such as ¾. This will require close attention to discussion and variation to allow them to understand fundamental ideas at a deeper level. They also start to experience fractions as part of mixed numbers such as 2½ and 3¼.

In lower Key Stage 2 they experience a much wider range of denominators and they are expected to be able to solve problems involving addition and subtraction of fractions with the same denominator. They now start to experience fractions through shape, measure and numerical amounts. This is often effectively managed through objects and situations that the children are familiar with.

In Year 4 children start to be engaged in strategies for calculating equivalent fractions as well as exploring connections between decimals and fractions. They begin to investigate the impact of multiplying and dividing by 10 and 100 to support decimal understanding and in preparation for understanding common percentages. In later Key Stage 2 they experience a range of strategies. They use numberlines initially to explore remainders and relate this to improper fractions. They learn to compare fractions with different denominators. They need support to understand the difference between strategies to add and subtract fractions (through common denominators) and problems involving multiplication and division of and by fractions. Teachers here would want to know how to cover such concepts through understanding rather than formulae and procedure only; or else the preparation for further understanding will be compromised. This will involve multiplicative reasoning and require some understanding of how ratio is a significant feature of how these processes work.

Background context and theory

Fractions relate to so many contexts: part wholes, division, ratio, positions on numberlines and continuums, proportion, and as an operator: a part of a group of something. As teachers we would serve children well if we were able to help them to understand how they interrelate. The aim of this chapter is to explore some of the reasons why teachers have struggled to teach these concepts effectively and therefore why children have often struggled to understand, beyond a certain point. A fraction can be used for many purposes. Those purposes are linked. The links are not always made clear to children; teachers can sometimes stick to what they know or what they feel safe to put out there. This is understandable but can limit development.

Why can fractions create confusion?

If fractions are experienced in an operational way, as part of visual, everyday experiences, with a teacher with enough confidence to distinguish between what they are confident in and what they are less confident in children should prosper. Problems with fractions tend to start with children learning isolated methods that work for the task in hand but don't act as a building block towards deeper understanding.

Terminology

Familiarity with fractional terminology is vital. Children are less hung up about using this terminology if guided appropriately at an early age. Fractions, such as $^3/_4$ or $^{11}/_{20}$, show both the result of a division and a link between equal part wholes and the total part wholes that make a single unit. Even a statement such as this involves some BIG IDEAS.

A fraction has a *numerator* and a *denominator*. The denominator, numerically, is denoted by the number beneath the line; the numerator by the number above it. The denominator indicates how many equal-sized parts make up the whole. The numerator indicates how many of those equal parts make up this particular fraction.

The line itself can be seen as signifying the process of division. It can also be seen as signifying a term such as 'out of' to link the numerator and denominator. So ¾ is then seen as 3 'out of' 4 as well as 3 divided by four, or divided into four equal-sized pieces.

Linked to these definitions of fractions, Derek Haylock (2014: 204) identifies contexts and meanings for fractions. In addition to a division and a representation of part wholes he identifies a fraction as a ratio, a fixed point, either on or between two whole numbers such as 0 and 1. In addition to these definitions fractions can also be used as a means to describe the relationship between a smaller and larger amount in differing situations. For example, 10 is $^1/_2$ of 20. On Wednesday we will be $^3/_4$ of the way through our cycling holiday.

The way in which we capture this amount as a link between two numbers is what defines a *rational number*. It is an amount that can be described thus, with a numerator and denominator. Similarly, an amount that cannot be described in this way, such as π or √5 is known as an *irrational number*. Pi and root 5 have a meaning but it isn't one that can be described exactly through such a division with a digital numerator and denominator, only an approximation.

Early teaching and learning experiences with fractions

Young children generally, by instinct aren't looking at a relationship between what is there in front of them and how much of something there is or was altogether. They tend to be interested in the more simple ideas of 'How many are there?' or 'Are they for me?'. As such, this relationship between the fractional and whole amount is significant and can be more complicated than other early experiences.

Big idea

One of the key purposes of fractions is to give us an idea about the relationship between two amounts. How much there is here and how much there is altogether.

The idea of being able to establish this link between the whole and the amount being reviewed relies on several relationships and ideas that we need to allow the children to understand as being significant. This includes the idea that part wholes have to be captured and referenced as being an *equal* size.

Children need opportunities to explore the amount of part wholes in different-sized sets or groups. They benefit hugely from discussion about what the fractional amount is and whether or not the part whole units are an equal size.

 ## Activity: What fraction is left?

Learning intention: To apply knowledge of part whole fractions in meaningful contexts; to link addition and subtraction to numerator adjustments

There needs to be agreement about how many equal parts the whole group has. For example, the class has 25 children. The egg box has 6 eggs. The cake has 12 pieces, the orange has been split into 10 pieces. The netball team has 7 players. The jigsaw has 24 pieces. Then the activity will show only a certain amount of each. The 2 numbers sought are how many are left and how many were there altogether. There are 2 out of 6 eggs used for an omelette. There are 2 out of 25 children away. There are 3 out of 7 netball players wearing their kit.

Smartboard presentations can reference how many items are missing or covered up. These can be revealed. Children are quick to make connections and can be encouraged to work these out before those missing are revealed. A typical learning scenario could be as follows.

Teacher: 'We have 7 out of 10 pieces of orange left … so how many of the 10 have been eaten (hidden). You think 3? Let's have a look … There we are – let's count them … 1, 2 … 3. Yes there are 3 left out of 10. Well done.'

The relationship being expressed as a fractional amount is between the amount of part wholes available, left or in view, and the total amount of equal parts that make up the whole. Gradually children can be encouraged to record these amounts, initially without the division line. When the teacher feels the children are ready to use the line denoting the equal part wholes it can be introduced. The relationship between the equal parts observed or left *and* those not there, missing or removed is relevant but would be shown as a ratio comparing two different part wholes.

So, early work and activities with children should have these things in mind. Children have in the past been encouraged to interpret pictures with part whole partitions and told to shade a half by colouring in, for example, 1 of the 2 parts or 1 out of 4 parts. This can have merit but only if discussion is taking place about why they are doing this. Each part must be an equal size. Rather than simply having one section shaded and the other not, children should experience shapes with more than one shading (Figure 8.1).

Figure 8.1   A partitioned shape

Figure 8.2   More partitioned shapes

- How many out of how many are blue?
- How many out of how many are red?

Figure 8.2 gives some further examples using other arrangements and colourings which give the opportunity to explore a range of key points very much needed in early fraction work.

Big ideas

- The need for equal sized parts is to allow us to compare the amount in question with the overall amount.
- Some equal sized parts are smaller than others.
- A small fraction of a large cake could be bigger than a larger fraction of a small cake (Figure 8.3).

Figure 8.3 Using cakes as a visual aid

The last BIG IDEA listed here is a mind blower! Such visual representations about known contexts – cake, pizza, chocolate bars can generate deep discussion at a fundamental level. The skill comes in the choice of questions and the visual representations. Before such discussions can come a range of other relevant activities to clarify the need for equal parts and the ability to identify them.

Big ideas

- Not all equal part wholes are the same shape or size.
- Equal part wholes can be the same size and shape but look different if a shape is orientated at an angle.
- Shapes can be halved and quartered in different ways. Children will benefit from both seeing this and finding their own ways to do this. A series of congruent shapes can be presented for children to discuss whether or not they have been quartered.

Children should be encouraged to use shape templates at different angles. Squares look like diamonds at an angle (Figure 8.4).

Discussion is needed to clarify that they are still the same shape. Children need the chance to identify a range of shapes that have been quartered or halved in

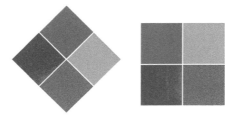

Figure 8.4 A square or a diamond?

different ways. This has strong links with Chapter 10 about orientation and identification. Children can benefit from a focus on equal part wholes. This will be more meaningful if they are able to discuss a range of shapes that are correctly identified mixed in with shapes that are not. For example, they could be asked: 'Find all the shapes that have $\frac{1}{4}$ shaded red or $\frac{3}{4}$ shaded green'. If children are encouraged to look carefully at whether equal-sized part wholes have been used they are *very* good at identifying inaccuracies.

Big idea

Children are very motivated to take on responsibility and apply knowledge.

This can be developed further, for example:

> Well done you two. Now I want you to make a number of shapes that have a quarter of the shape coloured in. Remember the different ways you have tried and been shown. Make sure two or three of them are incorrect and we will try to spot which ones. See if you can use the common mistakes we were talking about earlier this week to help you choose mistakes that some children might at first think are correct.

These mistakes might include four different-sized parts to the shape, one part shaded and four not, rather than one out of four — confusing ratio and proportion. It may include shading two out of five but the two parts shaded are half the size of the rest (see Figure 8.5).

This can generate good discussion. Some children may think the yellow part isn't a $\frac{1}{4}$ because it has two parts shaded ... and yet if the line were removed they would agree it was a quarter. It is the chance to confront confusion that deepens understanding after new understanding has happened.

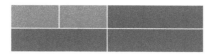

Figure 8.5   An alternative way of colouring ¼ of a shape

This whole pedagogy of confronting misconceptions using carefully chosen examples to draw out key features and visual or concrete resources is a rich one. It is not new to understanding how children learn. It builds on Piagetian principles of cognitive challenge. It uses teacher understanding of children's errors (Hansen, 2014) and common misconceptions (Ryan and Williams, 2007). What is slightly new in this discussion is the idea that teachers need to know at a fundamental level how to deepen young children's understanding. Active experiences such as these at a young age really do increase children's readiness to apply fractional knowledge and let them experience fractions in ways that don't put up barriers to understanding. Discussion is to be encouraged. This draws out children's ability to reason and to justify their thinking. It requires only that a teacher keeps attempting to deepen the way they understand what they know. Nothing less or more.

Other contexts for developing an understanding of 'part whole' fraction work

Alongside the colouring-in examples we have discussed, there are many other ways to introduce part whole fraction work into your classroom:

- *Balls in the bag*. Using different coloured balls, the amount of each colour would need to be made clear, for example 3× white, 2× blue, 5× red. Each ball is a tenth of the total.
- *Cards in the suit or in the pack*. Variations occur with picture cards. This does have links with probability, which, although not a specific curriculum theme, is still covered in data handling as it provides rich meaningful contexts.
- *Cuisenaire rods* provide a good manipulative resource to both create and interpret part whole fraction representations (Figure 8.6).
- Making a design with a total of 10 or 20 is meaningful as children have associated the rods with a number (numerator). The total of the rods provides the denominator. This can greatly assist the conservation of fractions in as much as fractional amounts of a given area can vary, significantly, in shape but remain the same value.

 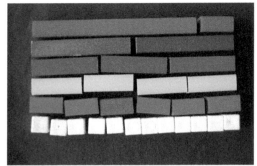

Figure 8.6

- Ruth Merttens (1989) recorded a very useful addition to this. Using squared paper she reasoned that any square whose sides were an even number squares long would have an area of whole squares that would be in the 4 times table. Therefore the calculation for a $\frac{1}{4}$ of that area, for example, would be straightforward. A 6×6 square, for example, would be 36 cm². A quarter of 36 cm² would be 9 cm². Children's different representations of 9 shaded squares would show how different a quarter of that shape could look, even though each shading represented a quarter of the whole (Figure 8.7).

 **Big ideas**

- As many variations as possible on simply showing standard shaped fractions on standard shapes with standard orientations of shapes are *very* much to be welcomed.
- Children's standard errors about representing fractions should provide a basis for discussion as much as possible.

Figure 8.7   Different representations of ¼ of a 6 × 6 square

For example, they should discuss a range of shapes with errors and correct representations to clarify which have the correct fraction attributed to them and what might be the flawed thinking behind the mistakes. These would include:

- Attempting to use the classic perpendicular bisector quartering that works well on squares (see Figure 8.8) for other shapes such as triangles.

Figure 8.8   A square quartered by a perpendicular bisector

- Pursuing the parallel line divisions even when the shape doesn't allow that (triangles, circles) (Figure 8.9). The parallel line divisions work for rectangles but not for circles.

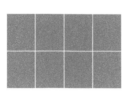 

Figure 8.9   Parallel line division can work on some shapes (such as rectangles) but not others (circles)

- Inadvertently chasing the ratio rather than the proportion. For example, they would see Figure 8.10 as having $1/3$ or $3/1$ of the squares coloured red because they are exploring the ratio of those that are red against those that aren't rather than seeing the link between the red squares and the total number of squares.

Figure 8.10   Although the ratio of yellow to red is 1:3 this should not be confused with the fraction of $1/4$ that the yellow shading represents

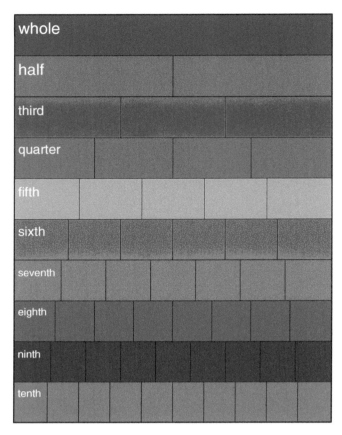

Figure 8.11 This fraction wall models well the interconnections and equivalent values of different sized part wholes

Visual representations as a basis for understanding fractions (Figure 8.11)

Cakes, pies and pizzas score with modelling fractions for a number of reasons, not least that the shapes support showing equal part wholes fairly easily. Also they are popular items that invite focus, imagination and real world understanding. As children become clearer about terminology regarding fractions, including what a fraction as a part whole actually is, the need to discuss, model and deepen understanding continues. The fixed whole object such as a pizza or cake allows an understanding of a key discovery to emerge through being able to develop mathematical reasoning using real world understanding. When analysing meaningful contexts such as these there is the chance to help children make sense of the role of denominators in the context of comparing similar-sized wholes (units) with differing denominations. The pizza or cake with more denominations will have smaller pieces. In a context such as this the idea is indeed a big one.

Big idea

The larger the denominator the smaller each piece will be.

Or:

The smaller the denominator the larger each piece will be.

This trail of modelling, discussion and hopefully understanding seeks to redress the common misunderstanding that children can bring to denominators; namely that a third ($^1/_3$) must be smaller than a quarter ($^1/_4$) because 3 is smaller than 4. A child, when asked if they would prefer a piece of cake cut into three pieces or a piece from one cut into four, will choose the former if they are fond of it. Thus, they are in a healthy mindset to make sense of this BIG IDEA. The issue becomes more complex later when dealing with a third or a quarter of differing amounts. The responsible teacher should seek to make sense of the main issues about fractions and to address them head on as best as they are able.

Equivalent fractions

Big idea

Equivalent fractions differ from equivalent amounts in as much as the former require multiplicative reasoning whereas the later require additive reasoning.

Consider these two problems to relate to this. Firstly, if my brother is 3 years older than me then when he is 20 I will be 17. In 30 years' time I will be 47 and he will be 50. I have used additive reasoning and simply ensured the same difference exists between our two ages. Secondly, if I decide that $^1/_4$ of a large pizza is a suitable size for a portion then I would take a slice from a pizza cut into four equal pieces. If a similar size pizza has been cut into 8 pieces I will need to use multiplicative reasoning. I cannot say that there are now 4 more pieces to a pizza, therefore I will have four more pieces to restore parity. Multiplicative reasoning is needed to allow me to deduce that because there are now twice as many pieces I will need twice as many to have an equivalent amount. One in every 4 pieces is what I should take.

These kinds of problem become much easier to discuss with children if there is software or an interactive program where these connections can be modelled. Progression when comparing fractional amounts of similar sized wholes is generally thought to take the following form:

- Interpreting and creating simple fractions.
- Interpreting and creating fractions where the numerator is higher than 1 (these can be dealt with simultaneously using the kinds of examples discussed earlier).
- Comparing fractions with the same denominator.
- Comparing fractions with denominators that are different but in the same table, for example $^2/_3$ and $^5/_6$, thirds and sixths.
- Comparing fractions with different denominators that need to be solved by finding a common denominator. For example, $^2/_3$ and $^3/_5$, thirds and fifths. Both numbers go into 15 and so 15 is the common denominator, so that

$$2/3 = 10/15$$
$$3/5 = 9/15$$

When covering this kind of work it is important that the examples chosen allow discussion of key points without creating unnecessary problems. If necessary $^2/_3$ and $^3/_4$ could be compared so that less emphasis is placed on mental calculation and more opportunity is given to what the process is helping to achieve. Ryan and Williams (2007) link an understanding of equivalence to the mid-stages of Key Stage 2. It is clear that children need to be comfortable with several BIG IDEAS to make such comparisons effectively, but particularly this one.

 **Big idea**

Equivalent fractions require understanding of multiplicative rather than additive reasoning.

Fractions as a point on the numberline

Fractional values exist as part wholes and as mixed numbers with a value greater than 1. The mixed number representation of $1^1/_4$ can be described as an 'improper fraction' $^5/_4$ where the numerator is bigger than the denominator. Do children need to know this? In the end they do. There is a strong link between division, fractions and algebra when solving equations and learning how mathematical equations are solved. Even practical situations in life regularly use such knowledge. If a team has 6 a side and there are 23 children, some deduction is required. Each child is $\frac{1}{6}$ of a team. All the children represent $\frac{23}{6}$ which equates to 3 and $\frac{5}{6}$ teams. This is an outcome of 3 remainder 5. It is possible to say that we will get the children and group them in sixes and find out one team is one short. One approach is trial and error. The other is about taking control of the problem, representing and solving it mathematically and then putting the mathematical answer back into the original real world context. This latter strategy is highlighted in the Maths Mastery approach in Singapore, currently underpinning a lot of maths teaching in academy schools in England. It is being looked at closely by policymakers, emphasising the need to represent problems visually and numerically to calculate and then adapt to a real world context.

Children need to have some feel for comparison of fractions to use them in numberline contexts. Strategies for comparing fractions require the ability to order them. They also need to be able to distinguish between a fractional amount and a fractional difference. Alice Hansen (2014) references the error of a child incorrectly referencing a point on the numberline between 40 and 50 as $40\frac{1}{2}$. The value of $\frac{1}{2}$ has been confused with a half of an amount, in this case a half of ten, which is the way the numberline has been set out.

Fractional values and the links with percentages and decimals

Big idea

Children need to know that although a higher denominator means there are more parts the actual value of the fraction is dependent on the relationship between the numerator and the denominator.

All rational numbers are fractions; this is what defines them. Therefore numbers shown as percentages or decimals or whole numbers can be referenced as a division operation involving two whole numbers (integers):

$$0.12 = 12/100$$

$$23\% = 23/100$$

$$0.016 = 16/1000$$

$$11.3\% = 113/1000$$

The three representations of part wholes, fractions, decimals and percentages are interlinked and it is important to start to develop children's understanding of how this happens (Figure 8.12).

0	¼	½	¾	1
0	0.25	0.5	0.75	1
0	25%	50%	75%	1

Figure 8.12 The links between fractions, decimals and percentages

It is this kind of interconnected knowledge about part wholes that allows children to have a feel for maths. How are these connections made? Well, certainly varied experiences around fractions are important – fractions as visual representations and fractions as an operation, for example $^3/_4$ of a pound (£) or $^1/_2$ of 70.

Children can find halving 2-digit numbers with an odd value in the tens column quite challenging. They may even say that half of 70 is $30^1/_2$. Base 10 blocks and partitioning methods can assist. For example, children can be encouraged to halve 60 and then discuss what will happen with the remaining 10. The pattern of multiples of tens halved is quite instructive. The last digit pattern gives a clue (Table 8.1).

Every other multiple of ten ends in 0. Half of an odd number of tens will end in 5. The confusion is between $^1/_2$ as a fraction and half of something, in this case 10.

Table 8.1 Halving multiples of ten

Number	10	20	30	40	50	60
Halved	5	10	15	20	25	30

Table 8.2 Halving single-digit numbers

Number	1	2	3	4	5	6
Halved	0.5	1.0	1.5	2.0	2.5	3.0

Thinking can be developed for other group sizes including 100 and 1000. The pattern around single digit numbers is also instructive (Table 8.2).

The odd numbers don't divide exactly by two but the even ones do. That is what defines them. Hansen (2014), amongst others, has critiqued a number of ways children can fail to appreciate the place value issues related to understanding decimals in terms of fractions. Indeed Ryan and Williams (2007) name a number of the misconceptions that Hansen and others cite.

These include:

- Treating decimal values as whole numbers. So 0.12 would be seen as being bigger than 0.7 (this problem occurs again in comparisons such as 0.099 and 0.71).
- The shorter the decimal the bigger its value because decimals are tiny bits and so fewer tiny bits means a bigger number.
- The longer the decimal, for example, 0.81243, then the smaller the value of each digit.

Many misconceptions here have their roots in understanding decimals as a part of our place value system (see Chapter 3 for a detailed discussion of place value). Decimals, percentages and fractions are closely linked. It is often easier to represent decimals as fractions, for example, 0.1 is 1/10, 0.27 is 27/100. Conversely $^{324}/_{1000}$ can be recorded as 0.324, and $^{32}/_{1000}$ as 0.032. Issues about understanding these links often relate to subtle nuances around column values. Obviously, percentages have already been linked to fractions, the numerical percentage having been derived from representing the amount out of 100, per 100, per cent.

The Key Stage 2 teachers among you are looking to create understanding over this four-year period that allows children to understand how these part whole references are connected. The meanings of 'whole' come in different contexts. Fractions can refer to single units – an hour, a cake or an orange – or they can be referring to a part of a whole set or multiplicity of things: $^3/_4$ of a class of 20, or $^2/_3$ of £60. It is important that by the end of Key Stage 2 children can evaluate in broad terms the value of fractions, decimals and percentages and that they have the ability to make sense of answers relating to these three areas regarding validity. This means they will have to have some understanding of how the three areas match up.

Fractions with decimals

The equivalence lines (see Figure 8.13) are the start of a process of matching up understanding. In developing in this concept children should also explore how to place fractions on a numberline.

Big idea

The denominator relates to how many equal parts the whole (unit or set) has been split into. The bigger the denominator, the more parts make up the whole. This means that fractions with the same denominator are spaced out evenly on a horizontal representation of the distance from 0 to 1 (see Figure 8.13), much like a magnified section of the numberline.

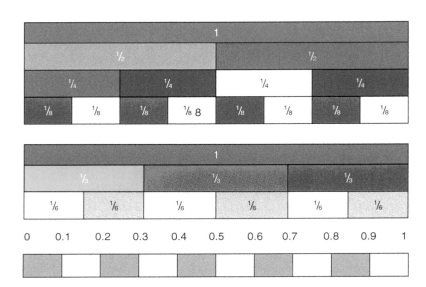

Figure 8.13   Horizontal representations of fractions and decimals

There are common issues here that can impede understanding. These can be the basis of taught lessons to remove some barriers to learning. For example:

- Some decimal equivalents to common fractions have more than one decimal place and others don't.
- Decimal equivalents are connected to other division operations.

It is important to highlight patterns between fractions and division, and that these are based on place value, for example:

$$5 \div 10 = 0.5 \qquad\qquad 3 \div 4 = 0.75$$
$$50 \div 10 = 5 \qquad\qquad 30 \div 4 = 7.5$$
$$500 \div 10 = 50 \qquad\qquad 300 \div 4 = 75$$

Place value is the connection. Children can be asked to record fractions as division sums.

$$^1/_5 = 1 \div 5$$

They can also use knowledge of other algorithms involving division to deduce the decimal equivalence.

$$100 \div 5 = 20$$
$$10 \div 5 = 2$$
$$1 \div 5 = 0.2$$

 Big idea

If the dividend is multiplied or divided then the quotient is similarly adjusted. This means that children can be encouraged to calculate decimal equivalents to a lot of fractions. Some fractions have more obscure connections. 7/9 will be 10 times smaller in value than 70/9 or 70 ÷ 9. However, the calculation is still quite complex.

Estimating from known connections

The fraction $^7/_8$ is a proportion; 7 out of 8 parts is indicating a ratio: 7 out of every 8 parts are present. As 7 is almost as big as 8 we know that the equivalent decimal will be quite close to 1, but just a little smaller. Decimal values continue with exactly the same underpinning as whole numbers. Two BIG IDEAS guide determining the size of the number. The column value and the use of a place holder to signify that a column has nothing in it.

 Big idea

Use of decimals is underpinned by the idea that ten in one column is worth one in the column to the left.

(Continued)

(Continued)

Therefore, fractions and decimals can be understood and ordered.

$$^1/_9 = 0.\underline{1}111111$$

$$^1/_8 = 0.125$$

$$^1/_6 = 0.1\underline{6}666666$$

It is the first decimal place that is the most significant regarding size.

1.25 is bigger than 1.1111 because the first decimal place is larger.

Clever question preparation can help to unlock such information.

100 square

The 100 square can be used as a resource to discuss the difference between 0.3 and 0.03 or 0.25 and 0.11 (Figure 8.14).

I would accept that a teacher needs to keep a clear mind when helping children to see that $^1/_{10}$ of 100 is 10, that $^1/_{100}$ has the same value as 0.01. However, children's understanding leaps forward when they can give a physical meaning to a complex issue. Each row is 1/10th of the whole. Each square is 1/100th of the whole. 1/10th of each square would be 1/000th of the whole. When we equate the 100 square to a chocolate bar children become really excited as they imagine and see the size of 1/1000th of a bar, or a 1/1,000,000th – literally a crumb!

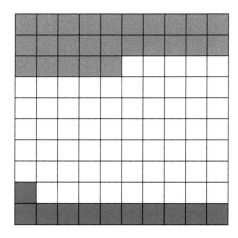

Figure 8.14 Using a 100 square to illustrate 0.25 and 0.11

Having understood these concepts they are ready to understand the BIG IDEA behind decimals that goes alongside place value.

 Big idea

The value of each decimal column decreases as you move along to the right. Now things can start to make more meaningful sense.

- 0.2 tells us we have two out of ten part wholes.
- 0.05 means we have none of the tenths and five tinier pieces.
- 0.007 tells us we have no 1/100ths and only 7 very small pieces.

As David Fielke (1997) states: 'The first decimal place is where each fractional part is worth the most'.

 ## Activity: Estimation with fractions and decimals

Learning intention: To derive approximate values of fractions as decimals

Get children to discuss different fractions and decide whether they feel a given fraction is worth less than ½ or more than ½ of a whole. Extend this so that they also decide whether it is much more or much less than ½.

Finally, when they are ready, ask them to indicate the value as a decimal, using just 1 decimal place initially. This can be extended by using a calculator to find the exact decimal value of a fraction. It can be extended still further by allowing children to use a numberline marked in tenths between 0 and 1. It can be marked with small marks between each tenth to indicate hundredths. Fractions and their decimal equivalents can then be marked to help children develop a feel for size. It is probably a significant step towards realising that comparing decimals is a lot more straightforward than other fractions; because the denominator is the same.

 Big idea

Decimals may be easier to order than other fractions because they use the same denominator. Certainly they use the same fraction family, involving powers of 10.

Fraction wall

The earlier example of fraction walls (see Figures 8.11 and 8.13) can be used to compare fractions and to establish the BIG IDEA that part wholes with larger denominators are smaller than part wholes with smaller denominators. The decimal patterns these fractions provide are instructive in developing further an understanding about how part wholes work. Table 8.3 shows fractions as decimals of up to five decimal places.

Table 8.3   Fractions as decimals

Tenths	0.1, 0.2, 0.3
Ninths	0.11111, 0.22222, 0.33333, 0.44444, 0.55555, 0.66666, 0.77777, 0.88888, 1
Eighths	0.125, 0.25, 0.375, 0.5, 0.625, 0.75, 0.875, 1
Sevenths	0.142, 0.2857, 0.4285, 0.5714, 0.714, 0.857, 1
Sixths	0.16666, 0.33333, 0.5, 0.66666, 0.83333, 1
Fifths	0.2, 0.4, 0.6, 0.8, 1
Quarters	0.25, 0.5, 0.75, 1
Thirds	0.33333, 0.66666, 1

Division, fractions, remainders and decimals

There is an understandable tendency for teachers to give children division problems that have answers, known mathematically as 'quotients', that are whole numbers. This can also assist with helping children to become secure about inverse operation links. For example:

$$6 \times 4 = 24$$
$$24 \div 4 = 6$$

At some point it is necessary to introduce the idea that division calculations do not always have whole number solutions, even those involving whole numbers. This differs from multiplication where whole number multiples will still be whole numbers. Therefore while 8 ÷ 4 and 12 ÷ 4 both have whole number solutions, the numbers in between, 9 ÷ 4, 10 ÷ 4 and 11÷ 4 will all have remainders. These can be expressed initially by simply indicating that the remaining one or more have not been able to be shared out, or it can be stated that the remaining ones are not enough to create another group of the size being formed; in this case fours. Ultimately, these calculations have both to be carried out accurately and understood. The remainder will be expressed as a part whole, either as a fraction or a decimal.

For example, $27 \div 4 = 6$ with 3 remaining. That is to say we can share 27 between 4 people 6 times with 3 left over. Or, we say 27 makes 6 groups of 4 with 3 remaining. We have 3 of the 4 required to make one more group.

$$\text{Thus, } 27 \div 4 = 6^3/_4 \text{ or } 6.75$$

Three quarters as a decimal is 0.75 which can be verified through deduction.

$$300 \div 4 = 75$$
$$30 \div 4 = 7.5$$
$$3 \div 4 = 0.75$$

We would want primary children to be comfortable moving between remainders, fractional and divisional remainders. Children can often find it difficult to interpret remainders as fractional remainders. I believe that greater emphasis on 'division into groups' rather than 'shared between' as the main model of teaching can assist their readiness to connect the remainder as a fraction with the denominator shown by the group size (the divisor). The discussion here emphasises the need for specific vocabulary. Dividend (the amount you wish to divide up), divisor (what you wish to divide it by), quotient (the result of division) and denominator all link up here. Although not widely used in primary classrooms, it would be wonderful to think that in 10–15 years' time the majority of children would be using these terms comfortably to both explain and show understanding.

Percentages: A short case study

Creating percentages is an example of equivalent fractions. It is rare that a given group size has exactly 100 parts. However, on many occasions the group sizes of a survey, a test score, the amount of possession a football team has, the price reduction, wages and taxes are changed into hundredths. Why? Hundredths form a key part of our counting system. Tenths would probably not give enough scope for converting large group sizes effectively ('8 out of 10 owners said their cats preferred it' is an exception!) therefore, hundredths are used. Children's worlds become increasingly surrounded by percentages and they should feel comfortable about using them and about examining the situations where they see and hear about them in terms of being able to evaluate the data linked to percentages and understand when and how they are used.

The 100 square is used to represent percentages in the early stages, for example, in Year 4. Equivalent fraction knowledge means secure knowledge needs to be achieved prior to using percentages effectively. This is fine. It helps children to become familiar with one version of what 30% or 81% looks like. It can also help to grow links between tenths and hundredths as well as common fractions such as $\frac{1}{4}$ and 25%, $\frac{1}{2}$ and 50%, $\frac{3}{4}$ and 75%. Crucial to applying knowledge are 1/10 and 10% itself. The part whole referenced earlier also helps to grow these connections.

$$1/5 = 2/10 = 20/100 = 0.2 \text{ or } 0.20 \text{ or } 20\%$$

The error in developing understanding for many in previous generations under traditional models for teaching percentages was the use of a formula for percentages that wasn't understood. There will be time for that formula when an understanding of what it means has been achieved. Understanding 25%, 50%, 75% and crucially 10% are key manageable skills to develop, particularly when it relates to something tangible such as test marks, increases in length or space, or a sale price or salary rise.

10% as a key skill

Finding 10% of an amount is equivalent to finding a tenth ($\frac{1}{10}$). This equates to dividing by 10. This skill is central to early Key Stage 2 place value and number work, which should sow seeds of understanding. If 10% of a total can be found by dividing a number by 10 then this is the avenue to a lot of other information. Here is an example.

Imagine a school of 400 pupils. Many aspects of the school are often referenced with percentages. For example, exam results, children with siblings, school dinner, numbers within a catchment area, increases in attendance and so on. When calculating some straightforward percentages 10% holds the key. If we know that 160 of the school pupils have siblings, we can use 10% to find out how much this is as a percentage. We know that 400 = 100% and from this we can divide by 2 to calculate that 200 = 50% and we can repeat this to find out that 100 = 25%. However, if we divide 400 = 100% by 10 we can immediately calculate that 40 = 10%. Now that we know 10% we can double this to find out 20%, by the equation 40 + 40 = 80 = 20%.

If we double this again we find out that 80 + 80 = 160 = 40%. So 40% of the school's pupils have siblings. Similarly the route to finding 10% also leads to finding 1%.

If 10% equates to 40 children then 1% will be a tenth of this. So 1% of 400 = 4.

Now we can go virtually anywhere. I can find 21% of 700 by finding 10% then doubling it and finding 1%.

$$10\% \text{ of } 700 = 70$$
$$20\% \text{ of } 700 = 140$$
$$1\% \text{ of } 700 = 7$$
$$21\% \text{ of } 700 = 147$$

The basis for understanding this lies in developing good discussion and understanding in place value work around multiplication and division. Knowing how to multiply and divide by 10 and 100 are skills that children know and understand much better nowadays. This means that time can be spent developing estimating skills and comparing different methods of solving percentage problems.

For example, the same steps that led us to finding 21% of 700 can also help solve 24% of 500.

$$10\% \text{ of } 500 = 50$$
$$20\% \text{ of } 500 = 100$$
$$1\% \text{ of } 500 = 5$$
$$4\% \text{ of } 500 = 20$$
$$24\% \text{ of } 500 = 20\% + 4\%. \text{ This equals } 120$$

An alternative way of arriving at the solution would be:

$$50\% \text{ of } 500 = 250$$
$$25\% \text{ of } 500 = 125$$
$$1\% \text{ of } 500 = 5$$
$$24\% = 25\% - 1\%$$
$$125 - 5 = 120$$

The whole process allows both estimation and understanding to be at the fore of children's work. Fairly soon they are ready to use a formula which they have already virtually understood anyway. That included dividing by 100 (to find 1%) and multiplying by the percentage required.

When extending children's understanding through work connected to percentage increases and decreases, we find that the percentage increase to get from, say, 80 to 100 (25%) is different to the decrease from 100 to 80 (20%). How come? This is because the numerical difference between the two totals is 20 in both cases. However, in the first instance 20 is calculated as a percentage of 80 and in the second instance as a percentage of 100, hence the difference. Captured as a BIG IDEA this would read as follows.

Percentage increases are greater numerically than percentage decreases because the difference constitutes a greater part of the original amount. So in the above example, the difference, 20, is a greater part of 80 than it is of 100.

Multiplying and dividing by fractions

This is an area that is much more in focus now than it has been due to the impact of the 2014 National Curriculum in England. The stipulation of children being required to be able to multiply and divide by fractions by the end of Key Stage 2 is interesting. What is important is that they aren't given formulae they don't understand. It is crucial that they are engaged in activities and discussion that, challenging though they may be, are accessible.

Student teachers are often able to quote the idea that when multiplying and dividing by fractions they remember being told to turn the numerator and denominator upside down and carry out the inverse operation. For example, when asked to consider the problem $6 \div \frac{1}{4}$ they will say that they know that if they multiply instead of divide and change $\frac{1}{4}$ into $\frac{4}{1}$ they should come up with the answer. Thus $6 \div \frac{1}{4}$ gives the same answer as 6×4, which totals 24. The fly in the ointment is that they are unsure why. Therefore they maintain they aren't really able to use the knowledge in any meaningful way, often shying away from algebraic reasoning.

Big idea

Understanding division by fractions relates to the grouping method of division.

From Chapter 5 on multiplication and division, you may recall that the 'share between' model of division makes little sense when applied to decimals or fractions. For example, 6 shared between $\frac{1}{4}$ of a person is not a realistic proposition, whereas 6 shared into groups of a quarter *is* fathomable. For each whole apple we can make four quarters. Therefore, on dividing into quarters there will be four times as many pieces as there were at the start.

Consider that 6 apples cut into quarters would mean that for every apple there will be 4 quarters. So when dividing by quarters the quotient is 4 times bigger than the dividend. When quartering, using apples in this example, there will be four quarters for every whole one. Four times as many pieces in quarters as there were whole apples. That is why previous generations of children were told they could turn the fraction upside down and reverse the operation. Remember, too, the other BIG IDEA.

Big idea

In division, the smaller the group size the more groups you can make.

$$10 \div 2 = 5$$

$$10 \div \frac{1}{2} = 20$$

Ratio and proportion

There are challenges to children developing a feel for ratio and proportion. Ratio explores the relationship between constituent parts. In Figure 8.15 we have some paint mix recipes. If we look at Paint #1 we can see that the ratio of pink to blue paint is that there are 5 pink parts for every 3 blue parts. In this recipe there are only two colours used. Therefore $\frac{5}{8}$ of the paint made will be pink and only $\frac{3}{8}$ of it blue.

Paint Recipes		Ratio	Proportion
Paint #1		5:3	5/8 Pink, 3/8 Blue
Paint #2		1:7	1/8 Brown, 7/8 Yellow

Paint Recipes		Ratio	Proportion
Paint #3		4:2	4/6 Green, 2/6 Red
Paint #4		1:5	1/6 Grey, 5/6 Purple

Figure 8.15   Paint mix recipes

Children need to learn and understand that ratio is about the relationship between the constituent parts not the relationship between one part and the whole.

Here is another example. In a class of 18 girls and 12 boys, we can say that the ratio of girls to boys is 18:12. However, this is rather literal. If we can find a common factor to both numbers we may express the ratio in a more intelligible way. Is there a common factor? Yes, 6 goes into 18 three times and 12 twice. Therefore the ratio between girls and boys can also be described as 3:2.

The class has 30 children. In every 5 children 3 of them will be girls and 2 of them boys. Because 5 goes into 30 six times then the six groups of 5 will take us back to our original figures of 18:12.

Why would we describe it as a ratio of 3:2 and not 18:12? The proportion will tell you how many of the whole class are girls and how many are boys. 18/30 are girls and 12/30 are boys.

With our ratio of 3:2 the numbers are smaller and easier to evaluate. Therefore with Paint #3 in Figure 8.15, the ratio of 4:2 can also be expressed as 2:1 because each constituent part has been halved. This way of thinking links to the multiplicative reasoning discussed in Chapter 5. We can apply this concept to larger numbers, so for example, 28:24 can be expressed as 7:6 as a result of dividing each constituent part by 4.

Why do we need to understand ratio? It is necessary in practical terms with recipes and situations that depend on the relationship between constituent parts. For example, on school trips you need an adult for every x children. As children take algebraic thinking further the idea of balanced equations and solving unknown numbers is dependent on this kind of reasoning. The need for the moment is to establish that it is multiplicative not additive reasoning that maintains the ratio.

Cognitive reasoning

Problems concerning ratios can easily be applied to real life situations and be used to help develop cognitive reasoning in children. For example, if we had 1 part Ribena to 5 parts water it is possible to explore the additive and multiplicative reasoning from first principles. If we have 1 litre of Ribena diluted in this way and we want to make 3 litres should we add 1 more litre of Ribena and 1 litre of water (additive reasoning) or should we make up another 2 litres in the way we made the first one if we want to maintain the same strength?

Conclusion

Part wholes and relationships between constituent parts occur throughout life. The BIG IDEAS highlighted throughout this chapter are worth emphasising through discussion. If you are aware or are becoming aware of key ideas that lie behind early fraction work, you can ensure children debate and discuss problems and situations and develop a deeper understanding of the mathematical concepts. This in turn would allow us, as teachers, to help children to understand fractions beyond simply learning rules that are open to being misapplied.

9

Statistics

 Learning objectives

By the end of this chapter you should:

- Be clear about the content requirements for teaching statistics in the National Curriculum.
- Have an understanding of how effective data handling can both represent information effectively and be used to emphasise key information.
- Know that children need to both interpret statistics through data handling and create their own data representations.
- Have a clear understanding of how children of all ages can be involved in several stages of the data handling process.
- Have some ideas about how to generate discussion with primary children that allows them to think of both what they want to know and how they might start to find it out.
- Understand how a teaching skill in handling statistics involves discussing multiple interpretations of data.

Why do we handle data?

Data handling procedures have existed for centuries and necessity is often the trigger for such developments. William Playfair, in the late 1700s, introduced most common graph types, more recently Tukey (1977) added box and whisker plots (Friel et al., 2001). Censuses, births, deaths and marriages have all been recorded now for two or more millennia. The purposes of these could be discussed at length and, depending on your viewpoint, it could be argued that governmental control, or managing resources effectively could be reasons to handle data. Beyond these purposes the pursuit of proving trends or knowledge is dependent on asking questions, learning and analysing results; hypothesising and concluding accurately are significant. Whatever the case there does need to be a purpose to representing data. Evidenced-based research is the key to finding what can be said to be true. This is deep territory. It requires thought about what is known and what it might be useful to get to know. So, data handling and the use and understanding of statistics are very big issues that begin as early as we are able to distinguish one thing from something else in some way.

Statistics to persuade

It is extremely common for organisations, companies and individuals to seek to persuade about a particular issue, product, event or action. Sometimes this is done through arguing logically. Sometimes it is done through the use of statistics that may appear to support the argument being made. Sometimes it is done through knowledge of the person being persuaded or an awareness about common behaviour patterns. Young children may not necessarily have extensive understanding of such forms of persuasion. Most children though have some emotional intelligence. They quite quickly become aware of the ways in which advertising and persuasion are around them. Their parents also quickly understand how the young can be manipulated by commercialism and by their peers as well as their own interests.

Therefore, it seems right that the role of the school and the teachers within it should be to work with this set of circumstances. Children should be supported to understand what statistical data are and how they can be used in the world, what possibilities and purposes there are in deciding what data should be collected.

As well as persuading, data can be used to understand events, marketplaces, opportunities for meeting demand and making better use of the world's resources. Achieving complete agreement on this point may always prove elusive, as the issue is dependent on your standpoint. So there is a lot at stake; a lot of responsibility and a lot of potential. Why then has primary school data handling over a period of time been of only a limited nature and limited use to children, and why are they unable to understand it more deeply? Let us look at the requirements of the National Curriculum, recently revised.

What does the National Curriculum say?

Although the National Curriculum statistics requirements in maths aren't formally recorded until Year 2 it is clear that throughout Key Stage 1 and beforehand young children need to be discussing and recording things related to statistical data handling. The need for this links quite closely with the need to have efficiency in how and why we record numerical amounts. In the real world the need for discovery seems essential, for example, to overcome or combat disease or illness or even to increase fairness, however that may be defined.

Young children invent their own ways of recording different amounts. For example, 3 and 4 year olds unfamiliar with the formal number symbols we use can still record evidence about who has how many sweets left on two plates so that they will know the next day whose plate belongs to who. This is not only personalised number work it is also early statistical data work. They count and compare amounts and begin to use formal representations such as 2, 5 or 10. They are also expected to begin to understand by how much the numbers are different. This quite complex early theme has real relevance to data handling.

By the end of Year 2 children are expected to be able to interpret a range of data handling methods; these are initially related to counting known objects but in time this moves on to representations of them, such as tallies or coloured squares. In Year 3 they continue to develop comparisons of amounts as well as totals, alongside using and interpreting scaled amounts. Year 4 expects children to broaden their range of data recording methods to include discrete and continuous data and time graphs. They are expected to use scale more efficiently at the planning stage and to interpret similarly. This work continues in Year 5 where children will also gain experience of collecting ongoing data over a period of time. This is consolidated still further in Year 6 where the interpretation of data becomes slightly deeper than the finding of difference and starts to encounter trends and patterns as well as worded interpretations of visual data involving two or more variables. Probability is no longer referenced specifically in the curriculum, although it does appear in a Key Stage 2 Level 6 paper published by the Department for Education in May 2015.

Purposes for data handling

Why then should the work taking place in schools be rather dry? Why should it not be focusing on developing the types of skills mentioned at the start of the chapter? Part of the answer lies in the outlining of the curriculum above. The content and skills are sound enough. They include clear development in both accuracy and scale; in creation and increasing complexity in data, and in calculating and interpreting data. The issue partly relates to the question of why are the children carrying out such data handling exercises? It is often the case that neither children nor teacher are really clear about where the work is going.

When adults and children are clear on what they are trying to achieve the bar is often raised significantly. A number of writers in the past few decades have started to stress how important the purpose is to children's understanding of maths and we can relate this principle to the handling of data, referenced as statistics, in the 2014 National Curriculum in England.

Patrick Barmby's work (Barmby et al., 2009) references the US National Council of Teachers of Mathematics' emphasis on formulating questions, gathering data and interpreting results. Haylock (2014) captures this process as collecting organising, representing and interpreting. Graham (1991) describes the process similarly with the skill of posing the question stressed heavily: what question will be asked and why? Graham also emphasises the role teachers have to play in turning, sometimes dry, data handling tasks into engaging issues that children may be more interested to debate. He also emphasises the cyclical nature of data research and interrogation. Sometimes the results of your investigation simply help you to realise that the question you originally asked has now led you to something else of greater interest than the original issue. Time is spent later in this chapter discussing how this may be done.

Unpicking National Curriculum content

Difference

A common question style in standardised assessments involves children interpreting a pictogram around the theme of difference. Children are asked to establish the difference between the number of one animal and the amount of another animal. Although formal statistics statements do not appear until Key Stage Two it is a chance to provide some sort of context for the earlier BIG IDEA from Year 1 involving difference itself.

Big idea

Visual data give a very good context for young children to establish an understanding of a range of vocabulary.

This vocabulary might include: more, less, biggest, smallest, more than, less than, difference. Young children cannot easily be told complex words like 'difference'. They can, however, experience a situation, make a statement and then find out that what they have discovered is the difference. For example, children can be asked to answer questions on the number of animals on the farm, relating to 'the most', 'the fewest' and difference (Figure 9.1).

For many children in Year 1 this is rather difficult. Although many will understand the number sequence and be able to count (either on arrival in nursery or

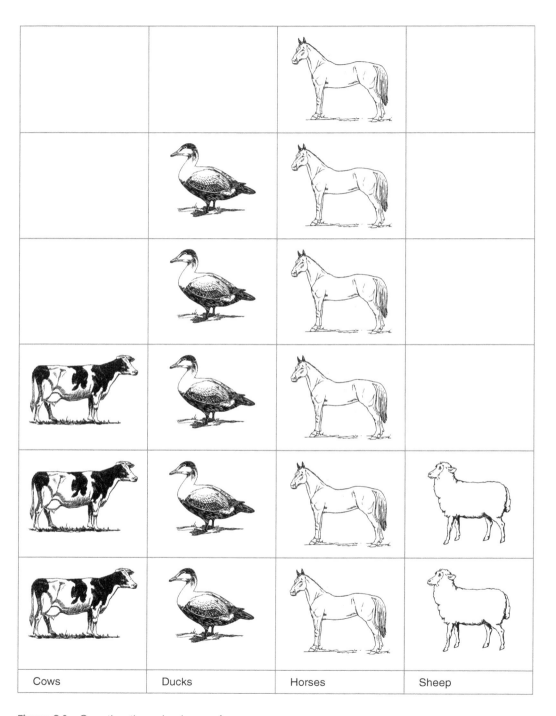

Cows	Ducks	Horses	Sheep

Figure 9.1   Counting the animals on a farm

Reception or soon after) others may not. This may be particularly true of summer-born children who only become 5 years old over the summer before Year 1 begins. At this stage it can be too early to really judge their progress or the ways they make sense of things. The concept of difference appears fairly soon after they are able to ascertain how many of a particular item there are and maybe whether there are more of one thing than another. One worry would be that if Year 1 children were asked to find the difference between the number of ducks and the number of cows in Figure 9.1 they would either be confused, count just one of them or add the two totals together by counting them all. However, if the task is presented in a way that means something to them the outcome may be different. For example,

Teacher: 'Now George, here are your ducks and Anisha, here are your cows. Let's spread them out so that the ducks are each above a cow. Well, like Jack in the story if you two were going to market each day to sell one of your animals who would sell all their animals first?'

Children's responses to this question could be that they don't know, or that the ducks will be sold first because there are more of them (this is logical but false). Or they may think the cows will run out because there are fewer (correct logic). They may or may not be able to say how many of the cows will be left at this point. What is common to all stages of understanding at this point is that they will benefit from carrying out the task as stated and discussing what is happening.

Teacher: 'OK, it's the first day. Take your first animal to the market and Lottie is going to buy the duck for 3 cubes while Farhad wants to buy Anisha's cow for 5 cubes because it's much bigger and costs more. Good … so are we finished? Have we run out of animals? No? OK. Let's move on to day 2.'

This type of scenario works on a number of levels as I am sure those of you who have worked with similar aged children will testify. When it is repeated with either the same or different children with some following, watching, predicting, guessing, then children can make real connections, although what each child gets from the task immediately may differ.

   If we turn back to our animal pictogram (Figure 9.1) it is possible to see the ones that will be left over. This is both the number of ducks left over after ducks and cows have been sold one by one and also the number of cows that would need to be added to make the amounts even. We can use questioning to check understanding, such as:

* 'How many ducks does George have left now that Anisha has sold all her ducks?'
* 'How many cows do we need to give Anisha so that she and George have the same number of their respective animals?' (Incorrect answers may mean the children need to be walked through the stages of the problem.)

Big idea

Young children have logical minds. It is easier to use practical contexts to grow an understanding of a concept than it is to tell them things that they don't really understand.

Richard Skemp (1976) and many writers since, would argue that the concept is more important than the terminology. I agree with this, although terminology in maths is very important because it allows for precision of understanding.

Big idea

Understanding usually needs to precede the use of correct terminology.

The value of discussion

In the scenario outlined above it is once again the quality of the discussion, provoked or managed by the teacher, that allows understanding to emerge and develop in children. The key features are meaningful situations that children can see and understand; ones that pave the way for active thinking, connections and ultimately more abstract thinking that has emerged from understanding. In these situations children may or may not come on board with conceptual ideas. However, every chance is being given for them to do so. It is important that we use appropriate questioning when asking children to engage with an activity such as this, and some useful teacher prompts could be phrased along the following lines:

- 'What do you think will happen when Penny has the horses and Raj has the sheep?'
- 'How do you know how many will be left?'
- 'After we found out how many more Raj had what did you do to see how many less Penny had?'
- 'Do you think the amount more and less will always be the same total? If so why?'

Instinctively, the opportunity to talk in pairs seems a useful outlet for children's ideas and thoughts. Now we are close to an understanding of difference that is fit for mathematical use in even more challenging circumstances.

Progression in handling data

As with other aspects of mathematics, typical progression for children should involve moving from counting with real objects to visual representations of them. Real life objects really need to be used with young children because that is the literal world that they know and are beginning to make sense of. Once this is secure they can be introduced to pictograms (such as our animal pictogram, Figure 9.1), which are simplistic examples of showing the objects being counted or compared, in reduced size. From there it is possible to move to block graphs, which draw on 1:1 correspondence just as the pictogram. However, the block graph and the pictogram can differ in two ways. On the block graph the objects can be represented through squares coloured in and there is the emergence of an axis which indicates numerically how many of an item there are (Figure 9.2). When being helped to learn how to interpret block graphs children are encouraged to read off the number of squares indicated from the number on the axis rather than count them up. In the early stages they will seek to manually count them, if only for reassurance.

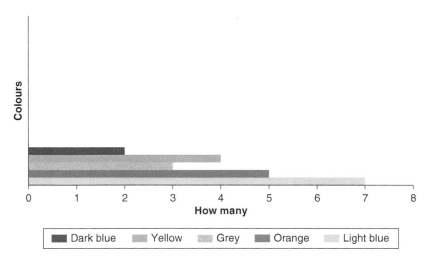

Figure 9.2 A block graph measuring favourite pencil colours in class

Criteria for sorting

In order to place and compare objects on a pictogram or block graph children need criteria for sorting. Children are inducted into sorting activities at an early age through shapes, size and colour amongst other things. Initially the emphasis is only on one criterion. However, as time goes by their understanding in this area needs to be extended. How can we tell the difference between two yellow objects, two dogs, two coats? The exploration of sorting through multiple criteria is tackled through, in particular, Carroll diagrams and Venn diagrams. Visual in appearance, Carroll diagrams allow for two criteria to be sorted (Figure 9.3). Venn diagrams allow more options to be considered (Figure 9.4).

Both types of diagram expand on the idea that there are ways to distinguish between fruits, numbers, animals and other sets that have some, but not all, things in common. In shape, for example, this is a key concept. The quadrilateral family includes some of the most commonly used shapes, all of which have at least one connecting feature. With younger children sorting would initially include colour and shape. Barmby et al. (2009) suggest that Venn and Carroll diagrams are more related to the process of reasoning about data, rather than data handling. While this is a valid argument they are in fact both valid examples of a BIG IDEA that relates to data presentation. Both types of diagram can really encourage understanding by offering a visual representation of different links.

	Legs	No legs
Alive		
Not alive		

Figure 9.3 A Carroll diagram

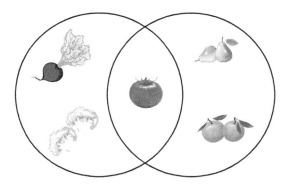

Figure 9.4 A Venn diagram

Activity: Working with Venn diagrams

Learning intention: Understanding Venn diagrams in context. Developing an understanding of sets and subsets

In this activity children should work in groups of three. Each of three children is allotted a circle of the Venn diagram (Figure 9.5). Get children to discuss a whole list of things that are either written down on cards or represented by pictures. Find out which items or themes are liked by 1, 2 or 3 of them. For example: scary films, broccoli, mathematics, heights. The card or picture gets placed in the right place on the Venn. The task can be scaffolded with a whole class demonstration. It can also be played by just 2 or even 4 children.

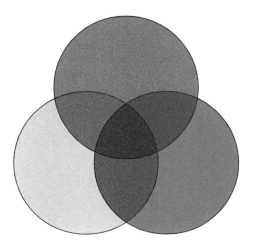

Figure 9.5 A three-circle Venn diagram

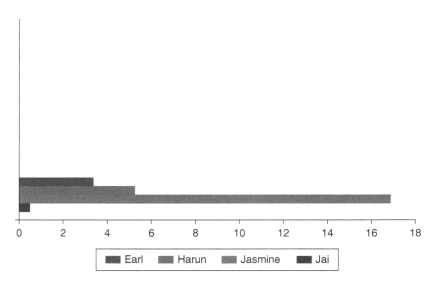

Figure 9.6   Journey times to school (km) – an example of a scaled chart

Scale

This becomes an issue when data relate to numbers that are too large to represent efficiently on graphs with squares. When this happens one square cannot continue to represent a whole object, too much space is taken up. Variations on how each axis is scaled allow part wholes to be referenced where necessary. Scaling can allow one square to be used to represent part wholes or multiples of one (Figure 9.6).

The journey times to school might be a useful way to begin to capture data related to part wholes. Local maps now are reasonably accessible online and can be adjusted to allow cm to represent kilometres and millimetres to represent 0.1 km or 100 metres. Other part whole data themes could include volumes of containers (litres) and weights of objects (kilograms). Debate can take place about how best to scale an axis based on the range of measures covered.

Line graphs

Although children grow used to the idea that there can be variations in height or length with pictograms and block graphs, they often need support and help to understand that variations in a line graph can equate to variations in other data representations. Figure 9.7 is a line graph showing weather temperatures in London across six days. Figure 9.8 gives the same information in a block graph.

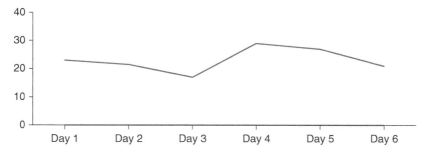

Figure 9.7 A line graph showing weather temperatures in London across six days (degrees Celsius)

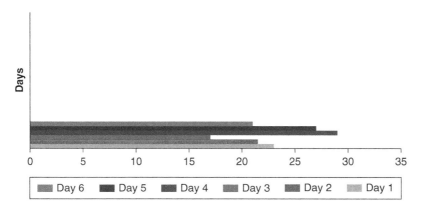

Figure 9.8 The same information in the form of a block graph

Decisions about how to show data

As these two representations of the same data show, selecting how to show data is an important decision. This depends on what the purpose for collecting these data was in the first place and what we are trying to find out. This is why children must and should be engaged in the full range of statistics and data collection. Without the purpose it is hard to say whether one method of representation is preferable to another.

Big idea

The purpose of the task helps to dictate which method of data representation is better.

Pie charts, histograms and scatter graphs

Pie charts are now an active part of data handling in primary schools. However, there is a danger of children achieving only a superficial understanding of them. A lot of time is spent with children interrogating pie charts. Sometimes they are asked to compare pie charts where the sample size is different, for example, in Figures 9.9 and 9.10.

Key Stage 1

Flavour	Number of children (out of 100)	Percentage
Chocolate	27	27
Strawberry	34	34
Vanilla	11	11
Orange	28	28

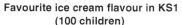

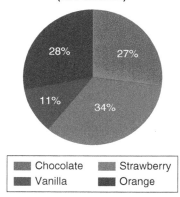

Figure 9.9   A pie chart with a sample size of 100

Children can now create fictitious pie charts using data software. This may mean they don't necessarily understand the links between the numerical amounts being referenced and the percentage conversions. Therefore, some questioning and opening up of understanding from the teacher can help them to overcome limited understanding.

Key Stage 2

Flavour	Number of children (out of 200)	Percentage
Chocolate	54	27
Strawberry	68	34
Vanilla	22	11
Orange	56	28

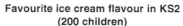

**Favourite ice cream flavour in KS2
(200 children)**

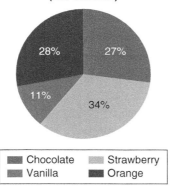

Figure 9.10 A pie chart with a sample size of 200

 **Big idea**

Pie charts relate to the link between the percentage of the pie shown and the number in the overall group whole.

Therefore, a large piece of a smaller group whole may have fewer people in it than a smaller piece of a larger group size. With the orange flavour in Key Stage 1 and chocolate in Key Stage 2 we find the following:

- 28% of 100 is 28 children.
- 27% of 200 is 54 children.

The percentage is smaller in Key Stage 2 but the number of children in that group is more because the group size is 200 rather than the 100 in Key Stage 1.

Histograms

Histograms are representations of group range sizes and are used to demonstrate how data are distributed across a range (Figure 9.11); for example, grade bands in examinations, sales figures for different months or times of the day. These data show how a range of children, merchandise, exam scores or whatever it is that you are measuring is spread across different boundaries.

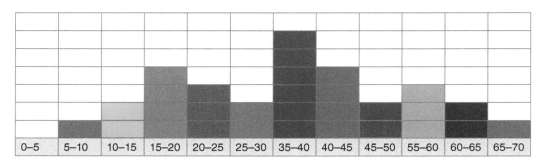

Figure 9.11   Histogram showing the distribution of children's exam scores in a test marked out of 70 (class of 30 children)

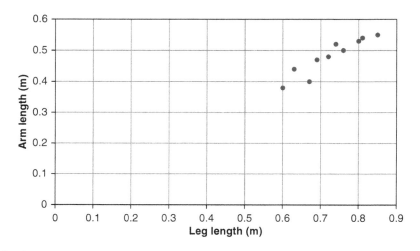

Figure 9.12   A scattergraph showing correlation between arm length and leg length

Scattergraphs

These are used to measure correlation. They can allow us to examine data relating to two variables to establish whether or not there is a connection between the two. In order to do so it is necessary to have data on two different variables relating to whatever it is you are analysing. For example, we might be trying to establish if people with longer legs have larger families. This hypothesis is unlikely and therefore the data should suggest this. Or we might be finding out whether people with longer legs have longer arms (Figure 9.12). This would be useful to know if we are making 'onesie' outfits in different sizes, for example.

Planning themes for data handling

Some pockets of very good stimulating data handling do exist in primary schools. Therefore, we need to start looking at what underpins it and how it links to the theories put forward earlier in the chapter. One way of examining what constitutes good practice is to look at fundamental flaws when teaching statistics and data handling that, as teachers, we need to overcome. Many of the following points can limit the value of data handling experiences:

- Isolated data handling tasks that don't seem to have an obvious purpose.
- A lack of involvement of the children by the teacher about what it is they want to find out.
- Small-sized sample groups generating insufficient data to examine. Barmby et al. (2009) and Shaughnessy et al. (1996) both talked about the key features of making data handling relevant. Time needs to be spent between, behind and beyond the data to ensure relevance and the possibility of discovery.
- A lack of discussion to deepen involvement and, crucially, understanding. Carefully orchestrated discussion can bring relevance to children's work.
- A tendency to allow similar kinds of data work and content to take place across a wide range of ages. Although I believe there has been some improvement here as many teachers seek to focus on requirements for standardised tests as the basis for shaping decisions about coverage.

How are these flaws overcome? By using appropriately selected examples as a means to develop understanding and by getting the children involved. Understandably, we may feel that if children are given too much choice the results can feel random, overwhelming or unmanageable, and sometimes all three. This will vary from class to class. It is possible to narrow the areas for discussion down in order to provide greater focus. However, some teachers do prefer to pose the question and then allow the debate to commence from there. We will now look at some key themes that can be used in lesson planning.

Theme 1: Children's favourite items

This could include favourite drinks, ice cream, school uniform colour, games in PE, books, fruits for breaktime snacks or school dinners. These topics could easily become unsatisfactory teaching and learning experiences if they are subject to any of the flaws mentioned above. However, when done with passion and purpose they can be very illuminating. Often, superficial 'find the favourite' questions, remain exactly that. Young children can be interested in initial data handling experiences of going around the class asking people questions. However, deeper thinking is required sooner or later. In a class survey of 30 perhaps 5 to 10 children will choose the most popular answer and the rest will be, to a greater or lesser extent, disappointed. Some teachers, possibly with lower Key Stage 2 children or above, may prejudge the issue as these children may well have collected data related to a 'favourite' thing before. Giving this data gathering a clear purpose is usually straightforward, for example:

Teacher: 'We need to decide which flavour ice creams we will sell at playtime. I want you to have a think about any considerations we will need to make.'

Usually there are some standard replies after thinking time and discussion. There may also be some leftfield responses. Children often cite cost, keeping it cool, not able to keep it for long. These are all sound ideas. Sometimes teachers ask if they can find out if there are any flavours children don't like or they allow children to rank their favourites as 1st, 2nd or 3rd. This can equate to point-scoring systems, such as 3 points for your first choice, 2 points for the second, 1 point for the third. The outcomes will vary. Some schools have more scope to actually run with the children's findings. Some are prepared to keep records on sales and costs long enough for tastes to change or for noticeable data changes that are then investigated. Some teachers guide the children to think up questionnaires that will allow them to ask a range of questions.

Big idea

A questionnaire only allows you to learn what the questions ask.

Understanding what questions need to be asked is a big issue in multimillion pound research. In business the skill is being able to find out what might help to make you more successful.

When using questionnaires in teaching the purpose should be clear and also provide a means to spark interest in the children.

Theme 2: Supermarkets

A good overarching theme that can encapsulate data handling and questionnaire work is that of supermarkets. What might children like to find out? When asked they will tell you. They sometimes just want to know which one is more popular, or which one is 'the best'. If pressed on how to find which one is best they may say 'the one most people say they like'. In this day and age it is now possible to find statistics about profit and customer numbers online to allow real world statistics to inform your discussion. Another area to explore could be online ordering, which many families are now using. A good questionnaire can provide some starting points and it is something children could take home to discuss with their family. For example, it could ask questions such as:

- 'Where do you shop? Why?'
- 'Do you only use one supermarket? What would make you change?'
- 'Do you use supermarket online resources? Why did you choose this one?'
- 'What would make you start to shop online?'
- 'How important is the time-saving factor?'
- 'Would you mind if it were only online shopping?'

Children often are interested in prices and choice, they may have favourite foods that other supermarkets don't offer. They can investigate shop layouts and compare prices; you may be able to arrange for them to talk with managers. Such work throws up new information that may make them curious about other issues. How are older or disabled people catered for? Where does the food come from? How much is from different countries? These are all rich areas for age-appropriate data gathering that has a stated purpose and a link to everyday life that can help children further their understanding. Whatever they choose to investigate in turn affects how they choose to present the information that they find. Why choose one method of presentation over another?

Points about different data presentation

It may be that pie charts are selected as an appropriate way of presenting the supermarket data that your class has gathered. These are both pleasing to look at and with simple software programs such as Microsoft Word or Excel fairly easy to construct. The link with percentages is important, the link with degrees perhaps less so.

However, the slice of the pie clearly relates to an angle through the size of the turn. Key aspects of pie charts that can be discussed include:

- Each section of the pie is part of a whole group that has been sampled, tested, surveyed or analysed in some way.
- Each part is a fraction that has a decimal and percentage equivalent. The size of the piece of pie relates not to how many people or objects there are, but to the link between the chosen group shown by the piece of pie and the whole sample group represented by the whole pie itself.

Table 9.1   Supermarket survey data

The supermarket your family uses most often		Fraction	Percentage	Degrees of a pie chart
Sainsbury's	16	16/60	26.66%	96°
M&S	4	4/60 **(1/15)**	6.66%	24°
Morrisons	11	11/60	18.33%	66°
Asda	9	9/60 **(3/20)**	15%	54°
Waitrose	6	6/60 **(1/10)**	10%	36°
Tesco	12	12/60 **(1/5)**	20%	72°
Other	2	2/60	3.33%	12°
TOTAL	**60**	**1**	**100%**	**360°**

Supermarket used most often

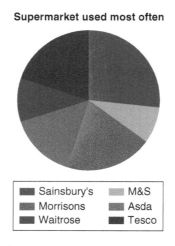

	Sainsbury's		M&S
	Morrisons		Asda
	Waitrose		Tesco

Figure 9.13   Supermarket survey data pie chart

Let's imagine the class has surveyed their families about the supermarkets. Table 9.1 shows not only these data but how this would be represented in terms of fractions, percentages and degrees on a pie chart.

If we then express this as a pie chart it would look like Figure 9.13.

Pie charts can only show only a limited number of choices effectively, beyond this the pieces become quite small where the comparative size of each slice of the pie is not distinctive enough. However, when dealing with a limited number of variables they can be very effective in showing how much a pattern has changed. For example, Figure 9.14 shows how a pie chart could express a change of school lunch preferences from one year to the next.

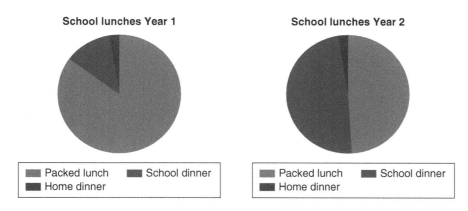

Figure 9.14 Using a pie chart to show data changing over time

Big ideas

- It can be instructive to use different data presentation methods, such as the ones above, to compare the impact of data.
- Allow children to think about whether or not one method could be better than another.
- As a teacher try to develop some knowledge or opinions about what different data presentation forms can and cannot achieve.

Alongside the examples discussed here do keep an eye out in newspapers, magazines, on TV and online about how data are presented and what impact it has. This can provide you with a wide range of inspiration for the classroom.

Profit experiments

At what age do children become savvy about prices? I suppose it varies but they should begin to make sense of prices by Key Stage 2, particularly when they get any freedom or opportunity to decide how to spend pocket money or funds in their possession. Price checks in supermarkets can assist this process. Many stores have online price checks which can be useful. This world of consumerism is a good one to involve children in. Are there commonly known shops near the school? Do children know prices of items in those shops? Do they know any other shops where the same items are sold at different prices? How much would they be prepared to pay for certain items?

You can supply children with figures related to sales and prices, and introduce the idea that the more that a shop or seller charges then the more profit they can make on each item. However, it may be that if they charge too much they don't sell as many items as they would at a lower price. It may be that for some items they could charge a little more without sales dropping very much. This could be modelled in an activity looking at the sales of milk at different price points (Table 9.2).

Table 9.2 Milk sales at different price points

Cost	30p	35p	38p	40p
Milk (per pint)	Sold 100	Sold 80	Sold 60	Sold 21

If, in the above example, we tell children that there is a production cost of 20p per pint there is much for children to discuss about profit, predicted trends from further reductions or increases and the kind of things that shopkeepers have to consider. These kinds of questions and activities have links with supply and demand. Most children would agree that £2.00 for a soft drink, whether Coke, fruit juice or water is quite a lot. Can they think of any situations when they, or their parents, might be prepared to pay such a price or more? Is it when it is very hot? Is it when they are visiting somewhere that you aren't allowed to take drinks into? If they are comparing supermarkets they can consider why people might not go to the cheapest one. Is it the location, or the quality of the products? Are they prepared to pay more for some items because it is more convenient than having to go to several different stores? Sometimes it is related to opening hours and the local store might be open later than the big supermarket. All of these situations and discussions take understanding and context into consideration. They are what Barmby et al. (2009) and Graham (1991) would term getting behind and beyond the data.

Experiments

Cress seed conditions for growth, water evaporation from puddles, rising dampness through different items such as bricks, insulation, identification of shapes through data bases – these are all areas where children can be involved in experiments that generate data. The level of involvement that children can have is sometimes dependent on the perception by the teacher of their own knowledge. This can mean that the teacher guides the activity rather than inviting children to decide what they want to find out and how they will do it, not wishing to compromise their own ability to control and influence. This level of teacher-led instruction is balanced out by the BIG IDEA about children's thinking determining their involvement, motivation and understanding. The two ideas go alongside each other.

 **Big idea**

Ideally, children shape their own learning and understanding with the teacher as guide and point of reference. This is affected by teacher knowledge and the desire to use available time productively to meet learning outcomes.

If we look at data handling questions in the Key Stage 1 SATs for 2015 we can see that there is a fairly standard offering. The emphasis is mainly on interpreting block and line graphs with the same starting point. Questions relate to 'most', 'fewest' and sometimes 'the difference between', all of which we focused on earlier. Figure 9.15 is a typical graph on a par with those offered in SATs papers. In looking at it we will also ask, how could such a data representation sample be opened up to offer an engaging learning opportunity?

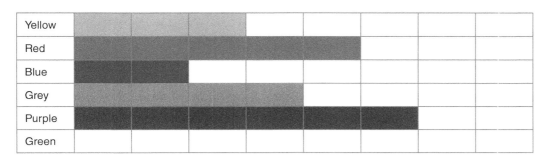

Figure 9.15 A block graph showing favourite jumper colours

Common questions for this block graph about favourite jumper colours would include the kinds of questions mentioned above. However, with a little adjustment the tasks and thinking required could be changed, for example:

- There are 25 children in the class so how many have green as their favourite jumper colour?
- If one person changed their mind how could this affect the scores so that two are the same?
- How many people would need to change their mind so that all the scores were the same?
- If we chose to represent the data in a different form (Table 9.3) does a new visual representation add anything to understanding? (In this table the data on 'grey' votes have been removed and a new total added, in order to set up a problem for children to solve).

Table 9.3   An alternative way of displaying favourite jumper data

Favourite jumper colour	
Yellow	3
Red	5
Blue	2
Grey	–
Purple	6
Total	**20**

You can also set questions without any visual aids. So for example, using a different set of variables: if there are 10 children who have to pick from four possible choices, work out how many chose which colour based on the following information. Blue is most popular. There is one more green than red and half as many black as red. (The answer here is blue = 4 votes, green = 3 votes, red = 2 votes, black = 1 vote.)

 Activity: Favourite colour data questions

Learning intention: Learning to reason and evaluate with statistical data

You could make up one of these tasks for yourself, or you could involve children in creating a problem for the class to solve. What age do you think children would have to be to think up a similar conundrum? You may be surprised. If they choose a distribution of cubes as their small data set, for example, 5 black, 3 green, 6 yellow and 1 orange, they can make the connections very well themselves and most children love having their ideas used for the class. Reasonably confident Year 1 children would do well at this and all children could achieve this in pairs or with appropriately scaffolded support. Key Stage 1 children are very comfortable analysing block and line graph omissions and variations between data tables and visual block graphs: they can become proficient at it and use it as a strategy themselves if they are given the chance to analyse as part of a group, through discussion and with teacher prompting.

The skill to develop their ability to think up insightful questions might be to give them the kinds of evaluative questions referenced with the favourite jumpers idea above.

Key Stage 2 SATs questions

If we turn to look at the types of questions on data handling set for Key Stage 2 SATs, we can see that they are still addressing standard interpretation issues related to amounts and difference. There are specific references to pie charts with differing group sizes, as we discussed earlier and some everyday contexts used for questions such as transport timetables. These are really good experiences for children. My strong advice would be to use known maps, such as the London tube map or local bus and train routes that the children may be at least partly familiar with.

A data table with bus or train times can be matched to a map outline. Children love fictitious travel routes and networks with their own names in or things they

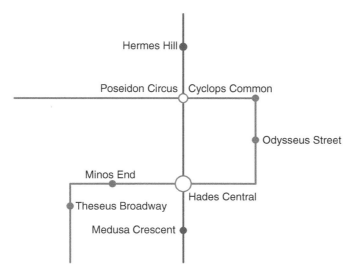

Figure 9.16 A fictitious map for a Greek-myth-inspired transport system

enjoy. For example, you could create a fictitious rail network for 'Harry Potter Land' or Greek Myth Transport System. A map is a good visual link to the numeric data and you should find that they are soon ready to create their own networks and timetables. Why? Because data handling is visual and because their understanding and motivation increase when they can relate knowledge and ideas to other things they are already familiar with.

Looking at the 2015 Level 6 Key Stage 2 SAT paper there is a much greater emphasis on 'between', 'behind' and 'beyond'. Rather than being the domain of the few, our children will all need exposure to this kind of thinking earlier in their time in school. They also need the discussion that these kinds of questions and tasks invite. A heavier emphasis on purpose and discussion can have a huge impact on confidence, achievement and willingness to use data.

Offering interpretations for line graphs

Figure 9.17 These two line graphs could be explained in any number of ways to describe how two variables are related. For example, time and the bath water level; or bank balance and time

As well as telling a story of information collected about journeys, temperature or weather patterns over a period of time, children benefit, in time, from discussing possible explanations to different shaped graphs (Figure 9.17). As well as deepening understanding this helps to overcome a common misconception where children interpret the line graph literally with regard to direction, going up or down, especially when travel is the feature of the graph.

Probability

Probability is not an area currently in the statistics National Curriculum guidelines and content. It is, however, rich with possibilities for generating and understanding data related issues. Situations exist where there are a specific number of ways that an event may work out, for example, in dice throwing, the sex of babies being born, coin spinning, and answering yes/no questions. Statistical predictions of likelihoods have nowadays been extended to predicted outcomes of more complex situations such as weather fronts and rain potential. The world is full of chance. Insurance companies use risk as the basis of their rates, fees and terms and conditions. Investment fund groups do likewise. The modern world relies on such business interactions. Children need to both experience the concept of probability in the real world and quickly understand several key things:

- Some events are more likely than others.
- How likely an event is will not necessarily correlate with how often this event happens. For example, 20 tosses of the coin may not produce 10 of each side.
- The larger the sample the more likely closer parity with chance actually is. For example, 1000 throws may ensure closer parity than 2 throws.
- 'Bias' describes the many considerations as to why the mathematical chance differs from the actual chance. Two teams play a match. 50:50 outcome. However, if one is Liverpool and the other is Canvey Island then this is probably not so.

Predicting winners when some teams or contestants are stronger than others helps this discussion. Trying to reason about the next vehicle to pass the school gate or the person in the class likely to jump the highest are also useful ways of exploring this concept. Whether something is 'likely' to happen and whether it is 'certain' are very different things. The terms 'never', 'always', 'likely', 'unlikely' are words that can support discussion of outcomes. For example, how could they apply to the following scenarios: School being closed for the next month? Snow tomorrow? Winning the lottery? Keira Knightley being your next teacher? Children like to argue to disprove or prove things. Finding 'certain' and 'impossible' statements is harder than 'likely' and 'unlikely' and therefore important.

Averages

In the recent past the concept of averages was covered quite widely in primary school. The notion of some definition linked to the centre or centralising incorporated the arithmetic mean, mode, median and range. It is currently the arithmetic mean that is in the curriculum.

The average referred to as the arithmetic mean is obtained by totalling a group of numbers and dividing by the total of different numbers that are in the group.

Thus, [3, 7, 8] would give an arithmetic mean of 6.

$$3 + 7 + 8 = 18$$

$$18 \div 3 = 6$$

Effectively this process centralises or 'evens out' the four numbers until they are equal. Sometimes the average will be in decimals if the divisor does not divide into the dividend exactly.

[1, 2, 48, 50] would give an arithmetic mean of 25.25

Big idea

Being able to estimate averages from a group of numbers is part of developing a feel for number and is a very valid life skill.

Looking at the scattergraph in Figure 9.18 we can see that the idea of gaining two pieces of information about an item, event or person to establish any overall deductions is scientifically an extremely important idea. It is often the basis of proof in discovery and establishing cause and effect in research. Here the theme is body part measurements (Table 9.4). The line of correlation establishes (broadly in this case) that the bigger the head circumference the longer the foot.

Other foci might include arm span against height, hand size against height, weight against waist size. Data collections about measurement allow children's hypotheses or interests to be followed through. They can be extended as children

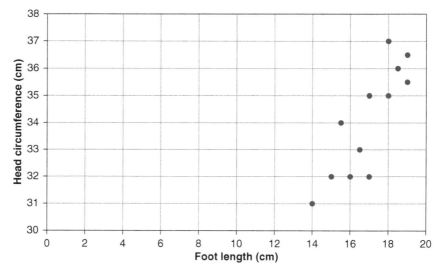

Figure 9.18 A scattergraph measuring head circumference against foot length

Table 9.4 A table showing the raw data that underpin our scattergraph

Measurements of head circumference and foot length for 12 children		
Child	Foot length (cm)	Head circumference (cm)
A	14	31
B	15	32
C	15.5	32
D	16	32
E	16.5	33
F	17	34
G	17	35
H	18	35
I	18	35.5
J	18.5	36
K	19	36.5
L	19	37

search for clues as to the profile of effective runners, throwers, gymnasts, sports-people, swimmers. For example, body mass index is an idea the teacher may want to throw in at some point, exercising due caution about children sensitive to their body profile.

 **Big idea**

If children are able to identify things that are likely to correlate, such as arm length and leg length, then they can learn for themselves what positive correlation looks like.

Interestingly by Level 6 in 2015 children were expected to identify positive–negative correlation and one variable changing while the other remained static.

We are now firmly into considering 'between', 'behind' and 'beyond' the data.

Framing questions for testing hypotheses

Big idea

Knowing how you are going to find out something is often more important than actually doing the data collection.

Tony Cotton (2013: 190–191), amongst others, stresses how enlightening and important it is for children to try to think how they would find something out. He cites a number of statements that would require serious fundamental thinking to decide how to find if they were true: 'You've worked well', 'France is quite hot', 'Our class is really good at swimming' and 'Indian food is pretty popular'.

All of these need some careful thinking regarding criteria that will decide if they are true or not. Children have their own examples of theories that may or may not be true such as 'counting sheep helps you go to sleep' or 'carrots help you see in the dark'. Discussion about how one might find out if these things were true is both fundamental, accessible and deep territory for children. It is to be encouraged even if the tests themselves do not always get carried out. It is the very essence of evidence-based research for which we all have reason to be grateful, such as medical discoveries and ideas that seemingly defied contemporary logic like the law of gravity.

Graham (1991: 106) emphasises the importance of framing the question that data handling activities will explore:

> The difficulties pupils have in handling and presenting data appropriately tend to be less in evidence if the investigation has been driven by a clear, purposeful question right from the beginning. In the adult world the endpoint of posing a question is, in general, finding a sensible and satisfactory answer.

This firm statement underlines how we can assist children to become much more secure in understanding and applying knowledge in handling data simply by allowing them to both discuss and plan for data handling based on greater involvement in thinking about four things. These relate to: what they want to know, how they are going to find out, greater curiosity about analysing what has been found out and how well it suits their goal. If this reasoning is also applied to how they approach all data handling tasks provided for them, they will progress well.

Misconceptions when handling data

Most of the established misunderstandings related to data handling have been referenced in this chapter. Young children will understandably get confused when different-sized objects are compared, for example, 3 large cows can seem to be greater than 4 smaller ducks. It depends if it is the amount or the quantity that is being evaluated. Children often need specific support and guidance to overcome the inclination to interpret line graphs as being related literally to travelling in a particular direction. The naming of zero on one or both axes is a path that sometimes needs exploring. There is debate as to whether all axes should start at zero or whether it is permissible to depict only a section of the axis, for example, from 500 to 700. Also, as discussed, the concept of difference can be confusing and can result in children identifying the amount a particular item totals rather than the difference between two items.

In all of these areas discussion that builds on previous experience wherever possible is advisable, ensuring that you hear how children are interpreting problems, even if they are wrong.

Conclusion

Generating discussion and dissonance is the key to moving understanding forward, using the curriculum as a content guide. Schemes of work sold by commercial publishers can have relevance; however, they are often limited in the way that they challenge thinking. Meaningful contexts and valid investigations such as those referenced in this chapter are fundamental to progress. They raise the bar and demand focus. The NRICH website (http://nrich.maths.org) is also a good source of inspiration. The book *Information is Beautiful* (McCandless, 2009) provides many thought provoking data representations that most teachers will find stimulating. Most children in primary schools can access the current Level 6 (May, 2015) content on data handling and statistics. They will need to experience data handling, and be able to relate it to what they know. Finally, they will need to be actively involved through extended discussion and by being encouraged to be curious.

10

Geometry: Shape and space

 Learning objectives

At the end of this chapter you should:

- Understand how to avoid limiting children's understanding through overemphasising shape names at the expense of recognising and articulating shape properties.
- Have a deeper understanding about the importance of teaching a wider range of orientations of the same shape.
- Realise the necessity of specific vocabulary related to shape and space. Shapes are named through their properties – not their orientation.
- Be clear that pathways to understanding shape and space often have to be grown through experience and discussion, including rotation.
- Be clear about a range of ways in which visualisation and strategies to decentre can be taught and developed through experience.
- Have more understanding of common misconceptions that can be addressed through whole class teaching and discussion.

What does the National Curriculum say?

In Year 1 children are required to recognise and name common 2D and 3D shapes. This knowledge should extend to different shape orientations, which will need to be developed through enlightened teaching. It also includes exploring variations on different shapes, which ought to mean focusing on shape properties as much as names as the key stage progresses. Children need to be able to describe movements and journeys using words such as forwards and backwards and involving part turns including a quarter, a half and a three-quarter turn rotations. Gradually this will involve clockwise and anticlockwise rotation. Children are expected to be able to apply fractional turn knowledge to clock hand movements. Vertical and horizontal orientation gradually extends to different orientations. Rotations at this point should include their own personal movements. They also start to use and hear related vocabulary to 2D and 3D shapes, corners and sides, vertices, edges and faces.

In Key Stage 2 pupils are expected to deepen this knowledge. Amongst other experiences this can include using and understanding right angles and giving and following instructions; this can and should include using Information and Communication Technology (ICT). In Year 4 angle knowledge includes understanding acute and obtuse as well as being able to distinguish between and discuss variations within shape families such as quadrilateral and triangle. It should also include a focus on comparing regular and irregular shapes.

Reflective symmetry is built on from Key Stage 1 and should include lines of symmetry other than merely horizontal and vertical lines. Year 5 extends this process as children experience other symmetries such as translation and rotation. Children's knowledge of coordinate use fits into the concept of transformations as accurate ways to depict movement, rotation and mapping. Increasing accuracy in measurement and estimation of angle is expected. Throughout upper Key Stage 2 children start to need to draw on more specific knowledge that they will need to remember, angles in a triangle or whole turn, part turns. They learn to use coordinates in all four quadrants, map and enlarge shapes as well as translate them. They can use technology to programme and design shapes and to navigate. They are reaching an age where they can start to discuss shape properties in some depth and theorise about patterns involving geometry, including angles of regular and irregular shapes.

Introduction

The real advantage about shape work is that it is so visual; it relates to our everyday world. Many children who can find abstraction and retention of key information difficult with number patterns and connections have a different mindset when it comes to shape and space. It is not always the same children who excel in number in primary years who are best equipped to thrive with shape and space work.

However, the teacher's mindset, as well as the children's, means sometimes they believe there will be a correlation. In reality shape and space is a natural, free area that as teachers we would do well to assume nothing about in terms of how little or how much children can achieve. It is also an area where active 'hands-on' experiences for younger children are needed for them to feel connected with 2D and 3D shapes.

Avoiding shape stereotyping

Shape work with young children is at its best when there is a focus on clear, logical discussion about shape properties rather than mere naming and shape recognition. Many children in early primary school build up a body of knowledge about shapes and shape names which is relevant but underdeveloped. It therefore hinders their subsequent development and understanding. Ryan and Williams (2007) have referenced one of these limitations as 'prototyping'. It doesn't just refer to shape and space but it is relevant here. This occurs when a rule that has some relevance is assumed to have universal relevance. For example, a child thinking that because most numbers seem to get bigger when multiplied, that would always be the case. In shape work there has been a tendency to present shapes in standard and regular forms and with a particular orientation. This has had the effect of children prototyping shapes by focusing on the name as a link to the orientation rather than the shape properties. Thus, the square has often been presented as a shape with a pair of horizontal and vertical lines rather than emphasising that the sides and angles are equal; so long as those properties are true on a four-sided flat shape it will be a square (Figure 10.1).

Figure 10.1

Ideas to develop shape property understanding

There are many strategies that we can use to help develop children's understanding of shape properties, these include:

- Using building blocks to create bridges, towers and designs and patterns fitting blocks together. The physical act of manipulating, joining together, selecting and choosing is one natural way to develop spatial awareness and spatial thinking.
- Potato (and other shape) printing. For example, by getting pictures that have used the same shapes in different ways with different orientations and colours.
- Shape identification games which allow children to search pictures to locate similar shapes with different orientations. Pictures and art designs are good for this.
- Environment recognition games. What examples of squares, circles, quadrilaterals, triangles can you find in the classroom, school or other environment? Magazines and online resources allow different pattern orientations to be experienced.
- Colouring *congruent* shapes in a particular colour. These could include shape templates and different orientations.
- Guess the shape of objects in a feely bag.
- Playing 'shape reveal' games on an interactive whiteboard (IWB) (www.mathszone.co.uk has some examples of this).
- Discussions about shape properties. These can be supported by rotating shapes on IWBs or by using flipcharts to hide and reveal shapes.

Big idea

Shapes only need different names when they have different properties.

Tessellation and prediction games involving shape are powerful stimulants to spatial thinking, especially when shape orientations extend beyond the horizontal and vertical side orientation; for example, 'reveal' games on IWBs with discussion and opportunity to complete partially revealed shapes. As the above activities show, there is such a huge opportunity to let children experience shape in a truly multisensory, experiential way. Before they can patternise or develop the ability to broaden recognition of different shapes in different orientations, they simply need activities that allow them to be around different shapes, using them, seeing them, manipulating them. Out of these opportunities come the opportunities, for us as teachers, to question and provoke deeper understanding of shape properties. This allows understanding to be measured at a level beyond simple memory-tag naming of other objects, like a chair, an apple or a tree.

Tessellating shapes

Visualisation

Which net won't work?

Figure 10.2

Useful activities and discussion opportunities with shape creations include allowing children to play with common commercially produced shapes including Polydron, straws and rods, as well as opportunities to make and use their own. This gives the chance to use *regular* and common shapes as well as *irregular* shapes. Alongside this consider *tessellating* shapes and finding out which ones do and don't tessellate (Figure 10.2). This is important for clarifying why squares are commonly used to measure flat shapes.

Useful questions to ask here can include:

- 'How many different shapes would you use to make a box?'
- 'Which of these (Polydron) objects has been made using the same shape each time?' (Solid shapes can be made solely out of triangles, squares, pentagons and hexagons.)
- 'Which is your favourite shape? Why?' (This can allow young children to relate shape to their own world and their own experiences.)
- 'Which of your patterns fits together without leaving any spaces?'
- 'Why don't these ones fit together in that way?' (In this example 'these ones' could be circles, footprints, stars, crescent moons.)

Discussions about tessellation and shape recognition can be guided by statements such as:

- 'I am going to choose some shapes to fit together and you can discuss with your partner if you think they will fit together without a gap, then we can try it out.'
- 'I will put some shapes up on the screen and you have to talk to your partner and tell me if it is one we have had already' (Here you could show pictures of different orientations of four or five shapes, these can, and should be, a mixture of well-known and irregular, random shapes. Children's eyes and minds are very sharp when they are clear about what they are trying to understand. If there were templates of each shape the children could test them by placing them over the designs on paper to test their thinking.)

Shape properties

Sorting games can be used to clarify and emphasise shape properties. These can involve sorting using one or more criteria. For example, does the shape have four sides? Does it have sides the same length? This active learning is well assisted by Logiblocs (a shape-based classroom resource using electronic components) and vast arrays of shapes that can be sorted and grouped in different ways. You could use a ring or a small hoop as a space for children to sort the shapes, with one category going inside the hoop the other outside.

Sorting shapes using a single criterion could involve activities such as:

- put all the blue shapes here;
- all the triangles here;
- all the shapes with no curves;
- shapes with more than four sides, or less than five sides, or an even number of sides;
- regular shapes;
- shapes with right angles;
- shapes with no right angles.

Sue Gifford (2005) references a number of examples of logical but false associations children can make with shape definitions through limited exposure to them, for example, thinking that 'triangles are blue' based on only limited experience. This sorting activity can also be turned on its head by asking children to 'guess the criterion'. Here you would place several shapes in the ring and ask children to decide what the rule is for being part of that group. Criteria that work well for this include:

- four-sided shapes (quadrilaterals);
- shapes with a curved side;
- regular shapes;
- shapes with less than five sides;
- shapes with a right angle;
- shapes with parallel lines.

This activity is well served by opportunities to share ideas with other children. Also children can think up their own rules for others to guess.

Big idea

Shapes are visual. They allow children to see and understand properties even if they don't yet know the appropriate vocabulary.

Sorting shapes by two or more criteria

When we use more than one criterion in our sorting activity the big question lying in wait is that some shapes will have common attributes (e.g. squares and rectangles both have four sides); however, there needs to be something different about a shape to mean that we would call it by a different name (so for the square all four sides and angles are equal). Furthermore, this new feature doesn't have anything to do with orientation.

This notion that to have a new name a shape must have a distinctive feature is a powerful one that applies to 3D and 2D shapes.

Figure 10.3   How are these shapes different?

Regular and irregular shapes

If we look at Figure 10.3 we can see a range of regular and irregular shapes. Children need a lot of opportunity to make, feel explore and discuss both regular and irregular shapes.

The shape families of triangles and quadrilaterals seem to have a range of different specific names within them (and we will discuss these in detail below). When shapes have five or more sides this is less common.

It is important to use common shape names early with children. This should be accompanied by the use of a variety of irregular shapes of differing numbers of sides, not just rectangles.

It is reasonably straightforward to use IWB photos of irregular shapes. This can be supported by constructing irregular shapes for discussion using interactive software. In addition it would be really useful to have a range of solid flat irregular shapes for discussion. These could be made of hard card or even cut out of wood using a jigsaw.

Further activities for developing language use and understanding with shape

Table 10.1

Activity	Learning intention
Geoboards with nails or plastic hooks to use elastic bands to form different shapes.	To allow children to explore different possibilities with shapes and to see how different shapes evolve to become new ones. (This is very useful for seeing, for example, that in triangles as one angle increases there is a corresponding decrease elsewhere.)
Feely bags with a range of regular and irregular flat and/or solid shapes for children to describe.	Children are to use the sense of touch to internalise shape properties further. To allow the sense of feel to link with the key geometry skill of visualisation.
Venn diagrams and other sorting devices to allow children to group shapes linked to common themes. For example, regular shapes, quadrilaterals, no curved sides, shapes with right angles, more than two right angles, parallel lines, symmetry, rotational symmetry, adjacent equal sides. These can be separate or overlapping groups.	To allow children to evaluate similarities and differences. To develop efficiency in naming and defining shapes and their properties. To allow visual comparisons that group shapes with similar properties. To allow further discussion to distinguish between different shapes that have been grouped together.

Table 10.1 lists useful ways to enable children to bond with shape and geometry ideas so that the understanding is part of who they are and not something they are being asked simply to remember. Most schools will have this equipment.

Shape names

- Children need to both understand and describe shapes effectively and be able to retain shape names. If they are only secure in one of these areas it should be understanding.
- Any shape that has different properties needs a different name. It does appear that triangles and quadrilaterals have a variety of known names within the one family (Table 10.2). Name changes relate to parallel lines, pairs of adjacent sides, opposite angles. Versions of these appear in shapes of different families but don't generate the same variety of names.

Table 10.2   Names and properties of triangles and quadrilaterals

Triangles	Quadrilaterals
Right angled: Triangle with a right angle in it.	Square: Regular quadrilateral; all sides and angles equal.
Equilateral: Equal sides and angles.	Rectangle: Two pairs of parallel lines and four right angles.
Isosceles: Two sides and angles equal.	Rhombus: All sides equal, opposite angles only are equal.
Scalene: Three different length sides.	Kite: Two separate pairs of adjacent sides are equal.
	Parallelogram: Two pairs of parallel lines.
	Trapezium: One pair of parallel lines.

There is a real need to assist children in discussing similarities and differences between and within shapes. Their understanding can easily be limited by under-exposure, causing them to struggle to recognise common shapes with a variation or to make assumptions which aren't true: For example, to think that a square rotated is a 'diamond' (Figure 10.4).

Figure 10.4   A square rotated is still a square

 # Activity: Shape 'Guess Who?'

Learning intention: Develop children's ability to articulate and interpret shape properties

Children need opportunities to compare different shapes and to identify differences. They also need opportunities to describe one of a wide range of shapes. For example, children could be shown a set of 20 different shapes and asked to pick a shape and record three clues about the shape they have chosen. They read the first clue. Other children discuss and come up with suitable possibilities. This narrows the field down. They read the second clue and so on until it can only be one shape. This can also be played as a shape version of the game Guess Who? where children will ask questions to eliminate shapes (Figure 10.5). In this context yes/no questions are the most straightforward way of eliminating wrong answers:

- Does it have three sides?
- Is it a quadrilateral?
- Does it have more than four sides?
- Are there any right angles?

Effective, relevant vocabulary is to be encouraged. In the end there may be several shapes with the same number of sides. One way or another the questions need to find differences between shapes to find the winning one (Table 10.3).

Figure 10.5   A selection of shapes for the 'Guess Who?' game, including regular and irregular quadrilaterals

Table 10.3   'Guess Who?' questions and possible shapes

'Guess Who?' question: 'Does the shape have …'	Possible shapes
All right angles?	Square, rectangle.
Parallel line(s)?	Square, rectangle, rhombus, parallelogram, trapezium.
Adjacent sides that are equal?	Kite, square, rhombus.
All angles equal?	Square, rectangle.
All sides equal?	Square, rhombus.
A reflex angle?	Deltoid.
Any acute angles?	Kite, rhombus, trapezium.

Developing understanding of shape properties through exploration

There are many names of logicians and mathematicians of countries hundreds of years ago that we still recall and cite: Euler, Archimedes, Pythagoras, Euclid to name but a few. I am quite sure they didn't launch straight into their more famous discoveries. They would have pondered and poked about, tried things out that were not so illuminating, moving to areas that were significant and then gradually refined their thoughts. As well as being compelled to teach a prescribed curriculum we need to allow children the chance to try things out that may not all be illuminating. As with the philosophy and ethos of developing problem solving you have to experiment and refine your thinking.

 ## Activity: Impossible shapes

Learning intention: To deduce why some shapes with certain properties cannot be made

Children need opportunities to make, interpret and explore shapes.

i 'Can you make a four-sided shape with one, two, or three right angles? Could you put into words why one of them isn't possible?'

ii 'Can you make a pentagon with one set of parallel lines, or two pairs?'

iii 'What is the most right angles you can have in a hexagon, triangle or an octagon? Is there a pattern?' (Geoboards are very good for this kind of exploration before drawing or making.)

Open and closed questions

There is a big difference between saying 'How many right angles are there in this hexagon or octagon?' and 'What is the most right angles you could get in one?' Further still, what can you say about the amount of right angles in polygons in general terms? Clearly the hexagon and octagon would need to be irregular as the regular ones don't have any right angles!

Angle as a measure of turn

Let us now explore how important this concept is to understanding: what skills need to be developed and understood and what activities can help this to happen?

 ## Big ideas

- Children need to understand how angle is actually just another unit of measure, around a fixed point. It is measured in degrees just like weight is measured in kilograms and length in centimetres and metres.

(Continued)

(Continued)

- Children struggle to understand protractors as measuring the size of a turn unless they are able to relate using them to the physical turns they make, relative to right angles. The relative size of angle can be explored using classroom space, for example: 'Face the door for both these instructions. Is it a bigger turn to face the window or a bigger turn to face the cupboard door?'

The research of recent years regarding primary school children's understanding of angle is depressing. Mitchelmore (1998) and Mitchelmore and White (2000) found two principal things: namely that most primary children were unable to give a relevant explanation as to what an angle was; also, they were unable to relate an ability to measure angle to meaningful contexts such as exits from roundabouts, the relative positioning of scissor blades and the degree of bend in an arm or a leg.

The source of such a set of circumstances may well inform us how to address the issue. It relates to understanding angle as a measure of turn. The idea of an angle being a measurement of the size of a turn around a fixed point is an instructive one. Haylock has termed this as the 'dynamic' view of angle (2014: 363). The two lines that meet capture the direction being faced both at the start and finish of the turn from a starting point on the corner (Figure 10.6). In the hurry to show and find right angles and learn to use the protractor this very important point is often forgotten or underemphasised.

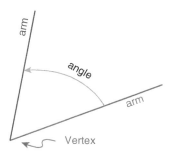

Figure 10.6   Understanding angles as a measure of turn

As such, it is almost inconceivable that many young children would be able to relate angle measuring to mental rotation and rotation situations in real life. It would run against a basic understanding of Piagetian child development. That is that children can only really learn to abstract as a result of experiencing and making personal sense of the real world. In many cases children have learnt to measure angles by gradually doing what they have been told to do as a procedure, captured by following instructions, possessing very little understanding. This traditional approach would include the following steps:

i   Place protractor over the angle.

ii Ensure the zero line is alongside one of the angle lines.

iii Read off the angle from the protractor.

iv Make sure you are clear whether the angle will be more or less than a right angle so that you don't read the wrong angle by mistake.

Such a set of instructions can accompany many lessons on angle measuring today. The use of the IWB does allow more discussion about the physicality of moving the protractor to measure accurately. However, we now need to grow an understanding in children of this active view of angle as a measure of turn.

Activity: Angle of turn in the classroom (Early years and Key Stage 1)

Learning intention: Understanding angle as a rotation around a point

Have a child face the classroom door and ask questions that require children to compare the angle of turn using aspects of the classroom layout, for example: 'Is it a bigger turn to end up facing the book corner or to turn the other way to end up facing the goldfish bowl? How could we find out?'.

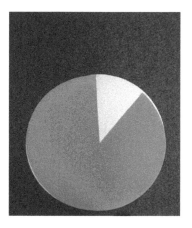

Figure 10.7

Child based understanding would need to understand that the angle measurer was capturing the size of turn they had learnt to create using physical, dynamic turning through a particular rotation captured by the white part of the circle (Figure 10.7); here the turn captures the rotation from the door to the trophy cabinet.

This is actually quite a lot of information for a young child to process. They would probably need to carry out each action separately and then be given the task of comparing to see which turn was bigger. Children are very focused on problem solving when they understand the problem. Here they may say things like: 'I could count how many times I turn my feet round' or 'We could measure to the goldfish bowl and the book corner'. This second idea shows that they are confusing distance to the object with rotation.

Using circle segments

Children do respond to the idea of standing in the middle of a circle and there being some kind of pointer to measure the size of the rotation either with numbers or by comparing the two turns (Figure 10.8).

Figure 10.8 Circle segments capturing the different rotations undertaken. Personal physical rotation by children is how this knowledge of angle can be understood

If we compare the early years activity above with the Year 6 style Standardised Assessment below we can see that a child who has physically experienced rotation through an angle will be less likely to confuse this with area.

Which colour is the spinner most likely to land on when it is spun?

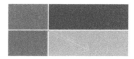

Figure 10.9   A spinner – you could make this out of coloured card

It is very common for a majority of children to believe the spinner is more likely to land on yellow because they are chasing the idea of the area rather than the size of the turn that the spinner makes (Figure 10.9). All four sections are of equal probability when it comes to predicting the destination of the spinner. Variations in area and shape orientation deepen the opportunities for understanding.

This process gets repeated in situations involving children and adults throughout life. Many of us struggle to predict outcomes involving mental rotation such as:

i   The direction we will face after a right turn on a map where we weren't heading north.

ii How to manoeuvre a car into a tight parking space where the ends of the car in which we sit are, for instance, two metres from our sitting position.

iii Manipulating furniture into tight spaces, around corners or through doors.

iv Giving instructions relative to the direction one is coming from: 'If you are approaching the crossroads from the church then you need to turn right…'

Some children, like adults, happen to be better than others at these decentring kinds of experience. This process can involve visualisation. Van Hiele's work on levels of understanding in geometry (Crowley, 1987) might be worth pursuing to determine progression. He valued visualisation. Also, he distinguished between shape association and recognition; he went beyond this into shape property awareness, moving into deduction and proof. Hegarty and Kozhevnikov (1999) identify skills and attributes that are possessed by people who are able to work in occupations requiring high levels of managing mental rotation of several objects. In short such people were able to compartmentalise the problems rather than hold all of the transformations in their head. One of the things this chapter is seeking to do is to provide relevant early steps to prepare for such experiences later in secondary and higher education.

These skills should develop with both experience and relevant discussion. Around activities such as those listed above we can all ensure two things. Firstly, we can ensure children experience a wide range of tasks that give them the opportunity to develop relevant understanding of the 'dynamic' view of angle including both the concept of decentring and being able to relate to seeing angle as the size of a turn, even when it requires a rotation in a different direction to the one we face. Secondly, we can provide opportunities, through visualisation and the discussion of visual problems, for children to articulate and to hear different strategies and interpretations of understanding and solving angle problems.

Further ideas to support this development

Real life direction games involving the compass points of north, south, east and west are useful ways of supporting children's thinking about angles. Let children explore $^1/_4$, $^1/_2$ and $^3/_4$ turns in the safe context of the classroom or hall where they can stand in the middle of a room or space and actually come to grips with what these size jumps actually do. Year 1 or more probably Year 2 children really benefit from these experiences. This may be due to their increasing ability to process information; or more controlled physical movements or a combination of these factors. Crucially, children learn by being active and they start to make sense of the order of the compass points. Mnemonics can help them remember how the compass points are arranged (NESW: 'Never eat Shredded Wheat' or 'Nearly everything sounds weird!'). These kinds of activities allow them to both understand rotation in context and develop thinking that prepares them for understanding decentring. By decentring, I mean actually starting to picture what a rotation outcome would look like, without having to carry it out in a physical sense.

An appropriate progression of questions for compass point activities could be as follows:

- 'Start at north and jump $^1/_4$ turn clockwise. Where do you finish?'
- 'If you end up at west after a $^1/_4$ turn where might you have started facing?' (There are two possible answers here, north or south.)
- 'If you end up facing north after a $^1/_4$ turn clockwise rotation, which direction might you have been facing to start with?'

If some of the questions are challenging then children can be encouraged to share their responses and discuss different answers. This process assists both Piagetian ideas of confronting knowledge that challenges your existing thoughts and Vygotskyan ideas about peer-assisted learning. It is such an active learning experience if discussing answers is part of the process. Closure on the solutions will take place at the end of the lesson; you want to extend and challenge as much as you can.

Further extensions can be easily achieved through introducing the compass points midway between north, south, east and west, namely northeast, northwest, southeast and southwest.

In doing so children may come up with questions such as: 'Why does the N or S come first?' or 'What compass point lies between N and NE?' or 'Can you get NNNNNE?' Ridiculous as some of them may seem they all show active thinking and understanding.

Children should be allowed both to carry out tasks that allow them to answer similar questions around $^1/_4$, $^1/_2$ and $^3/_4$ turn rotations from these alternative starting points. This is crucial experience for them to have at the earliest possible age because mental aptitude here is commonly not developed in children or adults. We get pretty good at dealing with rotation from a horizontal or vertical position but real life problems don't always work out like this.

Visualisation

The use of relevant active learning experiences across Key Stage 1 and lower Key Stage 2 will prepare children well for the challenge of visualising and decentring. For example, consider how the following problems can be solved through visualising the necessary turns:

- 'Imagine you are facing west and you turn $^1/_4$ turn to the right. Where do you end up facing?'
- 'If you end up facing northwest having done a $^1/_2$ turn where did you start off facing?'

Children can, of course, try the rotations out to try to find if their visualisation was accurate. All of this kind of work is deep but manageable territory for children of this age. The scaffolds to assist development and understanding include: compass points up on the classroom wall, collaborative working, multiple-choice questions and bringing some form of closure to the activity. In addition some children would be assisted by a 90° or $^1/_4$ turn segment, particularly for the more complex turns such as from southwest to southeast. So many connections are possible involving $^1/_4$ turns, degrees, clockwise and anticlockwise.

Acute, obtuse and right angles

All of this active rotating to understand angle does help children understand the standard taught ideas around angle sizes, which include acute angles (which are less than 90°), obtuse angles (greater than 90° but less than 180°) and right angles (exactly 90°). Children are often asked to find examples within the classroom or school of these kinds of angle. They learn much more quickly if they use templates through which they can physically rotate.

 ## Activity: Drawing angles

Learning intention: Children learn to understand angle through physical rotation around a fixed point

Get children to draw and cut out acute, obtuse and right angles, on sheets of A3 paper. Children physically rotate through the angle they cut out and compare it to a right angle to decide whether the angle they have drawn is an acute, obtuse or right angle.

 ## Big idea

Children need to be able to compare, clearly, a right angle template with other angles they are investigating.

In order to physically compare the different-sized angles that they have drawn children will need to have the bigger angle underneath in order to see the smaller angle above it. In time children can be given these kinds of task to estimate angle without the physical experience. This occurs when understanding of rotation has occurred. Sometimes children are asked to estimate angles that they don't really understand and are asked to do so with common orientations only, this is often of limited value and creates only limited or narrow understanding. It is a challenge for us as teachers to avoid this superficial approach. Many teachers constantly reflect on how to make their teaching create deeper understanding. These ideas are to assist them in that process.

Cross-curricular links with PE and geography

Working with angles offers us the opportunity to make cross-curricular links with other subjects. Clearly this kind of work links well to aspects of PE such as floorwork and apparatus gymnastics, which can combine aspects of rotation with height and balance. For example, a PE activity could be:

Teacher: 'Try to use the bars and stools to practice $\frac{1}{4}$ turn jumps."

Half ($\frac{1}{2}$) and three quarter ($\frac{3}{4}$) turn jumps are also very valid: they would need more space and jumping would need to be from a lower height. (This also has a scientific component as altering direction at speed affects balance.) Decentring can also be covered, for example:

Teacher: 'OK children. Look this way. If I am standing on the cushion here facing you and I jump $\frac{1}{4}$ turn to the right where will I end up?'.

If two young children who have just learnt to tell left from right (sometimes by looking at the L between their finger and thumb on the left hand) are doing a $\frac{1}{4}$ turn to the right they may end up in different places and if they swap places the situation may be reversed. This is instructive and worthy of discussion. They may even then be able to predict outcomes when other people jumping are facing the opposite way to them, having found out that *orientation* matters. Angle work can also be relevant for geography as it has strong links with map work, map reading, journeys, instructions, treasure location. Children can be encouraged to both experiment and to decentre.

 **Big idea**

The jumping activities above feed into the BIG IDEA that the right hand side as you look one way is the left hand side as you look the opposite way. This is vital when giving instructions. If you are asked to turn to the left it is dependent on the direction that you are facing.

There are harder pathways of understanding to grow, such as the concept of $\frac{1}{3}$ of a rotation (Figure 10.10), which lies somewhere between $\frac{1}{2}$ and a $\frac{1}{4}$ turn although not exactly (see Chapter 8 on fractions for discussion and ideas about understanding $\frac{1}{3}$).

$$\frac{1}{2} \text{ turn} = 180°$$

$$\frac{1}{4} \text{ turn} = 90°$$

$$\frac{1}{3} \text{ turn} = 120°$$

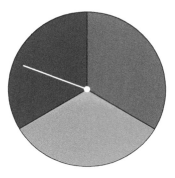

Figure 10.10 Working out ⅓ turn

In a circular rotation the more jumps you make to complete one whole rotation the *smaller* each jump must be.

Jumping activities can help further this understanding, for example: 'When we did ¹/₄ turn jumps with compass points then four jumps made the whole turn. Once we made the jumps half as big more jumps were needed to make the whole.'

This can lead on into introducing the concept of how many degrees make a circle: 'Now children, get your head around this! We use 90 small sized jumps to make up a ¹/₄ turn and 360 to rotate one complete turn.' It is this kind of discussion that feels child-friendly. It either produces understanding or gives you a real chance to see where children may be struggling. Such work paves the way for lots of estimating of angles as children begin to use angle measurers and there are many accessible, free, angle-estimating interactive teaching programmes which can be used in class. By using something that can measure angles children then have some idea what is being referenced: the size of the turn. If this key point is illustrated and developed by most teachers our children have a good chance of developing better spatial awareness and understanding than many of us had the opportunity to.

If you made a short video clip from overhead of a child making four equal jumps to complete a turn the idea of rotating would be enforced. If you made a second video where the same process took place but this time the child started off facing northeast instead of north you can enhance everyone's understanding by a discussion that explored that the four jumps still added up to a whole turn, even though the starting point was different and each jump was a ¼ turn.

Using technology: Following and giving instructions involving rotation

Children at a very young age can enjoy using computerised technology to give and follow movement instructions. This is because there is immediate, visually represented, cause and effect (Figure 10.11).

Figure 10.11   Bee-Bots, Floor Turtles and programmable cars (pictured here) all act as a meaningful context to secure understanding of angle turns, decentring and mental rotation

Children soon learn that programming the wrong instruction has the opposite impact to the one that they intended. The object or screen icon heads off in the other direction. They soon learn the adjustments of numbers needed when programming angles. Trial and error alone develops this. Playing and using the technology deepens understanding anyway, but tasks that generate active thinking related to children's current understanding can be even more effective.

Activity: Giving instructions to the Bee-Bot

Learning intention: Children learn to use left and right effectively when rotating and using directions

The follow sequence can be helpful in establishing a progression of understanding; it uses a Bee-Bot, a popular programmable robot found in many classrooms.

- 'Put in a direction and a number and see what happens.'
- 'Using left, right, forward and backwards try to navigate the Bee-Bot down this path (a created route on the desk or carpet) (Figure 10.12). You can try to navigate the path yourself if it helps.' (Facing the way the Bee-Bot moves can help orientation initially.)

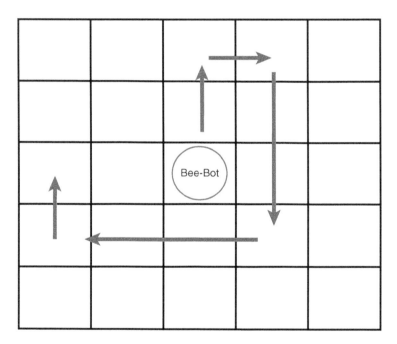

Figure 10.12   A Bee-Bot path

- 'Try to work out where the Bee-Bot will finish by following these instructions. Forward 2. Right. Forward 3. Left. Forward 1. Left. Forward 2. Right.'
- 'Try to write the instructions so that the Bee-Bot starts here and ends next to the plant pot.'

Once this has been achieved, set children the challenge of guiding the Bee-Bot without moving themselves, for example:

The pair of you have understood this really well! Here is the next challenge. I want you to write down the instructions to get the Bee-Bot from its position facing you [for example, on the other side of desk] through this route to the finish here by your pen pot. I don't want you to move from where you are siting. I want you to work out in your mind whether it's left or right and how far.

A question to check understanding here would be: 'What strategies do you use to work out left and right when the Bee-Bot is facing a different way to you?'. This is rich territory for discussion as children hear different ideas to their own and some will want to try them out.

This task is now a real challenge but within a context that the child knows well. The original learning intention would have been 'Children learn to use left and right effectively when rotating and using directions', by the end it can read 'Children start to apply knowledge related to left and right through mental rotation or by decentring'.

At a fundamental level this is deep, ground-breaking work, beautifully supported by physical resources and interactive scaffolded learning. With Floor Turtles and LOGO (an educational programming language) the opportunity is there to use software that educates and develops understanding about angle numbers (90°, 360° and more) A similar progression in understanding using these could be developed by using a set of questions and tasks as follows:

*   'What number angle makes a ¼ turn? Makes a ½ turn?'
*   'Try to make the pattern provided using LOGO or a Floor Turtle.'
*   A similar task using different orientations (northeast, northwest, southeast, southwest).
*   A similar task again showing random straight lines and various angles from 0 to 180°.
*   Beyond this there are possibilities to develop understanding of repeating instructions for which LOGO in particular is excellent. This can be very useful when developing an under-standing of *regular* shapes and their properties of repeated same-sized angles and side lengths.

Transformations

This concept is an important geometric concept. It covers the process by which a shape changes position but is essentially still the same shape. Figure 10.13 and Table 10.4 show how Shape A has been moved to different locations B, C and D but is still the same shape.

Symmetry: Reflection, translation and rotations

Many children and a number of adults believe symmetry to refer to reflections. It can do, but has a much wider meaning related either to reflection, rotation or translation as outlined above.

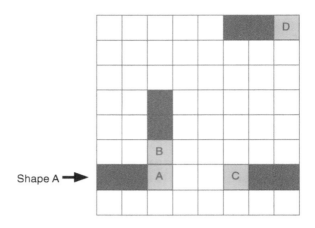

Shape A ➡

Figure 10.13 The same shape in different positions

Table 10.4 Discussion regarding the transformations in Figure 10.13

	Transformation	Discussion
Shape A to Shape B	¼ turn clockwise rotation around the point (3, 2).	Children find rotation around a point on a shape much easier than if the centre of rotation is not part of the shape.
Shape A to Shape C	Reflection in the line $x = 4$	The shape has been reflected in the line shown. The real challenge is to allow children to develop understanding of reflection when the reflecting line isn't horizontal or vertical.
Shape A to Shape D	Translation with a vector movement $\binom{5}{6}$ 5 squares across and 6 squares up.	Vector movements are recorded with the horizontal movement on top and the vertical movement below. This distinguishes them from location coordinates.

 **Big idea**

Try to ensure children get a range of experiences linked to symmetry including rotational and translational symmetry.

Activity: Tetronimoes, pentominoes and hexonimoes

Learning intention: To develop understanding related to whether shapes are different or transformations of each other

2D shapes made by joining together squares are known as polyminoes (you should be very familiar with dominoes), tetronimoes contain four squares (Figure 10.14), pentominoes contain five squares and hexonimoes contain six squares.

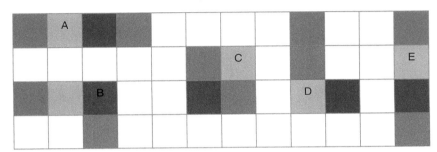

Figure 10.14   Tetronimoes have four squares

If we look at Figure 10.14 we see that Shape B and Shape D are in fact the same shape but with a different rotation. The same is true with Shapes A and E. Children can try to find as many tetronimoes or pentominoes as they can. They can score a point for any shape they make which isn't a transformation of one already shown by someone else.

A 3D version of this can involve using Multilink cubes to see how many different four- or five-cube 'homes' can be made that aren't transformations of each other; five cubes in a row with a vertical orientation (high rise flats) or a horizontal orientation (terraced bungalows) are very different to live in but they are essentially the same shape.

Common misconceptions with shape and angles

There are several aspects of shape and angles that can be commonly misunderstood, these include:

- Orientation: underdeveloped awareness of shape properties and over-reliance by children on orientation. Squares, kites and other quadrilaterals often suffer from this.
  Learning intention to overcome this: Ensure children experience shapes in different orientations so that it is the shape properties not the orientation that define their understanding.

- Triangles: overexposure to the equilateral triangle and isosceles triangles with the different length as the base.
  Learning intention to overcome this: Ensure children see, draw and discuss a wide variety of triangles distinguishing between similarities and differences.
- Regular shape emphasis: children can struggle to understand that many shape names refer to the number of sides a shape has and not that the side lengths and angles are equal. This can be caused by teaching that over-emphasises common shape names at the expense of shape properties.
  Learning intention to overcome this: Ensure there are challenges, activities and discussions that include regular and irregular shapes.
- Being only able to recognise reflective and rotational symmetry in shapes shown in standard orientation. The key is to help grow children's understanding of both at different angles.
  Learning intention to overcome this: Ensure children interpret and create a range of reflective symmetry experiences, including lines of symmetry that are different to the horizontal and vertical. Also, grow pathways in mental rotation and rotational symmetry that have the centre of rotation away from the shape.
- Angle not fully understood as a measure of the size of the turn: for example, children focus on area or fail to understand angle as a measurement size.
  Learning intention to overcome this: Ensure that young children experience angle rotation initially by physically turning through part whole turns before trying to measure angles with a right angle or an angle measurer.
- Children struggle to think spatially when it isn't from their own perspective. Thus they need to have opportunities both to do this in problem situations and to hear the strategies successful children use.
  Learning intention to overcome this: Ensure experience and discussion takes place about turning and rotation from different perspectives, such as Floor Turtles, Bee-Bots, Roamers, LOGO and instructions for journeys from different locations (see activities below).

If we are aware of such limitations in children's thinking we can plan for experiences that could extend and develop their knowledge on key geometric concepts. This may result in deepening children's understanding of shape space and angle quite quickly. It is important to use relevant vocabulary as children are better than we often think at using it. As always, be brave. Discussion is good, even if you are on the edge of your comfort zone. Being interested never adversely affected learning, even when teacher errors occur.

Relating spatial thinking to decentring and real life situations

In the middle of the previous century Piaget's 'mountain problem' (1956) was designed to measure how well a child could visualise or relate to other peoples' views and perspectives of a visualised scene – from a different angle (Figure 10.15).

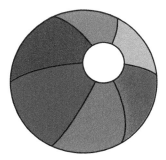

Figure 10.15 Our view of what the beachball looks like depends on the position we are standing in

Debate raged about the age when children can take on board the perspectives of others. Those who have challenged the age demarcations outlined by Piaget tend to do so by arguing and showing evidence that by using contexts that have some real life meaning we can generate more obvious understanding in children. As has been stressed with other mathematical topics throughout this book, children need to have many real, concrete experiences. This is the sense of the world that they draw on when they are trying to think through problems or imagine. Imagination, it could be argued, is dependent on adapting previous experiences and adjusting them. Thus, as teachers, we need to give children, at quite young ages, the chance to experience and discuss problems relating to spatial thinking and involving decentring in the way that Piaget's mountain task evaluates. Sue Gifford cites a passage from Gura (1992) which references the nature of children's early thinking and the need, as teachers, to cue into it. Children hearing scraping and banging noises in the room above are told that people are moving furniture around. 'What, on the ceiling?' is one incredulous reply. Even when taken to see it, they still found the concept hard to understand.

Small and real world

The solution is not to ignore children's thoughts and contributions but to use them as a catalyst to take their thinking further using discussions and activities involving seeing different perspectives through small world representations. In a small world scene, the object seen as being behind the dog will depend on which way the dog is facing and the position you are looking at it from. When you ask a child to put up the doll's left hand they may choose the hand on *their* left, but when they turn the doll around to face the same way as the child it is clear that this was an incorrect choice.

Small world representations of angle and perspective, for example, a car coming up to a roundabout, with bird's eye and side on views of the scene, all help to confront children's initially egocentric view of spatial representation. From such experience and discussion, visualisation, mental representation, landmarking, decentring can all be developed. Landmarking is the term used to work out the position of something relative to something or somewhere else. Some people find it easier to remember routes by landmarks rather than follow instructions. For example, 'turn left at the swimming pool' is easier to carry out than 'go down Dereham Road'. The familiar objects (landmarks) guide the way. These skills get used time and again in life so let's engage children in experience and discussion early on. Other real life situations involving angle interpretation can include compasses, scissors and clock hands. These generate variable angles that children can interpret, but only when they can relate the changing angle size to the experience of physically turning through an angle and are able to process orientation different to their own position. Games such as chess and Tetris as well as treasure hunt map reading all help to let children learn through experiences that deepen their understanding of angle rotation.

The beauty of all this work is that it is so visual. The development of spatial thinking, which relies on visualisation and relational understanding (such as being able to recall that the teapot is on the shelf, just after the blue cup and to the left hand side) is one that can be grown through experience, discussion and familiarisation. More complex visualisation is thought to link to making connections and not just memory, therefore experience and discussion are likely to be essential.

💡 Big ideas

- It is a key skill to be able to interpret direction instructions. Many adults turn the map upside down or around to achieve this.
- Orientation away from north, south, east and west needs more exposure as it is the least understood, recognised or acted upon by children and adults.
- Games and activities, like chess, Tetris, Boppit and moving target electronic games greatly increase spatial thinking and understanding. They may well increase confidence to tackle early STEM-related thinking and ideas.

Research shows that higher order spatial thinking needs to go beyond mental rotation. The process of breaking spatial thinking tasks down into smaller manageable steps is one that must begin at the primary level (Hegarty and Kozhevnikov, 1999).

 ## Activity: Spatial thinking with classroom objects

Learning intention: Developing the key skill of mental rotation through visualisation

Here are two possible activities that require children to engage with the positioning of objects on a board when the board is rotated. For the first activity, set up a board with a number of objects on it; on an identical board set up only one or two key objects and ask children to state where missing objects should be in relation to those they can see (Figure 10.16). For example: 'Here you see a collection of objects. On an identical board you can't see the plastic dog. Where would you place the dog to be in the right position after a ¼ turn clockwise?'.

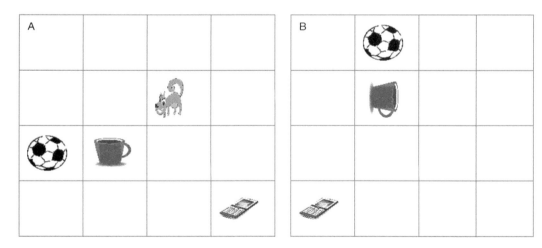

Figure 10.16   Board B has been rotated ¼ turn clockwise – where should the dog go?

This excellent visualisation opportunity would work well with real life objects on a grid. It would work really well to start at position B instead of A. The concepts of clockwise and anticlockwise support this well. This orientation change has gone from north facing to east facing. All compass point orientations could be used, including northeast, northwest, southwest, southeast.

We are then really growing pathways that have rarely been grown before at primary level. Children as young as 5 or 6 have shown themselves very capable of tackling this work because they have been inducted in a way that they understand. They have first-hand experience of it.

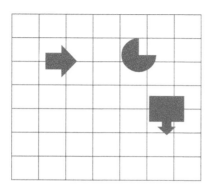 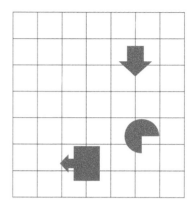

Figure 10.17 Two 7 × 7 grids, the second has been rotated by 90°

A second activity can involve growing mental rotation through landmarking. The second grid in Figure 10.17 has been rotated ¼ turn. The ability to predict what a rotated shape or collection of objects will look like is a key skill in many life situations: furniture and building design and arrangements, moving systems such as weather fronts, car engines, packaging, storing. Yet in order to provoke interest and active learning in children there needs to be a hook. Games such as covering up squares and asking children to predict the results of rotations raise the

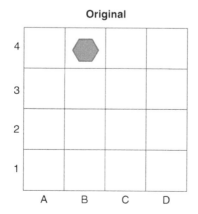 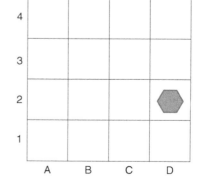

Figure 10.18 A rotational problem

stakes and can be accomplished on IWBs. A typical problem here could be a 4 × 4 grid that has an object in square B4 (Figure 10.18). Where will the shape be after a ¼ turn clockwise rotation? The challenge can be made harder by rotating the grid to a point that isn't horizontal or vertical. This involves significant application of thinking – either through mental rotation or by making other connections that assist the process (the grid and the numbers might need to be separated).

Conclusion

The ideas that we have covered in this chapter are to provoke your thinking and let you see that children really enjoy active tasks that they understand. Shape and space are both so visual that it becomes much easier to explain and engage them in these kinds of challenges when they can see a physical need to understand and solve problems.

The understanding that underpins most of the ideas and activities that we have discussed can be traced back to two key points. Firstly, more emphasis needs to be placed on shape properties in addition to names; secondly, understanding angle as a rotation about a point allows access to so many life related skills and situations. Children have to experience physical rotation themselves first before trying to tackle problems that reference it. As teachers of primary mathematics we should aim to develop these two key ideas in active experiences and discussion with children.

11

Measurement

 Learning objectives

By the end of this chapter you should:

- Understand the pedagogy of teaching measure through visual comparison; this is how young children come to understand it, initially.
- Appreciate how children can begin to understand measure beyond their visual world.
- Know the range of the theme of measure in the primary age phase.
- Be familiar with how non-standard units can both develop understanding and provide a platform for standardisation in measure.
- Relate place value directly to different units of measure.
- Be familiar with common misconceptions within the theme of measure, and know how these can be tackled through focused teaching.
- Teach for understanding so that formulae, when they begin to be used, can be understood and applied.

 What does the National Curriculum say?

Children begin school already curious about their world. They have probably had supervised experiences playing with objects, exploring space, fitting and matching. They will have had the chance to choose objects and food of different lengths and sizes. They know you can fill and empty containers and that sometimes this makes a mess. In their initial time in school they will continue with these experiences, not least because early years classrooms tend to be rich with objects to explore and experiment with. In addition to this, young children through their egocentricity often make comparisons with each other, such as 'My one's bigger', 'I've got more' or 'I'm quicker'. They can be engaged in discussion around these themes, for example, 'How could we see if you are right? How could we see if your bridge is longer (or higher or wider)?'.

By Year 1 they are expected to be able to compare measurements of different things with equipment and relevant comparative vocabulary: longer, bigger, smaller, shorter, heavier and so on. By Year 2 they are expected to be using formal, standard units of measure in weight, length, temperature and capacity and be able to demonstrate their ability to compare measures through symbols to denote 'is more than' (>), 'is less than' (<) and 'has an equal value to' (=). By lower Key Stage 2 children are required to be familiar with an increased amount of interconnections within measure, including metres, centimetres and millimetres as well as grams, kilograms, litres and millilitres. They are also expected to be able to add and subtract units of measure although representing part whole measurements with decimals isn't yet specified.

Gradually children are required to work with different units of measure and using decimals. They begin to tackle area and perimeter on standard shapes, moving onto composite shapes in upper Key Stage 2. They should be able to use units of measurement involving decimals by Year 6. They are required to be able to compare and estimate decimal and imperial measures. Pleasingly, it is specifically suggested that they are fully inducted into the conservation of area and its links with perimeter, developing a full knowledge of different ways area can be distributed and its impact on perimeter. By implication, it would make sense if this were extended to volume alongside surface area. Formulae are referenced for use in later Key Stage 2 and the vigilant teacher will want to ensure that deep understanding exists in children to avoid its misapplication.

Weight, length, capacity, volume and area

The concept of measurement involves many different strands. These relate to one-, two- and three-dimensional measures as well as weight, time, temperature and angle. Time is covered separately in Chapter 6, not least for the reason that the number groupings are different and that there are some distinct anomalies, particularly concerning analogue clock time. Angle is covered as part of Chapter 10 on geometry: shape and space. Temperature appears as a case study within Chapter 9 on statistics. Thus, this chapter will reference the measures listed above, one by one, with a repeating structure. It will track relevant early experiences for young primary children before moving on to more advanced application of knowledge. This will be followed by a discussion about common themes that relates to the three about place value (Chapter 3). It will endeavour to keep understanding at the centre of discussion at all times.

Length

Children are aware, at a subconscious level, of how long things are, almost from the moment they are born. If we also link understanding of length to feel and touch, as well as the visual experience, we can see that this is indeed a multi-sensory topic. Even in the dark, or with our eyes shut, length still impacts on our sense of the world. We can feel objects in a bag or in the dark and have a distinct sense of representing the feeling in our mind, even if the representation differs from what we can see in the light. It is also extremely likely that our images, linked to feel, are based on previous experiences that the sense of touch generates in our mind and thoughts. Long before they can speak, children are responding to the one-, two- and three-dimensional world around them. In a Piagetian sense the idea of length is a rich area for children's cognitive development in as much as Piaget (1954) stressed the need for them to have experiences that would challenge their current level of thinking and understanding.

Young children take time, and arguably, a structured focus, to ascertain certain key principles that affect their understanding of measure. On arrival at school they are likely to have encountered issues related to length through clothes, jigsaw puzzles and posting object experiences with different length spaces to feed things through. They often find it easier to get things out of boxes than to put them back in; gravity makes it easier to open the box up and tip things out. Subconsciously they find out that they are tall enough or have long enough limbs to reach certain things and not others. Often really interesting things are deliberately placed out of their reach, and sometimes out of sight too, such as Christmas presents.

Ginsberg (1986) argues that young children will often think there is more of something if it is spaced out; for example, a row of six cubes could appear to be longer than a row of seven or eight cubes if they are spread out. The surrounding context can make visual interpretation of things deceptive. A sofa in a small room can appear to be larger than it seems to be in a large empty room.

Progression

Piaget, and many people since, have realised that the visual world that is unavoidable for children, and often extremely interesting, needs to be used to move their thinking forward to what we, as adults, see as key features of deeper understanding. They need to be engaged in discussion and experience about how to decide length by considering it in comparison to something else.

Ryan and Williams (2007) and Haylock (2014) both stress the need for an early understanding of 'transitivity'. That is to say, children need to be able to compare objects for length and to start to use logic based on what they find. For example, a statement encapsulating this understanding could be: 'If the pencil is longer than the sweets and the sweets are longer than the crayon, then the pencil must be longer than the crayon'. Symbolically this could be represented as: $A < B$, $B < C$, therefore A must be smaller than C ($A < C$). This is actually a very relevant but sophisticated way of expressing a logical idea that young children can be provoked into understanding. At this point there seem to be three BIG IDEAS that are quite closely interlinked as children move through the early years into Key Stage 1.

Big ideas

- Transitivity as outlined above is a vital concept, involving early logical deduction.
- We can often find a way to compare the length of two objects through having a common starting point.
- We can devise ways of measuring a single object by matching it alongside a thing or things that occupy the same space (or length).

Activity: Transitivity

Learning intention: Children use deductive reasoning to solve length comparison (Figure 11.1) (this is a key feature of the new National Curriculum in England and a focus in Chapter 1 on problem solving)

When comparing three objects to test for transitivity only have two visible at any one time. Ensure the middle-sized object is used for the first two comparisons. Then ask the question about which one of the other two will be bigger, with one of them hidden. For example: 'You can't see the pencil but when we compared it with the sweets the pencil was longer. The sweets are longer than the crayon. Could you decide which will be bigger out of the pencil

 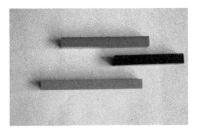 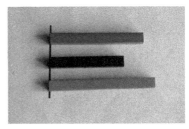

Figure 11.1

or the crayon without seeing it?' There are reasons why a child who actually is capable of deductive reasoning would still give the wrong answer. They may struggle to recall all the information. They may be more interested in the sweets anyway. Or the purpose of the exercise may not be clear so they lose interest, in which case it should be clarified. Perhaps three different-sized pencils could be used that can represent the three different-sized bears in the Goldilocks story.

Comparison

Comparison is a crucial feature of understanding length, and when teaching it to children there has to be a way of deciding which object takes up more one-dimensional space at its longest point. Ruth Merttens (1989) references a strategy that a number of teachers use that uses the law of gravity to decide the matter wherever possible; that is to stand both objects being compared upright to see which is effectively tallest. This can also be transferred to measuring horizontally by placing both objects against a wall or straight-faced static object.

You can get children thinking actively by comparing two objects where it is fairly clear which one is longer but placing them at different starting points so that the shorter object appears to extend further than the longer one (Figure 11.2).

Figure 11.2 Comparing sticks

'I thought Toby's stick was longer and yet it looks like Tilly's stick is longer. How can that be?' This is a good prelude to children carrying out tests to find out which objects are longer than others; for example, finding out the order of the size of different straws so that they can be used in different-sized glasses. Smart children may suggest just getting the different glasses and trying it out to see. However, it is good to have a real world purpose as often as possible with young children, as they can think actively to a high level when they truly understand the purpose of a task.

Alongside some early deductive reasoning and developing a strategy to compare lengths comes the task of specifying, in some way, how long something actually is. Children don't instinctively see the need for standard measures. Their world is, initially, quite a self-absorbed one. It relates to their understanding and their needs. So we need to have a way of describing how long something is to someone who isn't actually going to be able to see it but you can explain to them how long it is.

Even in this day and age of camera phones and internet photo attachments we can't actually tell how long something is through a picture. As teachers we will often need to stress that the gaps between items affect the comparison: 'What would happen if I squeeze these cubes up together. I think I can fit another one in'.

Children will experiment with different objects to match the same length whether it be their pencil, their teddy, a book or their shoe. They match up with logical comparative statements such as:

- 'My shoe is the same length as a pencil, 3 cubes and a pencil sharpener.'
- 'My doll is as long as 2 pens, 3 small bricks a pencil case and a pen-top.'

Indeed, building chairs, houses or other objects for toys or specific purposes teaches children a lot about transitivity, comparative and relative lengths. The 'trial and error' approach can come in the way of it but nevertheless has many commendable mathematical qualities.

Repeated non-standard measures

Ruth Merttens (1989) stresses the value of many different objects being used for comparison but with a gradual goal of getting children to use one particular standard-sized object repeatedly to ascertain lengths of different objects. Possible items could include: cubes, pencils, conkers, handspans or heel-to-toe feet measurements. Body parts have been used historically to measure with, particularly when the sale of animals has been involved, with horses measured in 'hands' traditionally. Such opportunities give the chance for children to compare different lengths through the use of a constant measure. They also give the chance to develop key learning points that will create efficiency and accuracy. Here are some important issues that can be used as learning intentions to underpin teaching:

- Comparing objects for length with a repeated non-standard measure (rather than simply by comparing two objects directly).
- Using a range of one kind of object to measure. For example, if cubes were used to measure objects a certain number would be put alongside and then all counted up. An extension to this would be when one object was placed heel-to-toe, so to speak, to calculate. This is often done with cubits (an ancient measurement based on the distance from fist to elbow) and feet lengths.
- Exploring how we can ensure we are accurate when we measure. This can be modelled in class by showing how a grossly inaccurate technique leads us to wrong answers and that we need clear strategies for achieving accuracy.

Big ideas

- The longer the item being used to measure, the fewer it will take to match the length. For example, it takes 3 exercise books to match the length of the desk but 32 Unifix cubes.
- The bigger someone's foot, cubit or handspan then the fewer of them it will take to measure something. 'I have just watched Ravi and Claire each measuring the length of the desk. They have used all of the measuring strategies we discussed well. However, Ravi has taken 10 handspans but Claire only 9. How can that be?'

This point is worth emphasising as it is slightly counter-intuitive. One might instinctively expect the bigger foot to be used more.

Moving to standard measures

In time, when children have had the chance both to experience and reason first-hand with physical objects and a range of non-standard measures, they are ready to engage in discussion about standard measures and their relevance. This should coincide with their ability to analyse the world from other positions than their own as they progress through the primary years. It will also be a process that is replicated in the other themes of measure, such as weight, area and capacity.

Units of measure

I would concur with a range of theorists, as well as schemes, that seek to engage children in experiences of standard units of measure viable for use in the classroom, to avoid those that are either too small to be operable with young children, such as millimetres and centimetres, or too large to be practical when measuring classroom objects, such as the metre or kilometre. The decimetre (10 cm) serves us well here. It is in between the centimetre and metre and scores well as a column name when we consider measure alongside place value. It could be recorded as a BIG IDEA.

Big idea

The use of the decimetre bridges the gap between centimetres and metres to allow manageable measuring of middle sized objects.

Estimation and the need for smaller units of measure

Children in Year 2 (and possibly Year 1) will use decimetres to measure a range of objects. The choice and purpose of such measuring by the discerning teacher can draw out the need for greater accuracy. For example, one way of introducing a need for smaller measures could be:

> Children. I am very impressed by the skill and accuracy of your measuring. Jasvinder and Kerry had a query that I wanted to share with you. They found that the chair and the desk both came out as measuring 4 decimetres and yet they feel the desk is wider. Simon noticed that his book was not quite 2 decimetres; it was more than 1 decimetre but less than 2. Maybe we need some smaller measures to help us.

Hence the need for centimetres and millimetres has arrived.

Once children have started to measure with repeated non-standard and standard units of measure, other BIG IDEAS come into consideration.

Big ideas

- There is really no such thing as complete accuracy with most forms of measure. It is only that some measuring is more accurate or uses more sophisticated equipment.
- Children need to learn the skill of choosing appropriate units of measures, relevant to the task in hand.
- They need a lot of experience of estimating with the different units of measure they use, even when they are non-standard. This feel for size and length is one that can be grown and should be encouraged.

Thus, we reach the point where children will be measuring objects that may require several different standard measures. This can be planned for with or without guidance. Likely combinations would include:

- decimetres and centimetres;
- centimetres and millimetres;
- metres and decimetres;
- metres and centimetres (taking decimetres into account).

(An issue with using metres and centimetres relates to decimal place value where the column next to the metre (100 cm) is not 1 cm. It is 10 cm. This is where the term decimetre is useful. Thus children would be given the chance to grow estimates to certain round numbers. This would include: nearest centimetre, millimetre, decimetre, $\frac{1}{2}$ metre, metre, 10 metre and so on.)

Big idea

The idea of an estimate is, in some ways, a conversation with yourself. How well can you develop your ability to estimate and what strategies do you use?

When discussing estimates an important point is to ensure that children aren't too focused on whose guess was the closest. What is more important is who has a strategy that they can share that helps them to estimate accurately. Children can get sidetracked by who was closest and miss the learning potential here. Possible strategies that children could offer include:

Kelly: 'Well, I know my pencil is about 10 cm so I think how many times would my pencil fit going across the desk and use that.'
Mohammed: 'My finger is about 1 cm so I imagine it going along the pencil.'

It can be useful to give other reference points for known objects that can be used. Visualisation is something children respond well to. It also involves a lot of relevant mathematical thinking, which has long-term benefits to their development and achievement.

Activity: Selecting the right unit of measurement

Learning intention: Identifying and consolidating understanding of appropriate units of measure

Which units of measure would you use to measure the following things: a pencil, a school corridor, a maths book, the playground, a pencil sharpener, a finger nail, the daily growth of cress seeds, the distance to the swimming pool?

When you are evaluating children's ability to choose appropriately it makes sense to mix up the areas of measure being referenced so that children make choices about length alongside weight, volume and other measures.

Activity: Giving children measuring that requires increasing levels of accuracy

Learning intention: Applying knowledge of measure in problem solving contexts

For example, we want to make a box that will fit five of these pencil sharpeners, length-wise, exactly and have three rows and be four layers high. So what will the measurements of the box need to be so that they don't wobble about in transit? A lot of packaging is now designed in such a way, so the question could have a specific outcome when the task is complete.

Although time is explored in greater depth in Chapter 6, measuring time is also relevant here. For example, you have to be at the station at 7:45am in the morning for a journey. You want to lie in until the latest possible time without stressing. List the tasks you have to do before leaving and estimate how long each one takes. Then decide your departure time to ensure you are in time.

Big idea

Increased levels of accuracy in measure are dependent on meaningful purposes that require such accuracy.

Gradually children's work should be leading towards the need to calculate measures through the four operations and will, by necessity, involve matching knowledge of those operations with the specific knowledge and skills connected to measure. They will need to reference measurements involving more than one unit of measure by using only one unit of measure and part wholes, often involving decimals. This issue is covered in Chapter 8 on fractions, drawing on one more BIG IDEA relating to only being able to record with decimals using one unit of measure.

Big idea

2 metres and 7 centimetres is *not* recorded as 2.7 metres. Column headings are related to the idea that 10 in 1 column is worth 1 in the next.

Weight

Connections and links can be made quite easily when exploring and using a range of different measures and the style of progress in weight, related to teaching and learning, will be similar to that in length. However, it may take a little time for children to distinguish weight (as a force) from size. In this respect it may be a slightly more challenging concept to grasp. Firstly, it is the case that a physically larger amount of one substance can weigh less than a smaller amount of something else. This is clearly true for less dense materials, such as feathers or foam, when compared to denser objects such as metal, concrete and granite. Secondly, and not often a subject for early primary school, the downward force weight of an object differs when there is a different gravitational pull. The further away from the gravitational force of the earth the less downward force objects have. This is the difference between weight and mass. Mass relates to the density of a substance or object, whereas the weight of an object is dependent on the gravitational pull on the object.

Big idea

Out in space objects weigh less but the mass is still the same.

Teaching weight to young children

As with length it is easier for young children to compare objects to see which is heavier or which pushes down with more force. These conversations begin, often, with a discussion about the effect of holding an object and letting go as a means of indicating how the strength of the downward force differs. Young children are able to begin to make sense of why small, dense, objects act with more force than larger, less dense ones. They are very logical. They need to feel objects first, weigh them and be invited into theorising about the outcomes. For example, 'Size can help us but look here. This 500 g weight is much, much smaller than the juice carton but it is heavier. How can that be?'

Progression of early experiences for children related to weight

Typical progress in understanding important principles concerning weight could include the following steps:

- Children have the opportunity to feel, investigate, build and fill up objects using a wide variety of things.
- They are encouraged to think how objects feel in their hand. Strong and weak objects can be used. Recognising whether objects are heavy or light should be encouraged.
- As with length, comparison and transitivity are to be encouraged. Which object feels heavier or lighter?
- Balance scales are good for visual comparison of two objects. The impact is immediate.
- Prediction and justification are parts of the process by which children deepen their understanding, including the ability to learn from incorrect predictions.

 Big ideas

- Young children, and older ones, can have their learning potential lowered by the need to be 'right' as opposed to being curious about why they were wrong. Therefore, mistakes are to be actively encouraged as learning opportunities. This takes real commitment by a teacher, and possibly by a whole school.
- Young children often associate being 'higher' with success. Therefore, on balance scales, they may initially think the bucket that goes up has more weight because it is higher. It may be useful to discuss this as a teaching example, interpreting the balance scale alongside predicting which object is heavier or lighter.

Transitivity is also useful for teaching weight, and a similar approach to that used with length can work well, for example, trying to find out the order of weight of three objects. This should, if possible, lead to being able to deduce some results without actually weighing objects. Object A is heavier than Object B. Object B is heavier than Object C, so Object A is heavier than Object C. This is a very worthwhile assessment task from Year 1 onwards. It is a very good indicator of early mathematical deductive reasoning, which is so crucial for maths work in later primary and secondary school.

Getting a feel for weight: Non-standard measures

Both balance scales and bucket balances provide a good basis for children to develop their estimating and measuring skills. A variety of different non-standard units can be used to evaluate the equivalent weight to different objects, such as: pots of pens, packs of sugar, balls of plasticine, tennis balls, plastic cups. They could, in turn, be measured using conkers, Multilink, pens, shells, with children having the opportunity to reflect on questions such as:

- 'Why does it take more Multilink to balance the plasticine ball than conkers?'
- 'Why doesn't the biggest object balance more of the non-standard units than all the others?'

These are all richer activities if they take place to a backdrop of discussion around estimation. This can be carried out in groups or possibly a whole class with two or three balance scales out the front and different children coming up to the front of the class to carry out the measuring. However you structure this, all children need to experience measuring at first hand, at some point.

Knowledge of equivalents to specific weights

In general, smaller standard weights (5 g, 10 g, 20 g) tend to be plastic because plastic is less dense and therefore lower weights are a reasonable size (5 g of iron would be really tiny). By the time we reach 50 g or 100 g the size of a cheap plastic weight would be quite big and metal starts to be used. This allows children at the end of Key Stage 1 to confront the situation of a small metal weight being heavier than a larger plastic weight.

It is a sound activity for children at about this age to see and experience collections of objects that are roughly equivalent to specific amounts, for example, 50 g balances a certain amount of cubes, pens, rubbers, books and sweets. Using amounts of 100 g and 200 g will have their own results. It is part of developing a feel for estimation and understanding. The same could be done for any weight. Such an investment of time does deepen the connections children can make. They are learning about equivalence and understanding of 100 g and other amounts in real, physical terms. This serves them very well when they come to consider the relationship between grams and kilograms where the amount of equivalent grams in a kilogram is 1000.

💡 Big ideas

- More dense objects take up less space proportionate to their mass.
- The fewer objects required to balance something, the heavier each object must be.

Just as metres and centimetres provide slightly inappropriate counting units of measure initially, the same is true for kilograms and grams. Thus the 100 g is quite a good grounding measure, for example, in setting the problem 'Do you think this will weigh about 100 g, more or less?'. In time this could be extended to 500 g and then 1000 g (1 kg). This level of measuring weight would likely be carried out around Year 4. Children's active experience of non-standard and standard weights should mean that they can use balance scales to both balance and compare objects, using non-standard, and then standard, weights.

Beginning to work with kilograms and grams

As children reach the point where they are using different units of measure they will need to be able to choose which ones are appropriate for the task in hand. The discerning teacher in upper Key Stage 2 will be doing two things in particular:

- Covering place value through different contexts including kilograms and grams, where there are some initial complexities (similar to using metres and centimetres in discussing length).
- Incorporating experience of different calibrations of scales so that children are able to interpret lines that are not numbered.

A BIG IDEA dealt with in Chapter 3 on place value is very relevant here – it relates to understanding the column values and how they are connected. The weight equivalent asserts that 2.1 kg is not 2001 g, as many children with insecure under-standing have stated.

Volume and capacity

Volume and capacity should follow a similar path to weight and length. Children need to have plenty of experience filling up a range of containers with a range of substances. These should include liquids, sand and solids that are different shapes. There are strong links with shape and space. Piaget spent a lot of time analysing volume related tasks; he felt a child's development went through different stages. A container with one long dimension was often considered to house more liquid than a more regular shape where the proportion of the shape is more balanced; particu-larly when the single, long dimension related to height.

A BIG IDEA from the weight section referenced that young children associate height with 'more'. Just as they mistake a bucket scale rising as indicating greater weight they will often think of a tall thin container as holding more than either a 3D shape with similar height, width and depth or a long thin shape with low height.

Piaget's work has been challenged regularly. This often occurs when theorists feel they have proved that the ages which Piaget ascribed for different stages of development are not relevant, and that development can be 'fast-forwarded' by confronting the issues Piaget raised as being hard for young children to understand. Such accelerated learning was often achieved through the use of specific contexts where flawed thinking was reduced (see Donaldson, 1978 and Hughes, 1986). Some of these ideas can be applied to volume and capacity.

 **Big idea**

Seek to meet common misconceptions related to conservation of volume head on. For example, engage young children in deduction of finding out which container holds more by pouring the contents of one full container into the second one. If the second container holds less then it will overflow. If it holds more it will not fill up. In some ways this is counterintuitive. Many of us may instinctively feel if the second container doesn't fill up it doesn't hold as much. Not so.

 ## Activity: Pouring with different-sized containers

Learning intention: Articulating understanding of 'greater than' and 'less than' through activity

Engage children in an exercise using very different-sized containers where they are to predict which container holds more water; the outcome here should be comparatively straightforward. Give them the opportunity to watch or test their predictions. Then ask them to discuss and complete statements such as:

- 'The first container overflows when the contents of the first are poured into it because ...'
- 'The second container does not fill up when the contents of the first container are poured in because ...'

What this does is several things. Firstly, the emphasis is not on the outcome, which is predictable. It focuses thought on what the visual outcome, overflowing or unfilled, actually means. Secondly, it emphasises the articulation of what has taken place and why. This involves reasoning and identifying relevant language to express understanding.

Non-standard measures

The relevance to estimating and working with different-sized containers remains valid. Smaller objects need to be filled more times than larger ones in order to fill a similar-sized container. Millilitres are tiny, with 5 or so to a teaspoon. Litres are quite large. 100 ml and perhaps 250 ml can be useful quantities to try to develop a feel for (much as with decimetres and 100 g in length and weight). Get children to see what 100 ml or 250 ml looks like in a range of different-sized containers. They can mark on them the point they thought the liquid would reach. When it comes to relating small quantities to filling larger containers, using 5 or 10 ml spoons to fill up cups or glasses can establish connections between the different amounts. Similarly 100 ml containers being used to fill larger vessels holding 1, 2 or 5 l also develops a feel for the connections between millilitres and litres. This point is grasped fully when the relationship between the two has been understood.

Big idea

There are 1000 ml in a litre. 1 ml is equivalent to 0.001 l.

Area and perimeter

Children often struggle to remember whether area or perimeter refers to the distance around the edge of something. This can be because some of their early experiences are limited to finding the distance around the edge of rectangles and counting the squares inside. An emphasis on more meaningful, related tasks can deepen their understanding and make the meaning of each clearer.

Distinguishing between one-dimensional and two-dimensional measuring

Who has the biggest sheet of paper? Which cake has a bigger base? These questions have real significance. There is a real challenge for children, as hitherto measure has been about one dimension only, in the main. Focus on the nature of the challenge is essential. For example:

Teacher: 'Although Kylie's cake is longer, Max's cake is wider. So which one is bigger altogether? If they were the same height which one would have more cake in it?'

Again the progression could, and perhaps should, involve natural objects being used to try to cover the paper or baseboard to the cake.

In measuring a flat space precisely, it is necessary to have a repeated, tessellating shape. There are many that could be used. The square happens to be the regular shape we use in standardised, flat shape measuring.

Ruth Merttens (1989: 85) suggests a 'cut and put' approach to tessellating shapes as a good way to deepen children's understanding of how and why tessellation works. Take any tessellating shape – regular or irregular. Cut out a section from its exterior and match it up on the opposite side to where it was taken (Figure 11.3).

 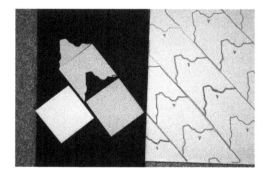

Figure 11.3 An example of 'cut and put' tessellation as a standard tessellating shape is adapted so that it will still tessellate

Activity: Measuring the size of flat shapes

Learning intention: To establish successful methods of understanding through the use of irregular shape

Young children need to use a range of objects to cover flat shapes to measure their size.

i   They can cover one object more than once using a different shape each time. For example, a book could be covered firstly with squares, then with hexagons or circles.
ii They can also cover several objects using the same shape to clarify that some shapes take up more space than others.
iii Squares can be used and their merits discussed and clarified.
iv Shapes can be drawn around on squared paper. A range of regular, straight-lined, irregular and curve-lined shapes will reveal additional issues about part whole squares. (Teachers can also use shapes on tracing paper placed over squared paper.)
v   It can be a good idea to let children use systems for approximating area such as counting all the whole squares and the part whole squares that appear to be at least half complete.
vi Discerning discussion can take place about whether or not there are more part whole squares that are more or less than half complete to ensure the approximation is as accurate as possible.

 ## Big idea

Discerning choice of example, task and discussion can ensure children encounter a range of issues related to a range of irregular and regular shapes.

Tackling length × width area calculation safely

Clearly there is a real advantage to seeing that rectangle areas are calculated by multiplying length × width. The aim is to avoid this understanding becoming 'prototypical' (Ryan and Williams, 2007) through ensuring it is one of a number of shapes children learn to calculate area for. There are a range of connections and strategies children can be helped to identify and use.

Activity: Compound shapes

Learning intention: Introduce children to compound shapes, right angled triangles, other triangles, squares and other rectangles almost simultaneously

Ensure children experience seeing rectangles as two congruent triangles with a single cut across the diagonal (Figure 11.4). This assists understanding of the later formula.

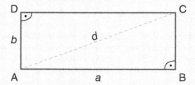

Figure 11.4 A rectangle consists of two congruent triangles

By doing this, children will get to see and understand any triangle as having half the area of the surrounding rectangle. Geoboards or nail boards with elastic bands are really useful for developing links with area. References to pi (π) with primary children are only relevant when they are underpinned through understanding. Pi is the irrational (undefined) link between the radius of a circle and its area and circumference. In reality the 3 and a bit times the square of the radius give the area of the circle. This is shown in the quartered circle in Figure 11.5. Approximately 6 and a bit radii are equivalent to the circumference of the circle.

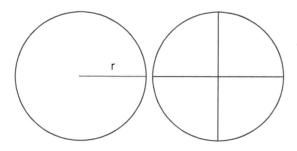

Figure 11.5 The radius of a circle

Activity: Measuring the circumference of a circle

Learning intention: Developing a conservation of length in the context of curved and straight lines

Ask children to estimate how many times the diameter of a circle would be the perimeter (circumference). The idea that it could be more than 3 times the diameter may be scarcely credible but a piece of string and several examples help to grow the belief that this is so.

Perimeter

Perimeter work can have a lot of good practical contexts such as picture frames, fences, sports pitches, fields and boundary markings. Here are some of the many learning goals that tasks to do with perimeter can address.

- Do all shapes of a similar area have a similar perimeter?
- Do all shapes with a similar perimeter have a similar area?
- Which area arrangements have the most efficient perimeter?
- Perimeters of rectangles can be found by doubling both length and width and summing together.

Misconceptions related to area and perimeter

There are common misconceptions that can come up when teaching perimeter as a topic, here are the most common:

- Children can believe that all area is found by multiplying length × width.
- Children can misunderstand perimeter to involve the outer layer of squares rather than the line or distance around the edge of a shape (see Figure 11.6).

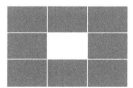

Figure 11.6 Calculating the perimeter of the white square does not involve the distance around the edge of the larger green square

- Children can erroneously assume that when the length of the sides of a flat shape are doubled then the area is also doubled.

This last point is not true because simply doubling the length of one dimension would double the area. Scale factor 2 enlargement results in the area being $(2 \times 2) = 4\times$ bigger. For example:

A square 3 cm $\times$ 3 cm has an area of 9 cm^2 (Figure 11.7).

Figure 11.7   A 3 × 3 square

A rectangle 6 cm $\times$ 3 cm has an area of 18 sq cm ($2\times$ the original area) (Figure 11.8).

Figure 11.8   A 6 × 3 rectangle (one dimension has been doubled in length)

A square 6 cm $\times$ 6 cm has an area of 36 sq cm ($4\times$ the original area) (Figure 11.9).
Doubling the length of the sides does, of course double the perimeter because they are in fact one and the same thing. You could explore this concept further by asking children to draw a small square, and then draw a new square making each side $3\times$ longer and wider. How many times bigger will the area be now? How many times bigger will the perimeter be?

Big ideas in primary mathematics

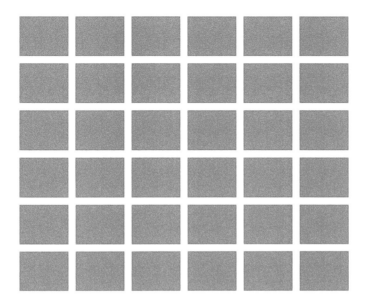

Figure 11.9 A 6 × 6 square (both dimensions have been doubled in length)

Shape enlargement

Although involving quite detailed work older primary children benefit from scale factor work. It is very visual. It builds on the previous ideas about area enlargement well.

Big idea

Scale factor enlargement requires two key facts: a centre of enlargement and a scale factor.

The increase in the area of the new shape will be the square of the scale factor used for the reasons stated above (Figure 11.10).

Big idea

The powers of recording measure of length and space relate to dimensions: 10 cm, 10 cm^2, 10 cm^3.

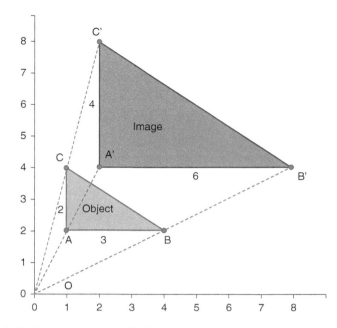

Figure 11.10   Scale factor enlargement with triangles

Calculating the volume of three-dimensional shapes

Primary school children are not ready for the use of formulae unless they understand why the formulae work. In the calculation of volume children need to understand two BIG IDEAS:

1   Volume is measuring the amount of space taken up
2   Shapes can appear to be very different even though their volumes may be the same.

Activity: Measuring volume with Multilink cubes

Learning intention: Understanding conservation of volume

Children should be given 24 Multilink cubes each and told to make different constructions using all the cubes. All the different creations will have the same volume. The choice of 24 is no accident. Multiples of 12 generate lots of factors, this impacts on volumes of cuboids and children may come up with cuboids consisting of the following arrangements:

$1 \times 1 \times 24$

$1 \times 2 \times 12$

$1 \times 3 \times 8$

$1 \times 4 \times 6$

$2 \times 2 \times 6$

$2 \times 3 \times 4$

Then they should be given a number of cubes to use to make cuboids of different dimensions. Any multiple of 12 gives multiple options. For example, 36 cubes = $2 \times 2 \times 9$, $2 \times 3 \times 6$, $3 \times 3 \times 4$, $1 \times 3 \times 12$, $1 \times 4 \times 9$ and so on.

Children should be shown a range of cuboids or other 3D shapes and asked to place them in order of how big the volume is. This can be done by counting each cube individually or by establishing a quicker way. This activity is significant. I strongly advise time is given to exchange of ideas on how volume is worked out. This could be extended to non-cuboid shapes made using cubes that might need to be broken down into layers or some other strategy.

 Big ideas

- Conservation of volume needs to overcome the idea that the longest single dimension necessarily creates the biggest volume, so $1 \times 1 \times 24$ (24) does not exceed $3 \times 3 \times 3$ (27). In fact the latter shape has a bigger volume.
- With 2D and 3D measurement it is the shapes that are the nearest to being regular that have the most efficient dimensions. The circle and the sphere have significant area and volume despite no one dimension being any longer than the others. The link between factors and area of rectangles is strong.

Conclusion

Measurement is an area of maths that involves several themes. Common to them all is the need to have tactile experience where physical manipulation of objects and resources deepens understanding, first subconsciously and then consciously. This chapter has explored how to scaffold the development of units of measure and place value issues. A number of common misconceptions have been explored with the intention that teachers should meet these head on through discussion and choosing appropriate problems for children to solve. By developing your ability to generate discussion that builds on children's active experiences you will serve them well.

Bibliography

Anghileri, J. (2006) *Developing Number Sense*, London: Continuum.

Askew, M., Brown, M., Rhodes, V., Wiliam, D. and Johnson, D. (1997) *Effective Teaching of Numeracy: A Report Carried Out for the Teacher Training Agency*, London: Kings College.

Barmby, P., Bilsborough, L., Harries, T. and Higgins, S. (2009) *Primary Mathematics, Teaching for Understanding*, Maidenhead: McGraw-Hill.

Blatchford, P., Bassett, P., Brown, P., Martin, C., Russell, A. and Webster, R (2009) Deployment and Impact of Support Staff Project. London: Institute of Education. (ISBN: 978–1–84775–515–5)

Bliss, J., Askew, M. and Macrae, S. (1996) 'Effective teaching and learning: scaffolding revisited', *Oxford Review of Education*, 22(1): 37–61.

Boaler, J. (2009) *The Elephant in the Classroom*, London: Souvenir Press.

Burton, L. (1984) 'Mathematical thinking: the struggle for meaning', *Journal for Research in Mathematics Education*, 15(1): 35–49.

Bynner, J. and Parsons, S. (1997) *It Doesn't Get Any Better: The Impact of Poor Basic Skills on the Lives of 37 Year Olds*, London: The Basic Skills Agency.

Carpenter, T. and Moser, J. (1984) 'The acquisition of addition and subtraction concepts', *Journal for Research in Maths in Education*, 15(3): 179–202.

Carruthers, E. and Worthington, M. (2004) 'Young children exploring early calculation', *Mathematics Teaching*, 187: 30–4.

Catterall, R. (2008) 'Doing time', *Mathematics Teaching*, 209: 37–9.

Cotton, T. (2013) *Understanding and Teaching Primary Mathematics*, Harlow: Pearson.

Crowley, Mary L. (1987) 'The van Hiele model of the development of geometric thought', *Learning and Teaching Geometry, K-12*: 1–16.

DfE (Department for Education) (2014) *Statutory Framework for the Early Years Foundation*, London: DfE.

DfEE (Department for Education and Employment) (2000) *Mathematical challenges for Able Pupils in Key Stages 1 and 2*, London: DfEE.

DfES (1999) *National Numeracy Strategy*. Available at: www.edu.dudley.gov.uk/numeracy/nns/Introduction.pdf (accessed 26/05/16).

DfES (2006) *Primary Framework for Literacy and Mathematics*. Available at: http://dera.ioe.ac.uk/14160/7/15f5c50f1b2f78d6af258a0bbdd23951_Redacted.pdf (accessed 26/05/16).

Early Education (2012) *Development Matters in the Early Years Foundation Stage Document*, London: Early Education.

Donaldson, M. (1978) *Children's Minds*, London: Fontana.

Fielke, D. (1997) *Extending Mathematical Thinking through Whole Class Teaching*, London: Hodder & Stoughton.

Friel, S.N., Curcio, F.R. and Bright, G.W. (2001) 'Making sense of graphs: critical factors influencing comprehension and instructional implications', *Journal for Research in Mathematics Education*, 32(2): 124–58.

Gattegno, C. (1988) 'Reflections on forty years of work on mathematics teaching', *For the Learning of Mathematics*, 8(3): 41–2.

Gelman, R. and Gallistel, C.R. (1978) *The Child's Understanding of Number*, Cambridge, MA: Harvard University Press.

Gifford, S. (2005) *Teaching Mathematics 3–5: Developing Learning in the Foundation Stage*, Maidenhead: McGraw-Hill/Open University Press.

Ginsberg, H. (1986) *Horizon*: Season 22, Episode 16. 'Twice Five Plus the Wings of a Bird' (28 April 1986).

Graham, A. (1991) 'Where is the 'P' in statistics?' in D. Pimm and E. Love (eds), *Teaching and Learning School Mathematics*, Sevenoaks: Hodder & Stoughton Ltd.

Gura, P. (ed.) with the Froebel Blockplay Research Group directed by Tina Bruce (1992) *Exploring Learning, Young Children and Blockplay*, London: Paul Chapman Publishing Ltd.

Hansen, A. (2014) *Children's Errors in Mathematics*, 3rd edition, London: Learning Matters/SAGE.

Haylock, D. (with Manning, R.) (2014) *Mathematics Explained for Primary Teachers*, 5th edition, London: SAGE.

Haylock, D. and Cockburn, A. (2008) *Understanding Mathematics for Young Children*, 2nd edition, London: SAGE.

Hegarty, M. and Kozhevnikov, M. (1999) 'Types of visual–spatial representations and mathematical problem solving', *Journal of Educational Psychology*, 91(4): 684–9.

Howe, C. and Mercer, N. (2007) *Children's Social Development, Peer Interaction and Classroom Learning* (Research Survey 2/1b). Available at: http://cprtrust.org.uk/wp-content/uploads/2014/06/research-survey-2-1b.pdf (accessed 26/05/16).

Hughes, M. (1986) *Children and Number, Difficulties in Learning Number*, Oxford: Blackwell.

Hutchins, P. (1989) *The Doorbell Rang*, London: Harper Trophy.

Koshy, V., Ernest, P. and Casey, R. (2000) *Mathematics for Primary Teachers*, London: Routledge.

Lave, J. and Wenger, E. (1991) *Situated Learning. Legitimate Peripheral Participation*, Cambridge: Cambridge University Press.

McCandless, D. (2009) *Information is Beautiful*. London: William Collins.

Merttens, R. (1989) *Teaching Primary Maths*, London: Edward Arnold.

Mitchelmore, M.C. (1998) 'Young students' concepts of turning and angle', *Cognition and Instruction*, 16(3): 265–84.

Mitchelmore, M.C. and White, P. (2000) 'Development of angle concepts by progressive abstraction and generalisation', *Educational Studies in Mathematics*, 41(3): 209–38.

Ness, D. and Farenga, S.J. (2007) *Knowledge under Construction: The Importance of Play in Developing Children's Spatial and Geometric Thinking*, Lanham, MD: Rowman & Littlefield Publishers, Inc.

Piaget, J. (1956) *The Construction of Reality in the Child*, London: Routledge.

Piaget, J. and Inhelder, B. (1958) *The Growth of Logical Thinking from Childhood to Adolescence*, New York: Basic Books.

PISA (2012) *Results in Focus: What 15-Year-Olds Know and What They Can Do With What They Know*. 2014-12-03. www.oecd.org/pisa/keyfindings/pisa-2012-results-overview.pdf.

Rowland, T., Turner, F., Thwaites, A. and Huckstep, P. (2009) *Developing Primary Mathematics Teaching: Reflecting on Practice with the Knowledge Quartet*. London: SAGE.

Ryan, J. and Williams, J. (2007) *Children's Mathematics 4–15, Learning from Errors and Misconceptions*, Maidenhead: McGraw-Hill/Open University Press.

Sarama, J. and Clements, D.H. (2004) 'Building blocks for early childhood mathematics', *Early Childhood Research Quarterly*, 19(1): 181–9.

Shaughnessy, J., Garfield, J. and Greer, B (1996) 'Data Handling' in A. Bishop, M.A. Clements, C. Keitel-Kreidt, J. Kilpatrick and C. Laborde (eds), *International Handbook on Mathematics Education*, Dordrecht: Springer, pp. 205–37.

Shulman, L.S. (1986) 'Those who understand: knowledge growth in teaching', *Educational Researcher*, 15(2): 4–14.

Siraj-Blatchford, I., Muttock, S., Sylva, K., Gilden, R. and Bell, D. (2002) *Researching Effective Pedagogy in the Early Years*, London: DfES.

Skemp, R. (1976) 'Instrumental understanding and relational understanding', *Mathematics Teaching*, 77: 20–6.

Skinner, C. and Stevens, J. (2012) *Foundations of Mathematics, an Active Approach to Numbers and Measures in the Early Years*, London: Featherstone.

Thompson, I. (2008) *Teaching and Learning Early Number*, Maidenhead: McGraw-Hill/Open University Press.

Vygotsky, L.S. (1978) *Mind in Society*, Cambridge MA: Harvard University Press.

Index

Page references followed by *f* refer to figures; those followed by *t* refer to tables.